RE/ORIENTING WRITING STUDIES

RE/ORIENTING WRITING STUDIES

Queer Methods, Queer Projects

EDITED BY
WILLIAM P. BANKS
MATTHEW B. COX
CAROLINE DADAS

UTAH STATE UNIVERSITY PRESS
Logan

© 2019 by University Press of Colorado
Published by Utah State University Press

An imprint of University Press of Colorado
245 Century Circle, Suite 202
Louisville, Colorado 80027

 The University Press of Colorado is a proud member of
the Association of University Presses.

The University Press of Colorado is a cooperative publishing enterprise supported, in part, by Adams State University, Colorado State University, Fort Lewis College, Metropolitan State University of Denver, University of Colorado, University of Northern Colorado, Utah State University, and Western State Colorado University.

∞ This paper meets the requirements of the ANSI/NISO Z39.48–1992 (Permanence of Paper).

ISBN: 978-1-60732-817-9 (pbk.)
ISBN: 978-1-60732-818-6 (ebook)
DOI: https://doi.org/10.7330/9781607328186

Library of Congress Cataloging-in-Publication Data

Names: Banks, William P., editor. | Cox, Matthew B., editor. | Dadas, Caroline, editor.
Title: Re/orienting writing studies : queer methods, queer projects / [edited by] William P. Banks, Matthew B. Cox, Caroline Dadas.
Description: Logan : Utah State University Press, [2018] | Includes bibliographical references and index.
Identifiers: LCCN 2018036071| ISBN 9781607328179 (pbk.) | ISBN 9781607328186 (ebook)
Subjects: LCSH: English language—Rhetoric—Study and teaching (Higher)—Social aspects. | English language—Rhetoric—Study and teaching (Higher)—Research—Methodology. | Academic writing—Study and teaching (Higher)—Social aspects. | Academic writing—Study and teaching (Higher)—Research—Methodology. | Queer theory. | Homosexuality and education.
Classification: LCC PE1404 .R394 2018 | DDC 808/.04207—dc23
LC record available at https://lccn.loc.gov/2018036071

Cover photograph by Michael Gaida/Pixabay.

CONTENTS

ACKNOWLEDGMENTS

The work of any edited collection is one filled with the contributions of so many wonderful people, and ours is no different. First, we wish to thank the contributors who trusted us with their projects; we know that giving their work to others to read, critique, and edit requires a great deal of trust, and we are so grateful that these brilliant scholars trusted us with their words and ideas. We hope we have done them justice.

When the idea for this collection first emerged, it came about because of what felt to us as a watershed moment in writing studies. When Will was writing his dissertation nearly twenty years ago, he could count on one hand the number of scholars in our field who were regularly researching and publishing LGBTQ work. A decade later, when Caroline and Matt were writing their dissertations, that number seemed to be expanding significantly, and their projects were a big part of that next generation of LGBTQ scholarship. What had not changed by then, however, was the paucity of methodological scholarship available in writing studies for supporting LGBTQ researchers and their projects. We conceived of this collection as a space for addressing that elision, and we thought the best people to do it were those scholars who had had to work so hard to conceive of and implement queer methodological frameworks and data collection practices in order to do the sort of research they needed to do. When we began this project, everyone involved in writing chapters was either finishing their dissertations or working on tenure and promotion, so they seemed to us the right people to ask about what changes we needed to see to our methods and methodologies in writing studies. Their contributions do not disappoint, and we're so thankful to them for all their hard work as we collectively built this project over the last several years.

We are also grateful to the brilliant staff at Utah State University Press for their encouragement and support. This book is one of the last projects that was initiated by Michael Spooner, whose work at the press has been one of constant support for writing studies scholars and scholarship, and we are thankful to him for meeting with us early on in the process and for encouraging us and this collection. Rachael Levay picked up this project when she joined USUP and has been a constant advocate for this collection; her kind attention seems proof that USUP will continue to support writing studies scholarship, and we are extremely pleased that our collection will be part of the USUP catalog. We are also thankful to Laura Furney and Dan Miller for their excellent work editing and typesetting the manuscript, and to Kami Day, whose careful manuscript edits are a model for how that sort of work should happen: they all seemed to understand the challenges this manuscript represented to traditional research and writing practices, and they asked us questions about choices that we and the contributors made rather than assume we had made errors; they did so much to help our writing be more clear and to communicate more effectively for readers. This collection is far stronger and more cohesive because of their support.

Will

In addition to those mentioned above, I would like to thank Matt and Caroline for their eager investment in this project and for being such phenomenal collaborators. Likewise, I will always be grateful to Cynthia Selfe, who was one of the first writing studies scholars to show me in word and action how much we need allies in our professional lives, and while her model of mentorship is not one I can always live up to, it is the one that I continue to look to for guidance. I'm grateful for the support of my department chair, Marianne Montgomery; for wonderful colleagues in the University Writing Program—Wendy Sharer, Kerri Flinchbaugh, and Rae Meads—who support and challenge me in equal measure; and for a dear friend and colleague, Rick Taylor, who never lets me get too down about any of the politics that are always part of working in the academy. I've also been fortunate in my life to be able to build the queer-friend-family I need, a lovely collection we have taken to calling, simply, The Council: Michelle, Shane, Erin, Andy, Matt, Josh, and Nikki offer endless encouragement, and they always seem to know the right time for a cocktail! I remain grateful and humbled by the love and support of my family: Jackson, Rachel, and Susan. And I'm especially thankful that so many hours of writing at home are accompanied by—and sometimes appropriately interrupted by—the calming and supportive snoozles of great dogs.

Matt

I would like to thank both Will and Caroline for the fantastic journey that has been this project. They've been so generous with their mentorship and so tireless in their efforts. I also want to thank the individual authors of this collection. Every time I reread these chapters, I'm blown away yet again by their discipline-changing queer scholarship. I also want to thank Utah State University Press for their steadfast support. We could not have asked for a more professional or encouraging press. I want to thank my department chair, Dr. Marianne Montgomery, for her steadfast support of this project and my group of ECU/Greenville close friends and colleagues, Dr. Michelle Eble, Dr. Nikki Caswell, Dr. Erin Frost, Shane Ernst, and Andy Frost. They kept me in laughs and in chocolate as I journeyed through this and other projects over the last few years. I want to thank Dr. Trixie Smith, my first and most profound queer mentor in the field. She has taught me how to be both a queer scholar and a sane and happy human as I move through this strange heteropatriarchal space called the academy. I want to thank two other scholars as well, Dr. Malea Powell and Dr. J. Blake Scott, who mentor and support me queerly year in and year out. I want to thank my family: my parents Joe and Brenda Cox, my sister Stephanie Demorest, my brother-in-law Matthew Demorest, my nephew Zeb Demorest, my niece Kristen Cox-Miller, my parents-in-law Kelly Crayton Lambert, Butch Lambert, Rick Gardner, and Jonathan Evans. As well as my grandparents-in-law Hilda Hatley Crayton and Johnny and Millie Gardner. I firmly believe family (both the ones you get and the ones you make) are what get me through life and their love sustains me. And lastly, I want to thank my husband, Joshua Gardner, who supports me and loves me day and night and who has taught me so much about what being a queer scholar and queer human in the early twenty-first century can be and who constantly teaches me about tearing down the boundaries and walls. There's just not much a late night dance and laugh with my husband in our kitchen can't fix. All of you teach me and care for me so much more than I feel I could ever give back. But you inspire me to always give back to my queer communities and to our unjust world.

Caroline

The process of editing this book was a joyful one, surrounded by queer family. Special thanks to Will and Matt and to all of our contributors for their imagination, intellect, and humanity. These chapters are ones that will contribute significantly to the influence of queer rhetoric on the field of writing studies, and it was a pleasure to watch them take shape. I am grateful to my friends and colleagues at Montclair State for their humor, indefatigable spirit, and passion for our shared work, especially Laura Field, Jess Restaino, Emily Isaacs, Ron Brooks, and Kira Dreher. My graduate experience at Miami University was crucial in not only shaping my sense of who I wanted to be as a scholar but also who I wanted to be as a queer-identified person. I am especially grateful to my dissertation chair, Michele Simmons, who mentored me and many other young queer scholars with endless patience and an openness to our needs. I learned the joys of chosen family through my relationship with Michele and my extended Miami family, especially Bre Garrett, Trav Webster, and Chanon Adsanatham. At Miami I also met my beloved Lisa Blankenship, whose laughter, intellect, and hope for a better future sustains me on a daily basis. I am grateful beyond measure for her role as my partner in life. I am thankful for my family back in Chicago, my parents and sister, for always having believed in me—they continue to be a source of great comfort. Finally, my wonderful cats were by my side throughout much of the work on this collection, and they continue to teach me important lessons about unconditional love, trust, and conviction to one's principles.

FOREWORD

Pamela Takayoshi

This book you hold in your hand or sit before on your screen is a signifi-cant (and at times playful) contribution to understanding how we make knowledge in the academy. Its focus is on the ways researchers build knowledge and in understanding the relationship among researchers, the questions they ask, their participants, and the data itself. In *Feminism and Methodology*, Sandra Harding (1987, 3) notably distinguished among methods (techniques for collecting data), methodology ("a theory and analysis of how research does or should proceed"), and epistemol-ogy ("a theory of knowledge"). Methodologies—as theories of how research does or should proceed—are conceptually quite distinct from methods—techniques for practice. The careful distinction between methods and methodologies is suggestive of the value queer method-ological theories offer any researcher committed to understanding how research practice works to create knowledge. Like the many feminist methodologists who took up Harding's call for paying explicit attention to the methodologies and epistemologies that inform our methods, the authors in this collection focus on the ways queer epistemologies impact methodological thinking about what is important in research and how it should proceed. The value of queer theory to revealing the invis-ible workings of knowledge making cannot be overstated. It is a *crucial* theoretical component if we researchers want to make knowledge that is accurate, honest, and just. In our cultural moment, this type of research cannot arrive fast enough. We must interrogate our biases—not only as people who work with and represent others but as researchers trying to create ethical and accurate interpretations of the world.

The authors in this collection examine qualitative, quantitative, and textual/rhetorical research in many different locations (the first-year composition classroom, academic publishing, cross-cultural rhetorics, the Digital Archive of Literacy Narratives, queer archives, infertility

DOI: 10.7330/9781607328186.c000

support groups, Grindr, writing assessment) through many methods (surveys, interviews, observations, rhetorical analysis, autoethnography). They carry with them foci drawn from a shared set of keywords that point to both oppressive and reparative experience:

normativity	radical	dichotomy/binaries
queer	power	in-between
disruption	oppression	queer
pleasure	visibility	worldmaking
possibility	desire	ambiguity
heteronormativity	affect	identity
homonormativity	ableism	orientations
orientation	trans	justice
difference	pleasure of failure	visibility

Here are the authors of this collection explaining the promise of queer epistemologies, methodologies, and methods for writing research:

- "Queer methodologies might trouble the (field's) valorization of normativity, firm stances, and conventional notions of ethos."—Hillery Glasby
- "Writing queer is possible in the most momentary and fleeting ways, but it is imperative—for queer scholars especially but perhaps for all scholars of writing—to resist the writing norms and assumptions that inform *how* we compose, to try to cup in our hands, however briefly and however impossibly, whatever water we can hold long enough for a small drink."—Stacey Waite
- "Queer and trans researchers can harness their disidentification . . . with quantitative methods to make productive interventions that can lead to more useful, more ethical research practices."—G Patterson
- "Interconnecting comparative rhetoric and queer studies . . . allows us to develop a critical framework for cross-cultural analysis that works to challenge, twist, and question taken-for-granted assumptions and knowledge."—Chanon Adsanatham
- "Queerness cracks and cleaves the normativity we wish to critique."—Jean Bessette
- "Queer theory, and in particular queer rhetorics, [is] a methodological entryway into . . . discussions of . . . all embodied nonnormativities, especially those that confront notions of ableism and heterosexuality."—Maria Novotny
- "By incorporating sex into the study of rhetoric, we can push the boundaries of rhetoric and writing studies and suggest that perhaps we need an anti-identitarian, impersonal approach to rhetoric. By *sex*, I want to be clear, I don't mean the category of one's biological sex

(male, female, intersex) but rather actual, embodied sexual desires and practices—those moments and practices that . . . challenge our subjectivity and bodily coherence."—Michael J. Faris

- "This is the primary purpose and benefit of a queer method: exposing the dominant sociocultural binaries and discourses and providing openings to questions that reshape those binaries, discourses, and the broader culture in the process."—Deborah Kuzawa

- "Those who are committed to assessment as a practice of social justice should embrace the politics and praxis of the feminist killjoy. . . . Queer validity inquiry [is] a method of ongoing resistance to the normative and normalizing practices of assessment."—Nicole Caswell and Stephanie West-Puckett

- "Queer rhetorics and professional writing can inform one another. Disrupting expected structures, making self and relationships visible, calling attention to normative structures, and embracing failure and unexpected processes and outcomes are just a few ways of queering professional writing spaces."—Caroline Dadas and Matthew Cox

Look at these assertions about the value of queer theories for writing research and ask yourself, aren't these matters to which *all* researchers should be attentive?

This book is for queer researchers—offering guidance in how to navigate queer research questions and subjects in ways traditional research methodologies do not address and which traditional methods do not scaffold. Researchers working from a queer epistemological standpoint reveal these hidden oppressions in research practices as limitations in knowledge making. For example, G Patterson (this collection) clearly reveals the ways even seemingly innocuous data-collecting tools such as surveys are ideologically imbued with practices that interfere with a queer worldmaking: without a queer epistemological and methodological perspective, the data collection not only participates in oppressive cultural identity structures but also produces incomplete and wrong data. It leads to bad research.

And this perspective is why this book is not *just* for queer researchers or researchers asking queer questions about queer subjects. All writing researchers work in heteronormative cultures and navigate normative binaries in making sense of the world—this book shows us how to be aware as researchers of those (often invisible) normative forces and how to navigate them in the conduct of ethical research. Queer theories, these authors assert, are foundational theories for anyone interested in writing and identity, in language and its uses, and in empirical research and our disciplinary practices for knowledge building. That is, queer theories are important not only for queer subjects. Queer theories reveal the processes by which we ALL function in our culture, which the authors make clear even in the brief bulleted list I've excerpted above.

As a feminist, I believe any feminism that is not intersectional is bullshit. As a feminist, I find queer theory's attentiveness to normativity, difference, oppression, and sexuality provides the radical illumination of concerns feminists have long held about the ways material bodies are read in culture. As a feminist, I have a clearer understanding of my position (as a cisgender, white woman) in the heteronormative, patriarchal culture thanks to queer theories and researchers; they have shown me a way I can work at being heterosexual without being heteronormative. As a feminist, my understandings of power and oppression are incomplete without queer theories. This book is a crucial contribution to thinking about methodologies for all researchers because as the editors tell us, "This work . . . can serve to reorient the field of writing studies, not so that everyone is engaged in work around LGBT/Queer objects/texts, people, or contexts but rather so that the discoveries and contributions of queer rhetorics and queer method/ologies can help us rethink the work of traditional data-collection methods and frames for inquiry" (6). To which I respond with a resounding, "Yes! And again yes!" This is a book about how we think, how we make knowledge, and how we interpret and analyze the world.

The editors identify a "fundamentally conservative strain in our field that has failed to recognize queer theories as important to our collective (and very broad) work with language and composition" (10). I wholeheartedly agree—the authors in this collection reveal the many ways queer theories shed light on language and discourse as they are implicated and involved in the uses of power. For readers unfamiliar with queer theories, this book provides a necessary beginning point, by which I mean it is necessary both that those readers become informed and that this book provides one sort of beginning introduction. For readers interested in queer theory, this book provides a detailed examination of the normative aspects of knowledge-making practices (research) a queer lens productively reveals and challenges. For readers interested in research methods, this book provides a theoretical window onto the importance of understanding the knowledge-making practices involved in research. For readers who are empirical researchers *and* queer theorists, this book reveals the detailed ways we must continue to examine our own practices in order to be better at them.

Any researchers who are self-reflective about their practices and their own subjectivity in the research process can benefit from thinking creatively about queering those normative practices that still haunt our work, from the research questions we pose to the analytic conclusions we draw—and beyond. Any researchers who want to produce *good*, accurate research should set aside striving for objectivity (a futile goal) and instead strive for transparency in the ways their identity, the identities of their participants, and the identity constructions of the broader culture impact the knowledge they make. The queer theories so meaningfully and clearly detailed in this collection can help them do that. And for those readers who worry about what happens to the *queerness* of queer theory when *all* researchers research/write/act queer, Stacey Waite (in this collection) offers the best reply I've seen, one with which I close this foreword:

> Sometimes I get tired of questions like these about who queerness belongs to and how it can't belong to everyone, or how it can't be moved off the queer body or away from sexuality—as if there is anything we do that moves *away* from sexuality and the body. But that worry, that worry that somehow everyone in this world will someday look at things in queer ways all the time, that worry that we will all just compose and teach in queer ways, that worry that then queerness will just be the norm, and therefore not queer anymore, that world is one I would love to see arrive—the truly impossible queer present. I would love to actually have this problem, to one day think to myself aw shucks, now everyone is writing in such queer ways, just what will we do now? (51–52)

REFERENCES

Harding, Sandra, ed. 1987. *Feminism and Methodology.* Bloomington: Indiana University Press.

RE/ORIENTING WRITING STUDIES

1

RE/ORIENTING WRITING STUDIES
Thoughts on In(queer)y

William P. Banks, Matthew B. Cox, and Caroline Dadas

Research is always about orientation, about how (and why and even to what extent) the researcher turns toward the objects, participants, or contexts of study. To stand in a classroom in front of twenty-five composition students is to stand in relation to others; usually, we stand there as their teachers, people charged with engaging these students in a host of activities intended to teach them about writing. But what if we're there not only as teachers but also as researchers, as teacher-researchers? Then while we might be oriented toward these students in the ways that a teacher typically is, we're also now oriented differently: we're seeing, being, engaging in more than one way, through more than one role. Our orientations as researchers mean we're in that space asking particular questions, looking for evidence to confirm or contradict working hypotheses; our being there as researchers means that we're operating on multiple cognitive levels, observing, yes, but also impacting that space through the ways our focus shifts.

The same would be true of any research site, whether that's the seemingly innocuous space of a nondescript room used for a focus group, the dusty and moldy space of a campus archive, or the bustling workplace we've chosen to observe as part of an office ethnography. When we enter a carefully chosen room to meet the five people who constitute a focus group, we engage that space and those people, we orient ourselves toward those people, as someone there to facilitate a focus group. We alter space by taking a seat near the video camera or the digital recorder; we ask the participants to move if they are not already sitting in the frame of the camera or near enough to the microphone to be heard and recorded. These orientations speak to our assumptions about who is in charge of collecting data, what counts as data, and which objects in the room have value. The same is true of the archive or the boardroom, or any other site where we show up and point ourselves toward

DOI: 10.7330/9781607328186.c001

objects of study. And we are also oriented from behind, as it were, by the discipline(s) we are part of, by the intellectual traditions and commonplaces out of which our inquiry questions have emerged—and to which we hope our own answers will contribute.

Experienced researchers know these things. We learned about these orientations in graduate seminars focused on research, or as we began to conduct our own research projects. But we also know that the methods and methodologies we studied and practiced in graduate school do not represent fully objective, ideology-free practices for studying objects, people, and spaces. Rather, each represents a way of orienting a researcher toward an object, a people, or a space. Where these practices—surveys, focus groups, observations, rhetorical analyses, and so forth—become commonplace, where they represent normative/ unquestioned activities or epistemologies, they demonstrate not only the ways that each has become an active method for orienting a researcher (and thus also preventing other orientations, other views from taking the foreground) but also how each has become a normative orientation for the field, a well-trodden path whose existence actively replicates itself from researcher to researcher, from discipline to discipline.

Reflecting on the "well-trodden path," Sara Ahmed (2006) writes in *Queer Phenomenology*, "Lines are both created by being followed and are followed by being created. The lines that direct us . . . are in this way performative: they depend on the repetition of norms and conventions, of routes and paths taken, but they are also created as an effect of this repetition" (16). These lines of motion are also lines of thought, of inquiry, of what is and is not permissible in the activities and frames that surround inquiry. In the intersections of the humanities and social sciences, where we tend to locate writing studies, these well-worn paths provide institutional and disciplinary validity; they become recognizable paths of inquiry and methods of discovery, and in their recognizability, their visibility as systematic processes, we take refuge in having developed (or co-opted) frames of empirical inquiry that lend our work certain kinds of validity as research. While one of the values of empirical research is that others can follow our methods for themselves and, ostensibly, validate our shared discoveries by reaching the same conclusions, Ahmed suggests that one reason other researchers find what we find is that they follow the line we established; our shared discoveries are as much about the lines we follow as they are about the data we collect or the methods we use to analyze them.

While writing studies has traditionally articulated research practices in terms of activities (methods) and frameworks (methodologies)

(Harding 1987; Kirsch and Sullivan 1992), this bifurcated approach can make it difficult for scholars doing queer inquiry work to see how best to approach and understand their research. What counts as queer work, after all? Is it the subjects of our research or the contexts in which we conduct research that make our work queer? Is it the way we collect data or the way we frame our collection methods? Or does *queer* work involve a more nuanced understanding of these concepts, concepts that guide so much of the way our discipline responds to and frames the work we attempt to do?

This collection represents our attempt to address some of these questions and to challenge the heteronormative orientations that have guided inquiry in writing studies since its inception. The scholars included here work to unpack the complex ways that queer scholarship has impacted the field of writing studies by disrupting not only the subjects and contexts of inquiry but also the frames and activities (and activity systems) in which inquiry occurs. In her groundbreaking study of lesbian, gay, bisexual, and trans (LGBT) students in a writing classroom, Harriet Malinowitz (1995) asked the powerful question, "Which of our theories of writing don't explode when we consider their ramifications for lesbian and gay writers?" (39). The writers included in this collection turn that question toward research method/ologies to ask the field of writing studies, how might queer rhetorics and research "explode" our working theories of research methods and methodologies?

The writers included here also represent an emerging generation of scholars who are poised to address some of the key challenges that established scholars in the field have identified as kairotic for researchers in writing studies. For example, as part of introducing the recent collection *Writing Studies Research in Practice: Methods and Methodologies*, Gesa Kirsch (2012) identifies three specific challenges she thinks worthy of our collective attention. Writing researchers, she believes, should be

1. "adapting different research methods to diverse settings and reporting this research in genres that best reflect these methods" (xi);

2. engaging in "interactive, collaborative, reciprocal, mutually beneficial, nonhierarchical relations with research participants and their communities" (xii);

3. and recognizing that the "increasingly collaborative nature of research" means that "as writing studies has expanded its scope and breadth to include the rhetorical activities of those whose voices have been neglected, silenced, or rarely heard, scholars are showing a renewed concern for representing participants with respect, care, and complexity" (xiii–iv).

These challenges are large and complex, but they also reflect a set of values central to the work of queer rhetorics and, we argue, to queer methods and methodologies. The writers included in this collection attempt to address these challenges in nuanced and rigorous ways, from engaging a diverse set of partners in research to playing with nontraditional genres in order to make their cases or represent their findings. Several authors also directly address the ways queer theories have helped them rethink language use so they can enact the sort of collaborative, nonhierarchical relationships that Kirsch believes our discipline should value. Through engaging new research sites and participants, and by framing and articulating their work through theories somewhat new to writing studies, these scholars offer insights into research practices in our discipline that we believe will help shape the next generation of writing researchers.

In this introduction, we attempt to situate the work that follows by articulating how these projects emerge at the intersections of queer rhetorics and queer method/ologies. This work, we believe, can serve to reorient the field of writing studies, not so that everyone is engaged in work around LGBT/Queer objects/texts, people, or contexts, but rather so that the discoveries and contributions of queer rhetorics and queer method/ologies can help us rethink the work of traditional data-collection methods and frames for inquiry. The projects and experiences reported on in this collection demonstrate how early-career researchers in writing studies have had to rethink our well-disciplined paths in order to do the work they need to do. We believe these pieces will be especially helpful to new and beginning researchers as they begin to think through the complex and often difficult practices of research.

THINKING QUEERLY ABOUT IN(QUEER)Y

Any book that attempts to explore queer theories, queer rhetorics, or anything we might want to label *queer* begins its work in a complicated, in fact quite "messy," place (Dadas 2016; Law 2004). For many, even most, researchers in writing studies, queer theories appear useful or applicable only if the research project involves LGBTQ people, objects/texts, and/or contexts. At the 2013 conference of the Council of Writing Program Administrators, for example, which took place in Savannah, Georgia, the theme for the three-day event was "Queering the Writing Program," and while there were three queer-focused plenary sessions, all delivered by queer-identified researchers who were engaged in queer-focused work, there was very little else about the conference that was queer. William remembers counting fewer than thirteen sessions in which it was clear from the title or session summary in the program that the papers from the session would actually engage queer work at all. More common was that the researchers who attended the event simply ignored the theme. Part of the reason for this disregard is that writing studies has mostly refused the "queer turn" that Jonathan Alexander and David Wallace suggest has occurred in our field over the last couple of decades (Alexander and Wallace 2009). They note that the emerging work of queer scholars in our field has produced a "better understanding of how heteronormativity operates in society at large, in our classrooms, and in the pages of our books and journals" (W301), and no doubt that's true. But as the WPA conference presenters demonstrated one after another, it's one thing to recognize heteronormativity and quite another to see how queer rhetorics shape, disrupt, or challenge our daily practices as writers, researchers, or, in this case, writing program administrators. One presenter admitted what we suspect was true of the majority in attendance: "I know this session doesn't really address the conference theme, but it turns out, we don't really know anything about queer theory, and we didn't want to embarrass ourselves by reading one or two articles and then trying to make our presentation connect to them." While the "queer turn" in the field for queer scholars has been about much more than simply adding *gay* or *lesbian* to our menu of identitarian concerns, much of the field, we suspect, has struggled to get past this sort of inclusionary mindset. In this section, we attempt to define queer rhetorics and queer methodologies such that the field of writing studies can better see how these theories of language and writing—about self and other, about agency and its failures—are foundational theories for anyone in writing studies to know and to engage. These theories do not merely explain how to include LGBT people in our discipline or our research, nor simply how to treat LGBT students or faculty; rather, these theories, like all theories, help us to see our work differently, to challenge what has come before, and to offer alternative ways of being in the world, regardless of sexual orientation.

Queer Theory, Language Theory

Early articulations of queer theory focused on two concepts that should have been both recognizable to and welcomed by writing studies scholars at the time: discourse and performativity. Borrowing heavily from the work of Michel Foucault, who posited that discourse, like power, is difficult to pin down in simplistic language structures, early queer theorists came to understand discourse as a method for both enacting power and disrupting it. Foucault (1988) writes, "We must not imagine a world of discourse divided between the dominant discourse and excluded discourse, or between the dominant discourse and the dominated one; but as a multiplicity of discursive elements that can come into play in various strategies" (122). Part of what queer scholars appreciated about Foucault's notions of discourse and power was that they made sense based on our own embodied experiences with language. Like other groups fighting for civil rights, queer people had experienced language hurled at them in rage so as dehumanize and belittle them, the same language they then flipped so those hurtful words, in queer spaces, became discourses of camaraderie, innuendo, and/or humor (Bergman 1993; Chauncey 1995; Cleto 1999; Meyers 1994). We're reminded of that infamously uncomfortable scene in Mart Crowley's *The Boys in the Band* (2008) in which Harold hurls the words *Jew* and *fag* around in ways intended to be both cruel and kind, aware of both how the world treats these two groups and what it means to play with those terms at parties like the one the characters in the play are attending. For Harold and the other characters at the party, language—and the party itself—becomes a type of resistance to the language outside that space. "Resistance," Annamarie Jagose (1996) writes, "is multiple and unstable; it coagulates at certain points, is dispersed across others, and circulates in discourse . . . [that is] endlessly prolific and multivalent" (81). For many LGBTQ people, there is a felt sense, as much as a theoretical one, that one resistant method for maintaining our existence involves not being bludgeoned by languages intended to hurt us but pushing back, even in small ways, in order to maintain our own senses of self and community. Ultimately, this is a recognition that language itself is unstable and that within that instability, marginalized groups can attempt to assert agency.

Another attempt to find agency outside the spaces provided by normativity came about in queer theory's early adoption of performativity as a key concept. Performativity, like Foucauldian notions of discourse, foregrounds that which is "multiple and unstable" (Jagose 1996, 81), in this case referring to gender and sexuality. Early feminist and queer theorists (e.g., Diana Fuss, Luce Irigaray, Judith Butler), according to Jagose, began to recognize that *woman* represents "a regulatory fiction, whose deployment inadvertently reproduces those normative relations between sex, gender and desire that naturalize heterosexuality" (84). Woman—and man, girl, boy, lady, gentleman—doesn't represent a direct relationship between biological or anatomical demarcations of sex systems or sexual organs and language but rather a set of social, cultural, and (at times) biological beliefs that have solidified over time into concepts of gender that suggest individuals, based on anatomical sex, have essential and largely immutable behaviors, experiences, and mental functions because of that anatomy. Judith Butler (1993), however, recognized gender as "a ritualized production" (231) that never fully succeeds but that is always grounded in a language of its own undoing.

> The practice by which gendering occurs, the embodying of norms, is a compulsory practice, a forcible production, but not for that reason fully determining. To the extent that gender is an assignment, it is an assignment which is never quite carried out according to expectations, whose addressee never quite inhabits the ideal s/he is compelled to approximate. Moreover, this embodying is a repeated process. (231)

Key to queer theory's early articulations of gender performativity is the awareness that gender, like language, is systematically unstable, constantly in flux, endlessly repeatable. What this means for LGBTQ people, as well as those occupying and embracing more heteronormative bodies and experiences, is that these performatives are fundamentally antibinary (Bornstein 2013) and that they demonstrate our shared human experience of "being implicated in that which one opposes" (Butler 1993, 241): genders are known in relation to the many genders they are not. The same might be said for race, class, nationality, ethnicity, and so forth. The realization that language and identity are interwoven and interanimated means that any discipline focused on the study of language must engage theories and rhetorics grounded in such a realization. Likewise, our research practices must also be built out of such understandings.

What has this realization meant for writing studies so far? What might it mean for writing studies in the near future? For a field that trades in language study and language practice, it sometimes seems that queer theories have had little impact outside the study of language practices specific to LGBTQ people or to queer-as-identity scholarship. We're thinking here of Harriet Malinowitz's (1995) *Textual Orientations: Lesbian and Gay Students and the Making of Discourse Communities*, of course, but also Jonathan Alexander's shift from focusing exclusively on LGBTQ students to acknowledging a need for sexual literacy in *Literacy, Sexuality, Pedagogy: Theory and Practice for Composition Studies* (Alexander 2008), and Zan Gonçalves's (2006) exploration of queer students and rhetoric in *Sexuality and the Politics of Ethos in the Writing Classroom*. These important texts—as well as a host of articles in our field's major journals—helped to make queer texts, people, and contexts meaningful to the field of writing studies. At the same time, we fear that the field has walked away from these texts with the assumption that queer theories and queer rhetorics start and end with identity-oriented projects, and that if one is not studying LGBTQ students, texts, or contexts specifically, queer theories and queer rhetorics may have little to contribute to one's projects. While these authors would likely not identify their own research as only identity based, it seems to us that our discipline tends to take them up in just that way. That was certainly the feeling William had when he left the 2013 WPA conference. This shortsightedness, of course, is not the fault of these early queer projects, which served to open the door to connections between queer theories and writing studies; rather, we argue, it stems from a more fundamentally conservative strain in our field that has failed to recognize queer theories as important to our collective (and very broad) work with language and composition. Just as Martha Marinara, Jonathan Alexander, William P. Banks, and Samantha Blackman recognized that LGBTQ authors, texts, and topics only rarely have a place in our first-year composition readers—and if they do, they are often included as "issues" about which to argue (e.g., gays in the military, gay adoption) (Marinara et al. 2009)—more recently, Banks has been surveying graduate courses that serve as either (1) introductions to the field of writing studies and/or teaching writing or (2) courses on writing program administration and found that very few (5 percent or fewer) include texts that explicitly address issues of sexuality/queer theory and writing studies or writing program administration.

It seems to us that any set of theories that addresses language/discourse should be given serious consideration in writing studies. The essays in this collection have all been informed by queer theories and queer rhetorics (which we might define as queer theory in action). Some of them (Adsanatham) demonstrate why we need to bring queer theories together with other cultural theories in order that each might be sharpened by the other. Other writers demonstrate how queer rhetorics can help us to rethink long-held assumptions about research methods central to writing studies like those used in historiography (Bessette), autoethnography (Faris), and writing assessment (Caswell and West-Puckett), while still others discover meaningful queer research practices in spaces that remain understudied like the Digital Archive of Literacy Narratives (Kuzawa) and fertility narratives (Novotny). Given this rich diversity of methods, methodologies, and research contexts, rather than ask, what has queer theory done for writing studies?, we might want to ask, what does this new generation of writing studies scholars see in queer theory that is helping them rethink the work of writing studies?

Queer Rhetorics, Queer Method/ologies

Part of what we're seeing more recently is a shift from queer theory to queer rhetorics, a deliberate and thoughtful shift toward an action-oriented, rhetorically infused set of principles and practices informed by several decades of queer theoretical work. While innovative rhetorical and queer work is now happening in non-Western contexts like Thailand (Adsanatham, this collection) and among scholars working through indigenous traditions (Baca 2008; Driskill et al. 2011; Driskill 2016; Morgensen 2011; Smith 2011), it remains that the majority of work done in queer theory in its first thirty years has involved an evolution of primarily Western and European thought. No doubt, this represents a significant limitation for queer work writ large, one noted by a diverse set of scholars (Cohen 1995; Love 2009; Muñoz 1994; 2011) and one we acknowledge at greater length below. While we recognize this limitation, we also find that articulating a queer rhetoric, or queer rhetorics, must start somewhere. For the purposes of this collection, then, we situate queer rhetorics, and the method/ologies that emerge from or are influenced by them, in the tradition of the new rhetorics. For rhetorical scholars like Lloyd Bitzer (1968), rhetoric represents a "mode of altering reality" through the "creation of discourse which changes reality through the mediation of thought and action" (4). Rhetoric is the "the *process* of using language to organize experience and communicate it to others"; as such, it is both the "distinctive human activity and the 'science' concerned with understanding that activity," C. H. Knoblauch (1985, 29) tells us. And Krista Ratcliffe (2003) reminds us that rhetoric is "the study of how we use language and how language uses us."

Queer rhetorics, it seems to us, are fundamentally about the interconnections of language and reality, as well as the ways language mediates reality, alters reality—in short, the way language makes reality an option at all. But rather than assume a primarily ontological nature for language and reality, queer rhetorics begin with the assumption that critique—the calling out of language as language—represents an initial and important destabilization of meaning, not to prevent meaning or to pretend that meaning cannot be made but to ask why *this* meaning at *this* time and under *these* circumstances; these are fundamentally rhetorical questions:

> To call a presupposition into question is not the same as doing away with it; rather it is to free it from its metaphysical lodgings in order to understand what political interests were secured in and by that metaphysical placing, and thereby to permit the term to occupy and to serve very different political aims. (Butler 1993, 30)

Scholars engaged in queer rhetorics recognize the social nature of language, as well as the instability of language as both "social" and "natural." This *queer* engagement with language and reality, with objects and experiences, led Banks and Stephanie West-Puckett (2015) to identify three specific queer rhetorics that we want to bring up here as examples of how these rhetorics can impact both methods and methodologies for re/orienting writing studies: rhetorics of intentionality, forgetting, and failure. All three of these rhetorics originate in the embodied thinking of queer scholars and theorists and demonstrate what it might mean if writing studies took queer theories and queer rhetorics more seriously.

1. Rhetorics of Intentionality

By connecting queer phenomenologies (Ahmed 2006) and theories of trans identity and embodiment (Salamon 2011), Banks and West-Puckett (2015) demonstrate an important rhetorical practice among queer persons in which intention is (often) valued over outcome. For example, consider trans bodies that do not "pass" as the gender they may intend. No doubt, queer studies has a long and complex history of trying to understand "passing"—passing as straight, passing as gay or lesbian, passing as male or female (for both drag/cabaret performers and individuals who identify as trans). When we take up this conversation as part of a heteronormative rhetoric that values outcomes, that privileges the finished product over ongoing processes and practices, Banks and West-Puckett argue, we force queer bodies and experiences to "fail" by engaging them in a discourse that presupposes their inability to "pass," to occupy a body or performance in a system always already looking for them to fail. This discourse also assumes that the *intended* outcome is a heteronormative notion of gender or gender(ed) performance. They write,

> Rather, the body becomes a complex and nuanced site of social and cultural negotiation that does not *mean* for a moment and then ceases to mean, or rather, does not *mean* a clear and determined meaning and then continues to mean that thing across times and contexts. . . . By disrupting the ubiquitous binary of male/female, masculine/feminine, trans (and intersex) bodies call forth states of being that are neither and both. Trans bodies may intend states of being that succeed or fail in various contexts—or partially succeed or partially fail, as even that binary is ultimately flawed. These bodies tend to value *intention over outcome*.

Ultimately, Banks and West-Puckett argue that "part of what makes queer objects queer . . . is that they disrupt directionality, calling into question the paths that lead toward them, as well as away from them."

In the context of this collection, we might ask, how does a queer rhetoric of intentionality shape methods of data collection or method- ologies for understanding research purposes and contexts? For one, a queer rhetoric of intentionality would challenge the very foundation upon which the WPA Outcomes Statement is based; it would challenge the veracity and the validity of any rubric based on abstract and disem- bodied outcomes; and it might ask, both pedagogically and method- ologically, what is the point of studying (evaluating, obsessing over) the products students create? When we consider how much writing studies research—the current micro-industry developing around threshold concepts and transfer, for example—is dependent on very particular notions of outcomes and seemingly observable data, any alternative rhetoric or methodology for studying writing that privileges intention over outcome would help us see our research from multiple and more nuanced positions. It might also help us think differently about what we mean by "outcomes" and "rubrics" (Caswell and West-Puckett, this col- lection). In the context of this collection, we also see how rhetorics of intentionality can be used to reframe digital tools (Faris, this collection) and to challenge both hetero- and homonormative assumptions about sexuality, digital spaces, and "hook-up" culture.

2. Rhetorics of Failure

Banks and West-Puckett (2015) also demonstrate, though obliquely, how a queer rhetoric of failure (Ahmed 2006; Halberstam 2011) could impact methods and methodologies in writing studies. In their CCCC talk, they focused primarily on the "C's the Day" game that has been part of welcoming newcomers to the conference over the last several years. In particular, they spoke at length about one of the prizes for "win- ning" the game, a small, hand-made artifact that came to be known as Sparklepony. While the story is too long to repeat here (deWinter and Vie 2014), part of what fascinated Banks and West-Puckett was the "fail- ure" of the Sparklepony object as a piece of remix culture. They note that, as with the rhetoric of outcome (rather than intention), the field typically articulates remix in terms of success and failure, praising the student artifacts that "get it," that do something interesting and innova- tive with the artifacts they remix and ignoring in its studies examples of remix "failure," which leaves researchers to ask the question, what do we do with the failures? Sparklepony, they note, is only momentarily useful or interesting as a *blazon* at the conference; it means little outside that context. In fact, as they note, several academic blogs have mocked and poked fun at writing studies for its embrace of or interest in this "silly object" (Berlant 2009). Using Sparklepony and building on Halberstam (2011) in particular, Banks and West-Puckett question writing studies' neoliberal obsession with success and ponder what a queer rhetoric of failure might mean for our discipline.

Failure? What role can *failure* have in research, in which the goal is the discovery of truth or knowledge? To some extent, we might argue that Cheryl Glenn's (1995) now-classic study of Aspasia represents a rhetoric or methodology of failure. By looking at Aspasia's *absences* in the rhetorical canon, which grew out of Glenn's inability to find primary source materials connected to Aspasia, Glenn discovers a powerful way of understanding Aspasia's place and impact as an important rhetorical figure in ancient Greece. Of course, that isn't quite the same failure Banks and West-Puckett are engaging with. As Jack Halberstam (2011) explains, through a discussion of Barbara Ehrenreich's *Bright-Sided*, "While capitalism produces some people's success through other people's failure, the ideology of positive thinking insists that success depends only upon working hard and failure is always of your own doing" (3). Failure, Halberstam writes, might represent "knowledge from below" (11), a chance to eschew "being taken seriously" in order "to be frivolous, promiscuous, and irrelevant" (6). These are adjectives and experiences often linked to queer lives. And these are adjectives and experiences that seem to fly in the face of research and scholarship. Queerness-as-failure offers promise in those spaces where we make "a detour around the usual markers of accomplishment and satisfaction" (186), where we make use of promiscuous methods. Some researchers in this collection have begun to make use of failure-oriented methodologies as ways of interrogating a host of important discourses, like the medical rhetorics around in/fertility (Novotny), or even what it means to engage language queerly as part of designing research projects (Glasby; Waite). Still others (Caswell and West-Puckett) engage failure more significantly as a frame for rethinking writing assessment methodologies. After all, any theory of writing assessment that does not engage *failure* is a theory at best only half conceived. In the more quantitative/mixed-methods areas of our research (Patterson), what might we do with the "long tails" of our data? Rather than construct these elements as "outliers," what if we embraced those moments of research failure? What might seeing the center of our data through its outliers do for helping us rethink what we are (really) searching for—and what we think we've found?

3. Rhetorics of Forgetting

It's hard to imagine a practice more antithetical to historiography—or perhaps any research practice—than forgetting. So many scholars in writing studies have spent countless hours in archives, pouring over original documents, piecing together the histories of our field. Who would suggest we forget these things? While Banks and West-Puckett (2015) do not encourage us to "forget" anything in particular, they do demonstrate how "strategic forgetting" has been an important queer rhetorical practice and why we might want to engage such a practice more carefully and directly. They invite us to re/consider Jason Palmeri's (2012) *Remixing Composition* as a project that "demonstrates how orality and image have always been part of writing and writing studies" despite any number of essays in the field that tend to operate under the assumption that multimodality and remix are twenty-first-century inventions. Palmeri asks readers to ponder why writing studies has forgotten the richness of its multimodal history, even as his text demonstrates several reasons, not least of which is that so much of the multimodal work has happened at the pedagogical or classroom level or in textbooks rather than at the level of research. To extend Banks and West-Puckett's argument, we contend that rhetorics of forgetting tend to function in strategic ways and offer at least two ways of engaging with research. One method, with which we're quite familiar, is to mine the archives for lost stories, lost composers, lost teachers, and to tell their stories, to welcome these prodigal figures back into our rhetorical canon and demonstrate the richness they add to it. Another method, similar to Palmeri's history, might be to ask why certain elements of our disciplinary past have been forgotten: with Jim Ridolfo and Dànielle Nicole deVoss's notion of "rhetorical velocity" (Ridolfo and deVoss 2009) in mind, we might ask why certain tropes, conceits, or values picked up steam in writing studies and came to occupy a central place in our journals and books and why others have been (strategically) forgotten? How has forgetting those things been advantageous to certain researchers, composers, institutions? Why? What is it about these shameful figures that has made us forget?

In *Feeling Backward: Loss and the Politics of Queer History*, Heather Love (2009) demonstrates why queer scholars, or historians who seek to queer historiography, might want to engage that second type of forgetting project. Love notes that while "many queer critics take exception to the idea of a linear, triumphalist view of history, we are in practice deeply committed to the notion of progress; despite our reservations, we just cannot stop dreaming of a better life for queer people" (3). We recognize that writing studies can also find itself overly committed to triumphalist stories that might eventually save those sad women from the basement. Love encourages queer scholars in particular to pay attention to the "texts or figures that refuse to be redeemed" because they may serve to "disrupt not only the progress narrative of queer history but also our sense of queer identity in the present" (8–9). Queers are not the only bodies whose histories involve a long "association with failure, impossibility, and loss" (21). The pressure to redeem the past or to tell only stories that "rescue" forgotten figures threatens the present by offering it dangerously incomplete and inadequate stories of the past. In this collection, Jean Bessette encourages us to ask, "When we look for queerness in the archive, what exactly are we seeking?" Put more broadly, we might pose the following methodological questions for writing studies: When we look for X, what are we strategically forgetting in order to keep X in focus? How could we acknowledge that tension in our work? Why might we need to forget X in order to discovery Y?

EMBODYING IN(QUEER)Y

These particular queer rhetorics—of intentionality, failure, and forgetting—are, of course, just a starting place for how we might engage queer rhetorics at the level of methodology, but each demonstrates how the embodied experiences and practices of queer lives have shaped theoretical questions that challenge the normative dimensions of our discipline. We're excited to showcase in this collection a set of essays by emerging and early-career queer scholars whose engagement with writing studies requires them to think differently about the methods and methodologies they were taught in graduate school. The authors in this collection make no claims that would suggest traditional methods of data collection are inherently flawed, nor do they suggest that only queer theories or queer rhetorics should dictate research agendas in writing studies. The essays in this collection do, however, encourage writing studies researchers to pay careful attention to the ways queer rhetorics and experiences have shaped our in(queer)y practices and our ways of engaging our discipline.

This collection begins by asking what *queer* might mean to researchers and whether or not it's possible to write (or study writing) from a queer/ed perspective. Hillery Glasby's "Making It Queer, Not Clear: Embracing Ambivalence and Failure as Queer Methodologies" picks up on both rhetorics of failure, briefly described above, and queer theories of language in order to posit important questions about how researchers construct their projects and their (embodied) relationships to those projects. Rather than remain yoked to notions of order, structure, and coherence, "what if composition functioned as a *dis*ordering agent?" (25). Similarly, Stacey Waite disrupts genre conventions in order to provide a "failing, impossible, contradictory" (43–48) list for queer writers. "How (and Why) to Write Queer" builds on past queer manifesto writing (Rhodes 2004) in order to explore the (dis)connections between queer writing practices and queer research practices. Perhaps one of the most challenging ways of posing the question about what it means to be/act/write/research as queer is to ask how one might queer quantitative inquiry. G Patterson's "Queering and Transing Quantitative Research" takes up that challenge by exploring some of the more numbers-oriented research methods in our field and unpacking some key questions around identifying and disidentifying data, designing surveys, and queering participant recruitment procedures.

After exploring definitions of queer and rethinking what it might mean to queer *writing* itself, two of our writers explore fairly traditional research topics and methodologies in writing studies (intercultural communication and historiography) in order to demonstrate why we might want more queer approaches to be part of the mix. In "REDRES[ing] *Rhetorica*: A Methodological Proposal for Queering Cross-Cultural Rhetorical Studies," Chanon Adsanatham highlights points of connectivity between queer theory and comparative rhetoric, particularly in their commitments to nonnormative thinking and interventions into the exclusion of the Other. He draws on both fields to develop a cross-cultural heuristic he calls REDRES: recontemplating epistemology and knowledge across cultures; destabilizing what's normative and privileged; respecting and critically reevaluating historicity; embodying the ethics of hope and care; surfing incongruities as productive disruption. Through this heuristic, Adsanatham addresses the Eurocentric biases that often infiltrate rhetorical studies, offering an important contribution to queer rhetorical studies. Adsanatham grounds his theory in a case study of transnational Buddhist bodhisattva Kuanyin, demonstrating how past analyses of this figure have unfolded via normative lenses. Jean Bessette turns her attention toward the archives and our diverse histories in "'Love in a Hall of Mirrors': Queer Historiography and the Unsettling In-Between" in order to explore questions of identity and what "counts" for researchers. Her contribution begins by exploring important binaries—silence and speech, evidence and ephemera, truth and fiction—in order to argue for what she calls a "more spectral . . . understanding of history writing" (97). What are the stories our archives tell us when we disrupt some of these binaries? And what, to borrow from Love (2009), do our stories forget?

Stories and storytelling, of course, have been central to much of writing studies, not just our histories. From case studies and ethnographies to teacher action research, from pedagogical inquiry to the significance they play in our administrative theory and scholarship, stories are a major part of how we communicate our experience and research. In "In/Fertility as Counter/Story: Assembling a Queer Counterstory Methodology for Bodies of Health and Sexuality," Maria Novotny explores her own experiences with in/fertility, as well as those of other women and couples, in order to construct a counterstory through "queer assemblage" methods. This project, Novotny notes, can be useful to writing studies researchers but also to professionals in other spaces, such as medical clinics and hospitals. Similarly, Michael Faris explores the limits of storytelling as part of his autoethnographic project "Queering Networked Writing: A Sensory Autoethnography of Desire and Sensation on Grindr." Faris argues that writing studies has taken up sexuality in identitarian and discursive ways, largely ignoring sex acts and sensuality (and by extension other embodied, if messy, experiences). Faris's autoethnographic approach to studying his own activity on the digital app Grindr offers innovative methods for tracing desire and affect. In doing so, this contribution stands as a rare example of queer scholarship in writing studies that focuses on sex, not simply the abstract sexuality. The implications of Faris's study are wide reaching, complicating the notion that rhetoric is preceded by identification. Faris asks whether rhetorical interactions might be based on sensuality and desire rather than identity, particularly in digital environments. Ultimately, Faris disrupts normative epistemological attachments by attending to sensory and affective ways of knowing and connecting. In "Queer/ing Composition, the Digital Archives of Literacy Narratives, and Ways of Knowing," Deborah Kuzawa turns to the stories of the DALN to demonstrate how a queer methodology can be applied to contexts apart from those having to do with sexuality or gender. Kuzawa illustrates how queer methodologies and methods can help illuminate the ways systems of power operate in relation to literacy and knowledge. Kuzawa argues that through the queer method of "surfing binaries," the DALN resists the kind of binaristic thinking common to archives, troubling the discourses of academic/personal, restriction/openness, and expert/novice. The DALN's openness, which resists clear-cut definition of what counts as literacy, stands as a queer way of making meaning, allowing those who contribute to the archive to offer their own definitions of what counts as literacy. Through this analysis of the DALN, Kuzawa argues that a queer lens can help make visible how archives and other repositories of knowledge function as living systems that exist in a constant state of flux.

This collection ends on a perhaps unexpected but certainly queer note: validating failure. In particular, Nicole Caswell and Stephanie West-Puckett rely on queer notions of failure in order to sketch out a methodology for conducting and engaging with writing assessment. In "Assessment Killjoys: Queering the Return for a Writing Studies Worldmaking Methodology," Caswell and West-Puckett encourage us "to see good writing less as a monolithic set of traits and more as a dynamic assemblage of cultural values, one that resists hegemonic notions of knowing, doing, being, and expressing." Their chapter highlights a host of failure-oriented practices built on a queer validity inquiry (QVI) methodology in order to show writing studies the significant and exciting possibilities that exist on the other side of success. In as much as writing assessment can seem like an odd place to encourage or look for failure, so too can professional writing contexts seem antithetical to the work we're meant to be doing. However, Caroline Dadas and Matthew Cox explore just that in their chapter, "On Queering Professional Writing." While scholars such as Angela Haas (2012) have argued for increased attention to cultural rhetorics within professional writing, Dadas and Cox argue that the field has not given much attention to queer contexts or methodological frames. Based on an analysis of journal articles and conference presentations published in the last five years, Dadas and Cox contend that queer methodologies are not well represented in the field. They then argue that queer methodologies can enhance professional writing studies by calling attention to normative binaries often implied in professional writing contexts, such as success/failure. Increased use of queer frames for professional writing work can counter the hypernormativity or hypernormativizing rhetorics we often see at play in the field.

CONCLUSION: HOW TO USE THIS BOOK

It may seem strange, given the antinormative drive that animates so much of queer work, and we hope this collection, to end this introduction by offering a user's guide or even to suggest one particular method for how best to use this book. But this isn't that sort of "how-to." This how-to is also a *when-to*, a *where-to*, as well as a *what-if* and a *why-bother-to*. Those of us who have pulled this collection together hope the projects ignite in readers an awareness that what may seem like boundaries and limitations to research are simply the starting points for a researcher's most interesting projects, questions, and entanglements. Now that the editors of this collection teach courses in research methods, we see in our own undergraduate and graduate students how easy it is for beginning researchers to find a method of data collection that feels comfortable, or one that seems to have clear boundaries, and then try to shove their projects into it. It's not all that different from the first-year writer who learned forms (e.g., compare and contrast, classification and division) and then talks about their projects based on those forms rather than their topics, interests, or inquiry questions. For some, this way of structuring knowledge making can feel comfortable and assuring; amidst the chaos of what might be, at least we know we're doing a "case study," even if we're not sure why or what that really means.

This collection of essays, whose authors at times make use of familiar forms or concepts like autoethnography, narrative/story, writing assessment, case study, and surveys, is not designed or arranged by such categories. Nor does it lend itself to being read cover to cover. The authors use overlapping theories in different ways, and they explore a number of different types of research and research contexts to do so. As such, we envision this collection as one that supplements any number of the excellent methods collections in the field, including Katrina Powell and Pamela Takayoshi's *Practicing Research in Writing Studies: Reflexive and Ethically Responsible Research* (Powell and Takayoshi 2012) and Lee Nickoson and Mary P. Sheridan's *Writing Studies Research in Practice: Methods and Methodologies* (Nickoson and Sheridan 2012), as well as more thematically focused texts like Jacqueline Jones Royster and Gesa Kirsch's *Feminist Rhetorical Practices: New Horizons for Rhetoric, Composition, and Literacy Studies* (Royster and Kirsch 2012) and Eileen Schell and K. J. Rawson's *Rhetorica in Motion: Feminist Rhetorical Methods and Methodologies* (Schell and Rawson 2010). Texts like these, as well as John Creswell's general overview of research methods, *Research Design: Qualitative, Quantitative, and Mixed-Methods Approaches* (Creswell 2013), provide important contexts for research, contexts the contributions from this collect help unpack, disrupt, or extend. We encourage readers to supplement the more traditional texts with the essays from this collection, as well as essays and texts that address some critical absences from our own collection, texts like Linda T. Smith's *Decolonizing Methodologies: Research and Indigenous Peoples* (Smith 2012), Chela Sandoval's *Methodology of the Oppressed* (Sandoval 2000), and Margaret Kovach's *Indigenous Methodologies: Characteristics, Conversations, and Contexts* (Kovach 2010).

In mentioning these texts, we also want to encourage readers to move the work of this collection forward. Earlier, we acknowledged the long history of Western thought that produced queer theory, as well as our most common definitions of rhetoric, and how much our own collection builds on that work. We recognize that this somewhat singular history creates a limitation to our collection; we hope writing studies recognizes this limitation as well and is encouraging more diverse scholars and scholarship. We believe our collection works well to encourage more diverse projects in writing studies, and we hope the readers of this collection will take up the work that was not yet available in writing studies when we solicited manuscripts for this collection. We know that, moving forward, this sort of complex and exciting research will come to define writing studies as one of the more progressive disciplines in the academy.

REFERENCES

Ahmed, Sara. 2006. *Queer Phenomenology: Orientations, Objects, Others.* Durham, NC: Duke University Press. https://doi.org/10.1215/9780822388074.

Alexander, Jonathan. 2008. *Literacy, Sexuality, Pedagogy: Theory and Practice for Composition Studies.* Logan: Utah State University Press. https://doi.org/10.2307/j.ctt4cgqkw.

Alexander, Jonathan, and David Wallace. 2009. "The Queer Turn in Composition Studies." *College Composition and Communication* 61 (1): W300–W320.

Baca, Damien. 2008. *Mestiz@ Scripts, Digital Migrations, and the Territories of Writing.* New York: Palgrave Macmillan. https://doi.org/10.1057/9780230612570.

Banks, William P., and Stephanie West-Puckett. 2015. "Against Re/Production: Trans Theory, Digital Objects, and a Queer Paradigm For Remix." *Conference on College Composition and Communication,* March 20. Tampa, FL.

Bergman, David, ed. 1993. *Camp Grounds: Style And Homosexuality.* Amherst: University of Massachusetts Press.

Berlant, Lauren. 2009. *The Queen of America Goes to Washington City: Essays on Sex and Citizenship.* Durham, NC: Duke University Press.

Bitzer, Lloyd. 1968. "The Rhetorical Situation." *Philosophy & Rhetoric* 1:1–14.

Bornstein, Kate. 2013. *A Queer and Present Danger: The True Story of a Nice Jewish Boy Who Joins the Church of Scientology, and Leaves Twelve Years Later to Become the Lovely Lady She Is Today.* Boston, MA: Beacon.

Butler, Judith. 1993. *Bodies That Matter: On the Discursive Limits of Sex.* New York: Routledge.

Chauncey, George. 1995. *Gay New York: Gender, Urban Culture, and the Making of the Gay Male World, 1890–1940.* New York: Basic Books.

Cleto, Fabio, ed. 1999. *Camp: Queer Aesthetics and the Performing Subject, A Reader.* Ann Arbor: University Of Michigan Press.

Cohen, Cathy. 1997. "Punks, Bulldaggers, and Welfare Queens: The Radical Potential of Queer Politics." *GLQ: A Journal of Lesbian and Gay Studies* 3 (4): 437–65. https://doi.org/10.1215/10642684-3-4-437.

Creswell, John. 2013. *Research Design: Qualitative, Quantitative, and Mixed-Methods Approaches.* 4th ed. Thousand Oaks, CA: SAGE.

Crowley, Mart. 2008. *The Boys in the Band: 40th Anniversary Edition.* New York: Alyson Books.

Dadas, Caroline. 2016. "Messy Methods: Queer Methodological Approaches to Researching Social Media." *Computers and Composition* 40 (1): 60–72. https://doi.org/10.1016/j.compcom.2016.03.007.

Driskill, Qwo-Li. 2016. *Asegi Stories: Cherokee Queer and Two-Spirit Memory.* Tucson: University of Arizona Press.

Driskill, Qwo-Li, Chris Finley, Brian Joseph Gilley, and Laura Scott Morgensen. 2011. *Queer Indigenous Studies: Critical Interventions in Theory, Politics and Literature.* Tucson: University of Arizona Press.

Foucault, Michel. 1988. "Power and Sex." In *Politics, Philosophy, Culture: Interview and Other Writings, 1977–84.* Translated by David J. Parent. Edited by Lawrence D. Kristzman, 110–24. New York: Routledge.

Glenn, Cheryl. 1995. "Remapping Rhetorical Territory." *Rhetoric Review* 13 (2): 287–303.

Gonçalves, Zan. 2006. *Sexuality and the Politics of Ethos in the Writing Classroom.* Carbondale: Southern Illinois University Press.

Haas, Angela. 2012. "Race, Rhetoric, and Technology: A Case Study of Decolonial Technical Communication Theory, Methodology, and Pedagogy." *Journal of Business and Technical Communication* 26 (3): 277–310. https://doi.org/10.1177/1050651912439539.

Halberstam, Jack. 2011. *The Queer Art of Failure.* Durham, NC: Duke University Press. https://doi.org/10.1215/9780822394358.

Harding, Sandra. 1987. "Introduction: Is There a Feminist Method?" In *Feminism and Methodology,* edited by Sandra Harding, 1–14. Bloomington: Indiana University Press.

Jagose, Annamarie. 1996. *Queer Theory: An Introduction.* New York: New York University Press.

Kirsch, Gesa. E. 2012. "Forward: New Methodological Challenges for Writing Studies." In *Writing Studies Research in Practice: Methods and Methodologies,* edited by Lee Nickoson and Mary P. Sheridan, xi–xvi. Carbondale: Southern Illinois University Press.

Kirsch, Gesa, and Patricia A. Sullivan. 1992. *Methods and Methodology in Composition Research.* Carbondale: Southern Illinois University Press.

Knoblauch, C. H. 1985. "Modern Rhetorical Theory and Its Future Directions." In *Perspectives on Research and Scholarship in Composition,* edited by Ben W. McClellan and Timothy R. Donovan, 26–44. New York: MLA.

Kovach, Margaret. 2010. *Indigenous Methodologies: Characteristics, Conversations, and Contexts.* Toronto: University of Toronto Press.

Law, John. 2004. *After Method: Mess in Social Science Research.* New York: Routledge.

Love, Heather. 2009. *Feeling Backwards: Loss and the Politics of Queer History.* Cambridge, MA: Harvard University Press.

Malinowitz, Harriet. 1995. *Textual Orientations: Lesbian and Gay Students and the Making of Discourse Communities.* Portsmouth, NH: Heinemann-Boynton/Cook.

Marinara, Martha, Jonathan Alexander, William P. Banks, and Samantha Blackman. 2009. "Cruising Composition Texts: Negotiating Sexual Difference in First-Year Readers." *College Composition and Communication* 61 (2): 269–96.

Meyers, Moe, ed. 1994. *The Politics and Poetics of Camp.* New York: Routledge.

Morgensen, Scott Lauria. 2011. "Unsettling Queer Politics: Whitman Non-Natives Learn from Two-Spirit Organizing?" In *Queer Indigenous Studies: Critical Interventions in Theory, Politics and Literature,* edited by Qwo-li Driskill, Chris Finley, Brian Joseph Gilley, and Scott Lauria Morgensen, 132–51. Tucson: University of Arizona Press

Muñoz, José Esteban. 1994. *Disidentifications: Queers of Color and the Performance of Politics.* Minneapolis: University of Minnesota Press.

Muñoz, José Esteban. 2011. *Cruising Utopia: The Then and There of Queer Futurity.* New York: New York University Press.

Nickoson, Lee, and Mary P. Sheridan, eds. 2012. *Writing Studies Research in Practice: Methods and Methodologies.* Carbondale: Southern Illinois University Press.

Palmeri, Jason. 2012. *Remixing Composition: A History of Multimodal Writing Pedagogy.* Carbondale: Southern Illinois University Press.

Powell, Katrina, and Pamela Takayoshi, eds. 2012. *Practicing Researching Writing Studies: Reflexive and Ethically Responsible Research.* New York: Hampton.

Ratcliffe, Krista. 2003. "The Current State of Composition Scholar/Teachers: Is Rhetoric Gone or Just Hiding Out?" *enculturation* 5(1). http://enculturation.net/5_1/ratcliffe .html.

Ridolfo, Jim, and Dànielle Nicole DeVoss. 2009. "Composing for Recomposition: Rhetorical Velocity and Delivery." *Kairos: A Journal of Rhetoric, Technology, and Pedagogy* 13 (2). http://kairos.technorhetoric.net/13.2/topoi/ridolfo_devoss/.

Rhodes, Jacqueline. 2004. "Homo Origo: The Queertext Manifesto." *Computers and Composition* 21 (3): 385–88. https://doi.org/10.1016/j.compcom.2004.05.001.

Royster, Jacqueline Jones, and Gesa Kirsch. 2012. *Feminist Rhetorical Practices: New Horizons for Rhetoric, Composition, and Literacy Studies.* Carbondale: Southern Illinois University Press.

Salamon, Gayle. 2011. *Assuming a Body: Transgender and Rhetorics of Materiality.* New York: Columbia University Press.

Sandoval, Chela. 2000. *Methodology of the Oppressed.* Minneapolis: University of Minnesota Press.

Schell, Eileen, and K. J. Rawson. 2010. *Rhetorica in Motion: Feminist Rhetorical Methods and Methodologies.* Pittsburgh, PA: University of Pittsburgh Press. https://doi.org/10.2307/j.ctt5vkff8.

Smith, Andrea. 2011. "Queer Theory and Native Studies: The Heteronormativity of Settler Colonialism." In *Queer Indigenous Studies: Critical Interventions in Theory, Politics and Literature,* edited by Qwo-li Driskill, Chris Finley, Brian Joseph Gilley, and Scott Lauria Morgensen, 43–65. Tucson: University of Arizona Press.

Smith, Linda T. 2012. *Decolonizing Methodologies: Research and Indigenous Peoples.* London: Zed Books.

deWinter, Jennifer, and Stephanie Vie. 2015. "Sparklegate: Gamification, Academic Gravitas, and the Infantalization of Play." *Kairos: A Journal of Rhetoric, Technology, and Pedagogy* 20 (1). http://kairos.technorhetoric.net/20.1/topoi/dewinter-vie/.

2

MAKING IT QUEER, NOT CLEAR
Embracing Ambivalence and Failure as Queer Methodologies

Hillery Glasby

As a queer rhetor, I often feel as though my identity is limited on the academic page. When I compose zines and multimodal/digital texts, and invoke narrative and queer rhetorics, I come through in the text in ways I cannot on standard, MLA-formatted 8.5 × 11 sheets of paper (whether tangible or digital). My thoughts—and the meaning I make—are often contained by these parameters. Similarly, my thinking is somewhat restricted when I am asked to take a firm stance; I prefer to take my time, write through thorny issues and play around in the messy stuff. That's where my best writing comes from. It's the kind of work that speaks not only to the kind of rhetor and thinker I am but also to my experiences as a queer femme. I've engaged and explored my own ambivalence through/with/in numerous writing tasks regarding my feelings about growing up playing with Barbie dolls; getting "married" despite my queer politics; and using silence to enact (usually very loudly) queer activism on the National Day of Silence. Exploring contradictions and tension helps me understand why it isn't always easy to come to a conclusion, and it helps me to feel a little more comfortable being uncomfortable. Mostly, I like to use my writing to fuck shit up. And I like to teach my writing students how to use some of the same queer rhetorical strategies in their writing. Witnessing them experience, for themselves, where the *compulsion to fuck shit up* comes from is exciting and, at times, transformative.

In the following chapter, I consider the potential of ambivalence and failure as two queer methodologies toward (rhetorical) resistance writing. I argue for ambivalence as a generative site for meaning making, particularly for queer and other marginalized subjects. Furthermore, I consider some practical applications for writers who want to resist and

DOI: 10.7330/9781607328186.c002

upset rigid academic conventions vis-à-vis queer failure. Using a multi-modal course project I assign as an illustration, I consider how these two queer methodologies might trouble the (field's) valorization of normativity, firm stances, and conventional notions of ethos. The project shows us what these methodologies might look like in practice, moving student-writers toward a more critical understanding of normative conventions as well as ways to re/mis/appropriate those to better represent their experiences and ethos—a failure-affirming methodology. And in asking them to write back/to/through, they learn how to engage uncertainty and conflictedness—an ambivalence-affirming methodology. The chapter is guided by the following questions: What happens when writing teachers encourage student-writers, particularly those who are LGBTQ or otherwise marginalized, to resist and refuse the compulsion to compose coherent, cohesive, and polished products (Alexander and Rhodes 2011)? What if, instead, we asked writers to use methodologies that muddle or reposition the argument(s) at hand? In other words, what if composition functioned as a *dis*ordering agent (McRuer 2006)?

METHODOLOGIES: AMBIVALENCE AND FAILURE

Most academic writing tasks across the disciplines ask writers to take a stand, to clearly articulate a position in order to persuade their audiences, then using logic and sound evidence, develop and execute a clear argument, what Gary Olsen (1999) calls "the rhetoric of assertion" (9). Logic, linearity, clarity, and coherence are typically considered strengths—even mandatory—in academic writing; as a result, polished products become "fetishized" in the writing classroom and mastery becomes the objective (McRuer 2006; Olsen 1999). Finished, "clean" drafts are intended to conceal and erase the messy processes behind themselves. But, as Robert McRuer (2006) points out, aren't those messy processes what writing and composition are about in the first place, rather than simply reducing writing to a tidy endpoint?

Numerous scholars have pointed to the ways in which composition reiterates these goals and practices, which tends to represent a small, exclusive section of writers—mostly white hetero men of the West (Anzaldúa 2015; Harding 1998). So what happens, then, when an unruly, marginalized subject(ivity) is compelled to write, as Harriet Malinowitz (1995) and David Wallace (2011) have encouraged? What tone and tenor do these voices invoke? For marginalized writers, nonassertive modes like illogic, love, ambivalence, and failure can be more organic and generative strategies. The academic research-based essay, a genre that often upholds tightly controlled academic conventions, has little room for these nonnormative strategies, however. The narrow, and often binarized, spaces writers are typically permitted to write from and within serve as a way to regulate and normalize not only texts but also persons and their identities. Academic writing can feel rigid, exclusionary, and uninspiring for authors who write from disenfranchised subject positions, particularly indigenous peoples, those of color, and lesbian, gay, bisexual, trans, queer (LGBTQ) individuals. Fringe subjectivities, those marked by difference, already always lack credibility in dominant discourse, which prizes normativity and male heterowhiteness. Nonstandard language use, alternative ways of knowing, different types of evidence, and unconventional rhetorical appeals can further complicate these authors' ethos. But marginal subjectivities offer unique insight because of the knowledge gained through lived experience. Knowledge made through alternate routes is just one reason queer methodologies are—dare I say—more appropriate for queer subjects and those doing queer work: queer methodologies allow for alternative identities, experiences, and rhetorical moves.

Both these queer methodologies—ambivalence and failure—grow out of queer theoretical applications and queer rhetorical practices and therefore resist and challenge the regulation and normativity upheld within and through composition studies and the academy at large. Jonathan Alexander and Jackie Rhodes (2011) push back against the field's reliance upon and perpetuation of the status quo. They explain, "We *do* feel a status quo at work in our field—the status quo of the *composed* text, of the drive toward polished writing, of using even the messy genres of digitally enabled communication for the generation of finished texts" (Alexander and Rhodes 2011, 194). Troubling the field means troubling its histories, values and practices. Numerous scholars have drawn connections between the control exerted over students in the classroom/field and in the heteronormative academy. For instance, in *Crip Theory*, McRuer (2006) calls the contemporary neoliberal university "literally disciplining," focused on efficiency, with a "slick, corporate feel" (166). He draws literal and metaphorical connections between the normalizing practices of writing instruction and the dictionary definition of *composition*, "a process that reduces difference, forms many ingredients into one substance, or even calms, settles, or frees from agitation" (147).

Composition and *composure*, after all, share the same root: *composure* means "being calm or in control"; *composition* is defined as "the act of pulling things together" in the New Oxford American Dictionary.

But what does that imply for subjects? In response, Alexander (2008) questions, "How does one compose oneself or become composed as a 'straight' person?" (106). What does the discipline require when it asks writers to "pull themselves together"? Drawing from Michel Foucault's work in *Discipline and Punish*, Alexander and Rhodes (2011) argue such a request "disciplines it [the subject] into a docile body" (189). By this logic, docile bodies are "possible" subjects, while noncompliant bodies are "impossible" subjects, thus their argument that queer, because of its deviation from the status quo, is an impossible subject (the school subject) and "subject" (the queer student subject) for composition. In a queer move, McRuer (2006) troubles the very definition of our field and its reinforcement of "safe, contained, composed" (168) authors and texts and asks, "What would happen if, true to our experiences in and out of the classroom, we continually attempted to reconceive *composing as that which produced agitation*—to reconceive it, paradoxically, as what it is? In what ways might that agitation be generative?" (148; my emphasis). Feminist and queer methodologies enable and promote the kinds of agitation McRuer (2006) speaks of, and in doing so, they open up and expand rhetoric for nonnormative subjects, which allows the subjects to push back against mainstream ideologies, epistemologies, and composing practices.

AMBIVALENCE: EXPLORING, EMBRACING, AND WRITING FROM UNCERTAINTY

Like the subversion and resistance from which queer rhetorical strategies draw their strength, ambivalence both constitutes and unsettles writerly subjects, their contexts, and (queer) subjectivities and ethos. As scholars like Gloria Anzaldúa (2015), Geneva Smitherman (1973), and Alexander and Rhodes (2012a) have discussed *and* demonstrated in their texts, enacting the very rhetorical moves mainstream discourse discourages can be powerful reclamation projects. And as feminist, queer, postcolonial, and transnational scholars have demonstrated, marginalized writers access incredible possibilities when they engage and create texts that write *back* to the forces that mark, misrepresent, and/or control them (Bhabha 1985; Micciche 2014; Trinh 2010). Writing *against* and writing *through* can be equally provocative and meaningful methods. Generally a marker of distress, ambivalence is normally understood as something to be avoided rather than desired. Numerous postcolonial and transnational scholars (Aciman 1999; Hoffman 1999; Marciniak 2006; Simic 1999; Trinh 2010) tell stories that situate ambivalence as a side effect, or a symptom, rather than a process or methodology. I see enormous potential in invoking ambivalence as a methodology because it reduces, or altogether negates, the desire for coherence and polished texts.

To gain a better sense of how ambivalence might function in terms of writing methodologies, I turn to "Reading Lauren Berlant Writing" by Gregory Seigworth (2012). He discusses the metaphorical excess of Berlant's writing, particularly her sentence structure. In her long-winded, tangential sentences, there is much to be learned from the "affective/sensorial natures of incoherence and ambivalence" (351). In other words, we ought to pay attention to the unfolding messiness rather than hesitate to approach. He explains how, for Berlant, ambivalence represents "a damp, tangled clot of incoherences. An unresolvable clog of curly ambivalences. Surplusage" (347). *Tangled, clot, clog, curly*: nonlinear, messy, overlapping, blurred boundaries of where something begins and another ends. Here, ambivalence draws its energy from a state of being unresolved, enmeshed, disoriented. Though writing outside a queer rhetorical framework, Robert Yagelski (1999) defines ambivalence in similar terms as "a troubling space between doubt and committed action . . . a space of both possibility and paralysis" (32). These authors position ambivalence as something at once generative and degenerative. Possibility is understood as emergence, growth, and forward movement, whereas paralysis might mean retreat, stalling, or stalemate. From a traditional writing studies methodological standpoint, possibility is what the field leans toward; queer writing studies method-ologies take us closer to those dark, stagnant places we tend to avoid or understand as nonproductive even though those places can offer insight and meaning through mess and dis-ease.

Rather than being perceived as a state that (further) diminishes authority, ambivalence—as a rhetorical move—can author-ize the marginalized subject vis-à-vis negotiation of their identities and lived experience. Here, both writer and reader can make meaning or become unsettled by bearing witness to the struggle to pull things together. This is the heteroglossic knowledge that the oppressed, rather than the oppressor, hold. Writing back, according to Homi Bhabha (1985), is made possible by the experience of multiple and contesting epistemolo-gies. He explains,

> Hybridity is the revaluation of the assumptions of colonial identity through the repetition of discriminatory identity effects. It displays the necessary deformations and displacement of all sites of discrimination and domination. It unsettles the mimetic or narcissistic demands of colonial

power but reimplicates its identifications *in strategies of subversion that turn the gaze of the discriminated back upon the eye of power.* (154; my emphasis)

Therefore, the goal of ambivalence-driven writing is simultaneously directed both outwardly (at the oppressor) and inwardly (at the oppressed): write yourself so that Others might know the Self. This can be critical self-care work since difference becomes internalized over time. For Anzaldúa (2015), writing back functions to "reconcile this other within us" (167). Facing and deepening difference can take the nonnormative writer to a provocative place, a place of resistance (writing *back*), a place of failure and refusal (writing *against*), and a place of ambivalence (writing *through*).

FAILURE: UNSETTLING AND DISRUPTING ACADEMIC WRITING CONVENTIONS

Inviting writers to engage rather than settle ambivalence, to open up rather than to close, could be understood as a sort of failure—a failure to follow traditional academic conventions. "The queer art of failure," as Jack Halberstam (1998) explains, "turns on the impossible, the improbable, the unlikely, and the unremarkable. It quietly loses, and in losing it imagines other goals for life, for love, for art, and for being. Failure can be counted within that set of oppositional tools that James C. Scott called 'the weapons of the weak'" (88). It is this description of failure I connect with my research, which, admittedly, leans toward the more positive connotations of failure Halberstam discusses. Although the deployment of failure in this chapter might be understood as more generative and positive than Halberstam or Lee Edelman (2004) intend (since generation and positivity imply production and futurity), my understanding of failure certainly welcomes and fosters those "darker territories of failure associated with futility, sterility, emptiness, loss, negative affect in general, and modes of unbecoming" (Halberstam 1998, 23). When it draws on both Halberstam's (1998) work with failure and Edelman's (2004) work with the death drive, queer rhetorics seeks to destroy notions of a secure, stable future—something conventions work so hard to uphold.

Invoking queer rhetorical strategies in the composition classroom is one way to push for the failure of these normative writing conventions and disrupt the ties the field has with composure and order. In this way, according to Halberstam, failure constitutes a refusal while still remaining an ongoing site for renewal and the existence of queer(ness). This line of thinking informs not only my methodology toward my own research and writing but also influences my pedagogy and approach to student writers. It isn't uncommon that like Othered writers, student-writers already feel excluded or distanced from their disciplines and academic writing in general. These alternative methodologies might invite them in or at least give them a different understanding of why they feel excluded in the first place. After all, critical queer pedagogical work has long called for teachers to examine the reasons for these exclusions, in addition to acknowledging the normativity they produce and reify. Because I tend to think of writing under erasure, I teach writing under erasure as well. In other words, I work hard to contextualize and upset academic conventions as I am teaching writers about the presence and importance of these conventions, in addition to how and why those conventions privilege and marginalize certain groups and individuals. Therefore, queer methodology is inherently linked to queer pedagogy for me as a queer femme writing teacher. My abstract understanding of queer and its rhetorical power have led me to teach resistance writing by way of more concrete queer rhetorical practices. Of course, not all queer and/or marginal writers employ queer rhetorical practices. In fact, some tend to write quite conventional texts. The key is paying attention to the rhetorical function, and affect, of queer strategies to locate those that allow writers to remain in control of their own texts by losing control of normative conventions.

QUEER RHETORICAL STRATEGIES: PUSHING FOR THE FAILURE OF NORMATIVITY

> We need not to restrict but expand.
> —Joseph Harris

Jonathan Alexander and Jackie Rhodes (2012b) explain queer rhetorical practices as those "that recognize the necessity sometimes of saying 'No,' of saying 'Fuck, no,' of offering an impassioned, embodied, and visceral reaction to the practices of normalization that limit not just freedom, but the imagination of possibility, of potential" (193). Narrow academic conventions are colonizing forces that linger in the writing classroom. Writers of difference sense, and ultimately internalize, that they are not "right." In her "A Letter to 3rd World Women," *mestiza* rhetor Gloria Anzaldúa (2015) says the white man tells her, and those like her, "*Don't cultivate your colored skins nor tongues of fire if you want to make it in a right-handed world*" (164). Those marked by difference are expected to reduce that difference throughout their education, remain distanced from it, and even abandon their home cultures and languages; these expectations carry over into the writing classroom (hooks 2004; Lamos 2011; Lyons 2009; Rodriguez 1982; Smitherman 1973; Villanueva 2009). Emotional appeals and the personal are seen as weak or too informal; logos and form remain king. According to Anzaldúa, we are expected to "bow down to the sacred bull, form" (165). As Victor Villanueva (2004) explains, "Academic discourse tries, after all, to reach the Aristotelian ideal of being completely logocentric" (12), but logos is often inadequate. He argues, "Personal discourse, the narrative, the auto/biography, helps in that effort, is a necessary adjunct to the academic" (17). He also calls for the literal and metaphorical inclusion of *memoria*/memory, for it not only links authors to their own experiences but also connects them with the experiences of Others like themselves. As Villanueva (2004) understands from personal experience as an assimilated subject of the academy, "Memory simply cannot be adequately portrayed in the conventional discourse of the academy" (12). While some conventional strategies are inadequate, others feel hostile to those who are/have been oppressed.

Similarly, in "Hello, Cruel World Lite: Beta 1.0.1: the Mini Guide," in a section inspired by Audre Lorde's point that "the master's tools will never dismantle the master's house," Kate Bornstein (2006) provides examples of oppressive tools used by mainstream discourse: force, either/or thinking, intimidation, capitalism, blame, and so forth (4). Bornstein challenges readers to avoid these more aggressive and orthodox measures. She then introduces alternatives—what she calls the "wrong tools for the job": magic, love, patience, illogic, culture-jamming, paradox, riddles, and so on (4). Bornstein's alternatives can also function as subversive rhetorical techniques for LGBTQ writers who find the master's tools counterproductive for their aims. Alternative rhetorics (like feminist, queer, and Other rhetorics; digital rhetorics; and multimodal and DIY composing) provide marginalized writers with a space to exist and explore, offering more expansive approaches to representation and ethos. Specifically, as Alexander and Rhodes's body of work demonstrates, queer rhetoric reclaims and asserts a dissident ethos. It is strategic in that it breaks away from, and even completely avoids, heteronormative, heterosexist, and conventional composing practices praised for being safe and legitimate.

Queer rhetorical strategies can serve as avenues of healing and moves toward decolonization for those who find themselves, their voices, and their experiences silenced or lost to regulation. As Anzaldúa (2015) encourages third-world women of color, like herself, to write, she decries the academy. She says, "I have not yet unlearned the esoteric bullshit and pseudo-intellectualizing that school brainwashed into my writing" (163). In resistance to the academy's uptight approach to writing, Anzaldúa (2015) is rhetorically resistant, and her intentions include justice and sovereignty. Taking up Anzaldúa's work, in her discussion of third-space zines, Adela Licona (2002) argues for the use of "Anzaldúan practices," which she describes as "rhetorical and material practices that allow people to reimagine and to reinsert themselves into processes of trans-formation, both of their own subjectivities and of the world in which those subjectivities may be called forth, ignored, or rejected" (101). As a result, a third rhetorical space is created where the subject's experience is welcomed and centered. In a move Pamela Caughie (1999) might classify as passing, Anzaldúa occupies "the space of an authority that is not authorized" (181). In doing so, Anzaldúa (2015) gives the following advice to those who struggle to author-ize themselves to write: "Throw away abstraction and the academic learning, the rules, the map and compass. Feel your way without blinders. To touch more people, the personal realities and the social must be evoked—not through rhetoric but through blood and pus and sweat" (171). This advice has guided me, not only as a writer but also as a teacher of writing. But how does that (de/re)materialize in writing studies and in the composition classroom?

PUTTING QUEER METHODOLOGIES INTO PRACTICE: THE PROJECT

These theories and methodologies have coalesced to inspire Writing *Back* | Writing *Against* | Writing *Through*, a multimodal project I devel-oped for LGBTQ Identities and Writing, a junior-level composition class I designed to teach at a midsize public research institution in Appalachia. The course is a special theme within the Women and Writing strand of required junior composition class offerings, with an enrollment capped at twenty. In addition to the institution's general junior-level course outcomes (set by the composition committee, under the advisement of the director of composition), the course provides an investigation into the following specific threads:

- the dynamic relationship between sexual identity, sexual politics, gen-der identity and writing
- how who we are influences not only *what* we write but also *how* we write and establish ethos for particular audiences
- the potential of alternative and queer rhetorics and multimodal, visu-al, and digital composition
- how nonnormative texts can challenge and subvert standardized genre conventions, as well as the ways they critique large systems of

power, social institutions, and mainstream ideologies—specifically
those that perpetuate normative sexual identities (Glasby 2016)

Throughout the semester, students read texts from various LGBTQ
and alternative rhetor-writers that invoke queer rhetorics, ambivalence, and failure-affirming composing practices. From foundational
texts like Leslie Feinberg's *Stone Butch Blues,* Hélène Cixous's "The
Laugh of the Medusa," and manifestos from Riot Grrrl, Radicalesbians,
Queer Nation, Julia Serano, and the Combahee River Collective to
newer iterations from Roxane Gay and Alison Bechdel, the course
texts examine how Others have been historically constructed, silenced,
and erased by/through dominant discourses. And in response, these
authors plead for other marginalized subjects to speak up, to write,
and to claim and articulate themselves through words and queer composing strategies.

In the same vein, in an attempt to take up those calls, the project
description on the assignment sheet reads, "This project provides you
with a space to document and analyze the ways you have been erased,
silenced, and written, along with the ways you (re)present and (re)write
yourself. In the spirit of Feinberg, Arenas, Gibson, Baggs, Cixous, and
Anzaldúa, consider the ways others see, understand, and define you;
then speak back" (Glasby 2016). I also include advice from Rhodes
(2015), who has argued on numerous occasions, along with Alexander,
that queer(ness) fails and is failed by conventional print texts, composition as a class and discipline, and the academy at large. In support of
these methodologies, she advises student-writers to "1. Resist mastery;
2. Challenge yourself to fail; 3. Compose as a composer, not as a critic;
and 4. Trust me that play is okay" (Rhodes 2015). Rhodes's references
to risk, failure, freedom from conventions, and play mesh well with
the queer methodologies students employ in their work for this project. When they are asked to write about how they have been written,
and they begin to see the impact of those messages and limitations,
students experience conflict—mostly within themselves. Rather than
asking them to sort through and process these feelings of ambivalence,
I invite them to engage these feelings and to use them for momentum
and insight. For me, the best way to do this is to invite students to
engage spaces or moments of uncertainty and to write about them,
without the pressure of "figuring it out" or delineation—to write
themselves *into* the mess and confusion rather than out of them. For
example, rather than writing about a point or issue they feel comfortable with or sure about, I ask them to instead explore places where
they feel uneasy, torn, or unsure. Of course, there are risks involved

in asking students to do this work, for not only are they expected to understand normative conventions and approaches, but they are also being asked to explore resistant methods that question and trouble academic discourse and its power. They also might hesitate to write about what they don't know since they have most likely been taught to write about what they *do* know. It is not easy, but it can be incredibly rewarding, for both writers and their audiences. Personally, I find this kind of work beneficial because it allows me to explore rather than settle my feelings. When I wrote about my own ambivalence regarding same-sex marriage and the marriage-equality movement, I realized it was okay for me—as a queer lesbian—to both want and not want to get married. Just because I'm queer doesn't mean I can't find some value in being married to my partner. This kind of writing provided me with a space to negotiate and flex my own queer politics rather than take them on, wholly and rigidly, from others. Students can benefit from the same kinds of moves in their own writing. And often, it gets them thinking far beyond the more simplistic black and white/pro-con approaches they tend to favor and rely on.

In an attempt to decenter my authority in the classroom, and to change the goal of my feedback from evaluation toward reader response and assessment, I use a grading contract in this course, inspired by Peter Elbow and Jane Danielewicz (2008) and my graduate school's composition program. Therefore, the project is assessed based on how well it achieves outlined criteria provided in the assignment sheet. Following are the criteria for the project:

- has a **thoughtful and generative focus** for exploration
- makes an **argument** (whether implicit or explicit)
- demonstrates **complex, critical thinking about yourself and your identity/subject position**, its portrayal, its potential, and the implications of that portrayal and potential through narration and/or discussion
- demonstrates an **understanding of the elements of arrangement and visual composition(s)** as well as the effectiveness of specific rhetorical appeals and visual composition strategies
- incorporates at least **four academic journal articles and two other credible sources**
- includes a **descriptive Cover Letter** that explains the project's rhetorical goals, aims, and composition/design strategies
- **responsibly cites and documents all sources** (images, sound, and other materials) in MLA format
- shows evidence of **substantial and thoughtful revision** that considers feedback from instructor conferencing and peer review

- considers or intentionally undoes **academic conventions** of grammar, punctuation, and spelling, appropriate for the medium and message at hand (Glasby 2016)

The project's process work spans four and a half weeks and is quite conventional, considering the methodologies I lay out earlier in this chapter. The project's process emphasizes writing to learn, using sources to find a way into/through conflict or ambivalence, and recursive drafting and revising based on continual feedback from classmates and myself. Students are first asked to write a short, one- to two-page proposal explaining how they will approach the following: their focus, audience, purpose, genre/medium, research questions, research methodologies, project design, composing strategies, and rhetorical goals (based on Jody Shipka's 2005 "A Multimodal Task-Based Framework for Composing"). After receiving feedback from their peers and me on their proposal and initial ideas, students dig more heavily into their research, chosen genre(s), and target rhetorical strategies. Once students complete the bulk of their preliminary research, they submit an annotated bibliography and storyboard/working draft. Afterward, I confer with them to touch base and troubleshoot in terms of form and content. Students are encouraged to continue their research and designing processes until the project deadline. In the final week before the project is due, I offer at least two in-class workshop days during which students revise and hone their projects alongside their peers. Every project is accompanied by a Descriptive Cover Letter, which describes their rhetorical goals and reflects on the process of meeting those goals. In addition, writers discuss the strengths and weaknesses of the final draft, along with the composing and design struggles they faced along the way. The intention here is to refocus their concerns from successful grades to writing strategies and their own composing—what works and what doesn't. In this sense, the grading contract helps reinforce a failure-affirming methodology since students are free to take more risks in their composing without fear of penalty or losing points. Students' projects may "fail" in terms of being perfectly polished products, but the students still create significant knowledge about composing and how to attain those rhetorical goals they set for themselves through firsthand experience. Maybe their videos and zines aren't exactly what they had hoped for when they submit them, but that doesn't mean they can't come out of the project having learned about the frustrating and time-consuming process of editing and provoking design elements. Or about writing, or themselves.

Consistently, students have used this project and these methodologies to (re)claim, explore, negotiate, represent, and understand their ethos in relation to their identity, sexuality, literacy sponsorship, and writing. Using the ambivalence-affirming methodologies I have discussed, their projects tend to center on significant sites of knowing and unknowing, being and unbeing:

- coming out—as feminist, LGBTQ, queer
- reclaiming a nonstandard dialect or home language through and in their writing
- negotiating hybridized and intersectional identities
- coping with sexual assault, disclosure/not reporting, and rape culture
- processing mental illness, anxiety, and depression
- writing from, with, and about the body
- exploring the effects of, and reasons behind, oppressions like racism, ableism, sexism, hetero- and homonormativity, (white) privilege, homophobia, and transphobia
- advocating for the inclusion of erased sexualities (like asexuality), identities (like third world, transnational, queer women of color), and experiences (like polyamory, BSDM, and sex work)

Exigencies like these, developed and explored through queer methodologies, are just one step in the right direction if the field values and works toward truly intersectional and queer classroom contexts, which understandably call for ambiguity rather than (or at least in addition to) intelligibility.

One point I try to reiterate throughout this project's process is that form and content are not separate but connected and interdependent, and they often work in conjunction to emphasize each other. In terms of failure-affirming methodologies and composing practices, students have used a variety of exciting media, genres, and genre blending to communicate their projects' goals and ambivalence positions. One student's project included poetry written in African American Vernacular English on a mirror to demonstrate how his poems reflect rather than avoid his identity as a black man of color poet; additionally the mirror-as-text invites the reader in, in a way that traditional paper or screens do not. Readers literally see themselves with/in his words, their faces marked by his transposed handwriting, home language, and words—in this design strategy, reader, writer, and text become one. Another student focusing on female body image used a female mannequin torso on which to write herself and her text. Being able to connect certain ideas and experiences with specific areas on the corporeal body emphasized the cognitive dissonance she experienced between the messages she had received about her body and the truth of her lived experience in her body. In addition, she hung a large sheet of butcher paper on the wall in a common area in her dorm, which invited other women to express their feelings about and experiences with body image and beauty standards. Collaborating with other college-aged women empowered her messages on the mannequin and demonstrated to both writer and reader that she wasn't alone in her struggle to love herself and her body. One of my favorite student projects to date is a handmade zine on asexuality composed on transparency paper. The student-writer intended to illustrate how asexuality represents an invisible and convoluted identity, something she felt daily. Using black, white/clear, and gray tones, she was able to emphasize and visually depict the vast gray area between how people understand asexuality and her specific experience as an aromantic ace. Every semester I am amazed at the incredibly creative and brave projects students compose using these methodologies. And I've noticed over time that they are writing and thinking in much more complex and sophisticated ways than I could have imagined.

REFLECTIONS ON THE PROJECT'S EFFECT AND AFFECT

Students have expressed that although these methodologies feel unfamiliar and counterintuitive in comparison to their previous learning and thinking about writing and research, they ultimately allow for creativity, meaning making, a sense of freedom, and empowerment. Once the students move away from more rigid rules and conventional expectations, they lean into flexibility and murkiness, ambivalence and failure. In addition, they seem to trust not only the methodologies more but also themselves as composers. They seem to appreciate a new-found sense of audience, too, one that moves far beyond the instructor as evaluator. The grading contract and emphasis on risk and play allow them to try things out without worrying about how taking a risk might negatively affect their grade. I've also noticed students tend to extend their writing beyond the class, whether it be pursuing publication or continuing on with the project for their own ends rather than the course's. Rather than thinking of a due date as an end point for an assignment, they see the project as an opening up in their thinking—one that doesn't end when the project is submitted for instructor review.

In terms of the project's and methodologies' impact on the students' lives, one student in particular felt the project gave her the space to negotiate her colonized subjectivity and two conflicting emotions of diaspora: a longing for her homeland, which she had come to idealize over time, and the harsh homophobic and misogynistic realities of returning home as an out queer woman of color. Another student-writer expressed appreciation for the project as a venue to finally understand, embrace, and advocate for her bisexual and fat identities, subjectivities she previously felt were impossible to explain and often not taken seriously, particularly because she was liminally sized (often read as not thin but also not fat). Yet another student used the project to speak back to her rapist and those who lambast survivors who choose not to report. She had decided against reporting her sexual assault, defending her right to not disclose; she was compelled to use the project to negotiate the tension she felt as a survivor—she wanted a space to process her assault, but she did not want her experience to be negated or challenged by law enforcement or a mandatory reporter; she wanted to remain in control of her story since her agency had been violated, as her body had been. In making this move, she refused the mainstream's expectations for rape victims' narratives that too often request and reinforce the "right" way to behave—to protect oneself, to resist assault, to fight back, to justify, to stay silent, to report, to forgive, to heal.

In this way, the most significant affect of this project's work entails the invitation of subjectivity, not only in terms of the students being able to express and negotiate their own subjectivities but also in terms of even having the chance to consider and identify their subjectivities in the first place. Ingrained in the minds and writing habits of some of these student-writers, especially those in the STEM disciplines, is that writing is always meant to be perfunctory, technical, and distanced from themselves. They have been taught to see personal writing as opinionated and biased. Some struggle to see themselves as writers; even more find it difficult to see themselves as composer-designers.

These queer methodologies—ambivalence and failure—and this course project have had a significant impact on me as a teacher of writing and as a queer writer-rhetor. Rather than beginning a writing or research task with a designated starting point, I tend to start in the thick of the middle: What don't I know? Where have I failed? What causes me discomfort? Where does my thinking and writing fail beautifully? Where is the pivot point, say between one perspective and another? What ideas about composing leave me ambivalent? These are the spaces I write and research from now. I've learned from students' projects that ambivalence is an effective way to implement the notion of writing to learn. Using writing to process and figure things out (even if they do not come to any conclusions) can be extremely powerful for writers who have been taught to only write from places of secure knowing. The project's framing—the metaphorical and literal writing of oneself, one's community and culture, and one's lived experience—can be transformative for reader and writer, for they bear witness to a journey toward knowledge rather than simply getting to the endpoint of a clear assertion. And, of course, this type of framing, and these methodologies, can function in the name of social justice and Lyons's (2009) notion of rhetorical sovereignty, which is timely and critical considering the field's move toward cultural rhetorics and identity and experience-based epistemologies.

~~CONCLUSION~~ AN UNRAVELING

Queer methodologies seek to expand not only representation for nonnormative individuals but also *ways* for representing them and their complexities and paradoxes. Drawing from feminist and queer theories, these methodologies work to identify and combat homophobia, resist and challenge the status quo, and reveal and dismantle oppressive institutions. For this reason, they can be particularly useful in writing classrooms that seek to explore, challenge, and/or disrupt the dominant culture; furthermore, they can be productive sites for subjects-in-process, fluid subjects, and those with hybrid and intersectional identities who find academic conventions narrow and inadequate. Moreover, these queer methodologies carry potential for the ways we tend to think about research and the intentions of that research.

Rather than conclude, I return to the beginning; rather than answer, I ask: What if, as these scholars recommend, composition was motivated to explore the tension of ambivalence and failure? What happens when we shift assessment's focus away from measuring success and traditional notions of achievement toward the failures in our students' writing? What might subversive composing practices offer marginalized students, and what happens when they learn about and deploy subversive composing practices with *rhetorical* and *political* intention? What is to be said for the deep ruptures and schisms between conflicting thoughts, ideas, and identities? What kind of meaning (and texts) can be made when writers are asked to engage unknowing and enact dissent rather than produce clear and logical thought? What if we failed to make sense of things in, and *through*, our writing?

REFERENCES

Aciman, Andre, ed. 1999. *Letters of Transit*. New York: New York Press.
Alexander, Jonathan. 2008. *Literacy, Sexuality, Pedagogy*. Logan: Utah State University Press. https://doi.org/10.2307/j.ctt4cgqkw.
Alexander, Jonathan, and Jacqueline Rhodes. 2011. "Queer: An Impossible Subject for Composition." *JAC* 31 (1–2): 177–206.

Alexander, Jonathan, and Jacqueline Rhodes. 2012a. "Queered." *Technoculture* 2. https://tcjournal.org/vol2/queered.

Anzaldúa, Gloria. 2015. "Speaking in Tongues." In *This Bridge Called My Back*, 4th ed., edited by Cherrie Moranga and Gloria Anzaldúa, 163–72. Albany: SUNY Press.

Bhabha, Homi. 1985. "Signs Taken for Wonders: Questions of Ambivalence and Authority under a Tree Outside Delhi, May 1817." *Critical Inquiry* 12 (1): 144–65. https://doi.org/10.1086/448325.

Bornstein, Kate. 2006. "Hello, Cruel World Lite: Beta 1.0.1., 1–4." http://katebornstein.typepad.com/files/hcw_lite_101.pdf.

Caughie, Pamela. 1999. *Passing and Pedagogy*. Urbana: University of Illinois Press.

Edelman, Lee. 2004. *No Future: Queer Theory and the Death Drive*. Durham, NC: Duke University Press. https://doi.org/10.1215/9780822385981-001.

Elbow, Peter, and Jane Danielewicz. 2008. "A Unilateral Grading Contract to Improve Learning and Teaching." English Department Faculty Publication Series 3.

Halberstam, Jack. 1998. *Female Masculinity*. Durham, NC: Duke University Press.

Harding, Sandra. 1998. *Is Science Multicultural?* Bloomington: Indiana University Press.

Hoffman, Eva. 1999. "The New Nomads." In *Letters of Transit*, edited by Andre Aciman, 39–63. New York: New York Press.

hooks, bell. 2006. "Keeping Close to Home: Class and Education." In *Conversations in Context*, edited by Robert P. Yagelski, 48–58. Cambridge: Thomson Heinle.

Lamos, Steve. 2011. *Interests and Opportunities: Race, Racism, and University Writing Instruction in the Post-Civil Rights Era*. Pittsburgh, PA: University of Pittsburgh Press.

Licona, Adela. 2002. *Zines in 3rd Space: Radical Cooperation and Borderlands Rhetoric*. Albany: SUNY Press.

Lyons, Scott Richard. 2009. "Rhetorical Sovereignty: What Do American Indians Want from Writing?" In *The Norton Book of Composition*, edited by Susan Miller, 1128–47. New York: Norton.

Malinowitz, Harriet. 1995. *Textual Orientations: Gay and Lesbian Students and the Making of Discourse Communities*. Portsmouth, NH: Boynton/Cook.

Marciniak, Katarzyna. 2006. *Alienhood*. Minneapolis: University of Minnesota Press.

McRuer, Robert. 2006. *Crip Theory: Cultural Signs of Queerness and Disability*. New York: New York University Press.

Micciche, Laura. 2014. "Feminist Pedagogies." In *A Guide to Composition Studies*, 2nd ed., edited by Gary Tate, Amy Rupiper Taggart, Kurt Schick, and H. Brooke Hessler, 129–45. New York: Oxford University Press.

Olsen, Gary. 1999. "Toward a Post-Process Composition: Abandoning the Rhetoric of Assertion." In *Post-Process Theory*, edited by Thomas Kent, 7–15. Carbondale: Southern Illinois University Press.

Rhodes, Jacqueline. 2015. "Feeling the Fear, and Doing It Anyway: The Risks—and Affordances—of Failure." Panel presentation at the Conference on College Composition and Communication, Tampa, FL, March.

Rodriguez, Richard. 1982. *Hunger of Memory: The Education of Richard Rodriguez*. New York: Dial.

Seigworth, Gregory. 2012. "Reading Lauren Berlant Writing." *Communication and Critical/Cultural Studies* 9 (4): 346–52. https://doi.org/10.1080/14791420.2012.733212.

Shipka, Jody. 2005. "A Multimodal Task-Based Framework for Composing." *College Composition and Communication* 57 (2): 277–306.

Simic, Charles. 1999. "Refugees." In *Letters of Transit*, edited by Andre Aciman, 119–35. New York: New York Press.

Smitherman, Geneva. 1973. "'God Don't Never Change': Black English from a Black Perspective." *College English* 34 (6): 828–33. https://doi.org/10.2307/375044.

Trinh, Minh-ha. 2010. *Elsewhere, within Here: Immigration, Refugeeism, and the Boundary Event*. New York: Routledge.

Villanueva, Victor. 2004. "*Memoria* Is a Friend of Ours: On the Discourses of Color." *College English* 67 (1): 9–19. https://doi.org/10.2307/4140722.

Villanueva, Victor. 2009. "Maybe a Colony: And Still Another Critique of the Comp Community." In *The Norton Book of Composition*, edited by Susan Miller, 991–98. New York: Norton.

Wallace, David. 2011. *Compelled to Write: Alternative Rhetoric in Theory and Practice.* Logan: Utah State University Press. https://doi.org/10.2307/j.ctt4cgnrd.

Yagelski, Robert. 1999. "The Ambivalence of Reflection: Critical Pedagogies, Identity, and the Writing Teacher." *College Composition and Communication* 51 (1): 32–50. https://doi.org/10.2307/358958.

3

HOW (AND WHY) TO WRITE QUEER
A Failing, Impossible, Contradictory Instruction
Manual for Scholars of Writing Studies

Stacey Waite

In 2004, Jacqueline Rhodes offered us a "queertext manifesto," a text that, at times, functions as a list of attributes or actions that might produce or be understood as queertext. In the spirit of this work, I want to imagine queer approaches to the practice of writing and to consider writing itself as a methodological process, one that—this essay proposes—must be queered in order to reflect the queer methods, subjects, or narratives our research in writing studies engages. Our assumptions about writing inform every step of the research process and often shape the very methodologies we take up as we imagine the form our research must (or must it?) take. I want to focus on the question of *how* we write—how scholars in writing studies compose, report, organize, position, and narrate scholarship and research. Essentially, this essay takes up the question, what would it mean to write in queer(er) ways, to (regardless of what our research may be *about*) formally enact queer subversions of the norms that dictate the ways we deliver and *write* our research?

In an attempt to both describe and enact its argument, this is an experimental exercise, one in which I imagine how we might practice, as writers in our field, composing our writing in queer(er) ways whether or not such composing is, in the end, actually possible. In their recently published *Techne: Queer Meditations on Writing the Self*, Jacqueline Rhodes and Jonathan Alexander remind us of the complexities and perhaps even impossibilities of queer composition; they write, "We understand queer *composing* as a queer rhetorical practice aimed at disrupting how we understand ourselves to ourselves. As such, it is a composing that is not a composing, a call in many ways to acts of de- and un- and re-composition" (Rhodes and Alexander 2015). And while being *composed* may not be possible or desirable in the realm of queer identity, politics, or methodology, this impossibility is not permanent and fixed;

DOI: 10.7330/9781607328186.c003

this impossibility, as Rhodes and Alexander suggest, doesn't mean we shouldn't try, shouldn't *try on* acts of resistance, shouldn't practice the kinds of "de- and un- and re-composition" they describe. After all, in their earlier article, "Queer: An Impossible Subject for Composition," Alexander and Rhodes (2011) assert, "We also want to make room for the kinds of writing—and the kinds of subjects—that challenge such composure, that offer rich, capacious, and (yes) excessive ways of thinking and writing" (183). I want to imagine the kind of writing that could "challenge such composure," the kind of writing that might move *against* fixed and conventional understandings of writing itself.

Of course, such writing is also impossible. In her video essay, "The Failure of Queer Pedagogy," Rhodes (2015) suggests that because of the heteronormative institutional locations in which teaching occurs, there may be no true "queer pedagogy"; there is only the possibility of teaching queer. She tells us, "Teaching queer means risking failure; it means opening conversation that cannot be closed." I want to argue the same for writing. There is no queer writing because writing itself is institutional—our language and its regulations always already constituted by dominant narratives and disciplinary conventions. But, this does not mean we cannot *write queer(er)*. This does not mean we cannot relish the failure of doing so. That failure, as Rhodes (2015) reminds us via Jack Halberstam, is a queer methodology itself.

To think of writing in terms of queerness is to grapple with the undeniable impossibility of writing, the undeniable impossibility of linear forms, singular voices, conclusions, dependable narratives, and discernable data. I offer here a kind of instruction manual, a list of demands, questions, and narratives that suggest some possibilities for writing queer; it suggests queer interruptions and subversions in many of our common assumptions about writing. It is also a failure before it begins.

PART 1: INSTRUCTIONS FOR WRITING QUEER
(which is impossible both because queer writing is impossible and because even if it were possible, there would definitely not be instructions)

1. Commit rhetorical disobedience.

2. Write from a position of failure instead of writing from the position of what you think you know. Certainty is only queer when you are certain your knowledge is partial, failed, and fragmented.

3. "Certainly, some will argue that it is perhaps impossible to construct writing . . . based on what is impossible to know—on

incommensurability, or unknowability. We maintain, however, that unknowability is the proper subject of writing itself" (Alexander and Rhodes 2014, 451).

4.   Don't stay "on topic." Drift gleefully off. Get lost.

5.   "Under certain circumstances, failing, losing, forgetting, unmaking, undoing, unbecoming, not knowing may in fact offer more creative, more cooperative, more surprising ways of being in the world" (Halberstam 2011, 2). And perhaps more surprising writing, more surprising forms, more surprising ideas.

6.   In fourth grade, I kept a treasured eraser collection in my desk. I was drawn more to erasing than writing. I wrote on my desk (a forbidden and elementary-school-detention-worthy blasphemy). I drew castles. I drew kings holding hands at the decorative doors. Always a drawbridge. Always a moon hanging over the scene. I almost always erased it all before Mr. Reardon or the class snitches saw.

7.   Imagine your writing outside the bounds of binary understandings: critical and creative, academic and personal, theoretical and practical. All of these all at once, or none of these all at once, which is a binary so nevermind.

8.   Get academic; get theoretical; get narrative; get personal. "The assumption, I suppose, is that the 'personal' isn't critical, isn't socially responsible because it encourages a solipsistic narcissism of knowledge production" (Banks 2003, 21). Solipsistic narcissism, why not? It might be fun.

9.   Don't we all have trouble distinguishing ourselves from external objects? Don't we all obsess about ourselves? Isn't that why we do whatever it is we do? Write queer because you're a huge queer or want to be or want everyone to think you are. Write queer because your writing and your self are not distinguishable. The self is all that can be known to exist. Solipsism. Also, there is no self.

10.   Approach writing as an act of discovery and experimentation. "I don't know what I'm looking for, really. I just have a bundle of 'interests' and proclivities. I'm really just screwing around" (Ramsay 2014, 117).

11.   Be irrational, hysterical even.

12.   Talk about your feelings; they are smart. Express and be curious about emotion, "foregrounding emotion as embodied and lived" and "vital for cultivating wonder" (Micciche 2007, 46).

13.   Show up in your writing as a body, an embodied force in the text, all the while keeping your reader aware that even the body is a contradiction: both an idea constructed and a real material thing that impacts the world: "Voice is produced by the body" (Elbow 1994, 3).

14.   My body is a moving target. Gender is a man holding a gun at a shooting range. He believes he has every right to bear arms.

15. Write with the knowledge this is all true, and all lies, all real, and all made up, which leads us to . . .

16. Write in queer voice(s). Contradict yourself. Queer writing "involves deliberately courting paradox" (Rhodes 2015).

17. Undermine your own authority, be certain in your uncertainty, develop a voice that can be trusted even as it is subjective, unreliable, and impossible to pin down, unless of course, you want to be pinned down in a sexy way.

18. Be promiscuous, neither married or monogamized to your discipline, your language(s): "A promiscuous approach does not seek to redefine norms—rather, it seeks to *disrupt normalcy altogether*, to intimately engage with and vicariously inhabit multiple perspectives, to live through the desires of strangers, to simultaneously invite and affirm the variety of human experience" (Branstetter 2016, 18).

19. Speaking of redefining and definitions, don't define your terms or pretend you can. And if you can, your terms are not very queer at all and . . .

20. Speaking of multiple perspectives, don't imagine your audience as some unified discipline, which is not real to begin with. Quote from people who should not be quoted from, quote from people who aren't in any disciplines.

21. For example, my father says sometimes it is not the actual consequences of an action that cause outrage but "the principle of the thing."

22. As a kid, I had no idea what he meant.

23. Speaking of quoting, attempt to develop (even though your ethical editors might insist otherwise) citation practices that don't pretend ideas are owned, that they can be traced back to their owners, that we are not all thieves in the night.

24. There is not one place, one body that ideas come from.

25. There is no origin so . . .

26. Cite queer, cite out of context, move ideas to places they never intended to belong.

27. Einstein said, or they say he said, that imagination is more important than knowledge, meaning that, in the end, fantasy (the wild things you can imagine) have more meaning than the truths you think you know—the truths of a field, of a self, of a history retold.

28. Don't outline your argument or say "In this essay, I will . . ." Promises can never be kept, or controlled: "When monogamy becomes labor, when desire is organized contractually with accounts kept and fidelity extracted like labor from employees, with marriage a domestic factory policed by means of rigid shop-floor discipline designed to keep the wives and husbands and domestic partners of the world

choke-chained to the status quo machinery—is this really what we mean by a 'good relationship'?" (Kipnis 2003, 19). Is this really what we mean by "good scholarship"?

29. In fact, you might consider *not* making arguments and thinking of a writing context that is less like a courtroom (evidence, argument, opening statements, etc.) and more like a carnival, or a nightclub, or a swinger's convention.

30. Don't be faithful or loyal to institutions, disciplines, or persons to whom others say you must be speaking.

31. "Resist the tendency to essentialize [your] respective affordances and constraints, which runs the risk of suggesting . . . that meaning-making is a simplistic, formulaic, or at best stable process" (Dadas and Jory 2015, 152).

32. "If you wish to make an apple pie from scratch, you must first invent the universe" (Sagan 2013, 180).

33. Don't become an authority on your subject.

34. Implicate yourself. You are an untrustworthy narrator (like Holden Caulfield and everyone else); you are an inadequate scholar (like everyone else); you are an implicated subject (like everyone else), in a precarious position, unable to speak for others, barely able to speak for yourself: "Within the conflicts of identification and desire, writers construct sel/f/ves through site-specific literate acts—one component of which is the articulation of positionality" (Monson and Rhodes 2004, 87).

35. "The act of composition, whether you are composing a work of fiction or your life, or whether you are composing reality, always means pulling off fragmented pieces and putting them together into a whole that makes sense" (Anzaldúa 1999, 238). Or sometimes it does. And sometimes it makes something else.

36. You can't quite write queer, but try: "Queerness is not yet here. Queerness is an ideality. Put another way, we are not yet queer. We may never touch queerness, but we can feel it as the warm illumination of a horizon imbued with potentiality" (Muñoz 2009, 1).

37. If there is not a word for what/who you are/mean/do, make one up: *queertext, genderqueer, bicurious, cisnormativity*. Words become words when we say, write, and circulate them.

38. Invent more words; we need them; more words for who we are/do.

39. Don't have a thesis, especially if by thesis you mean a linear argument that moves in logical, rational progression: this movement sounds an awful lot like the logic of heteronormative reproduction, which you should, in the end, do everything in your limited agency and power to avoid.

40. Get disorganized, make a mess.

41.   Try some queer(er) forms like . . .

42.   Become a "scavenger": develop "a scavenger methodology that uses different methods to collect and produce information" (Halberstam 2011, 13).

43.   Build "assemblages" (Puar 2007). Writing queer means paying "more attention to unfolding relations among what may initially appear as disparate and disconnected forces" (Palmeri and Rylander 2016, 33).

44.   Forces are ideas. Ideas are not ideas.

45.   Writing is "the salt in chocolate. It is not there to make sense; it's there to stimulate the senses" (Giovanni 2009, 51), and by senses I don't mean the five senses because we all know there are far more than five.

46.   Stop counting, evaluating and categorizing. Re-envision. Remix: "Whereas the critic would strive to sort art works into genres and periods, the remixer would seek to creatively recombine disparate materials—to make a new composition by juxtaposing samples from radically disparate artistic traditions and periods" (Palmeri 2012, 13).

47.   Repurpose—"a practice that further involves illuminating, and working within and against, the conditions that characterized a given situation" (Stenberg 2015, 2)—because . . .

48.   As Judith Butler (2004) notes, "That my agency is riven with paradox does not mean it is impossible. It means only that paradox is the condition of its possibility" (3).

49.   Write against as many writing norms as possible, meaning

50.   Value dark pasts, negative affects, and pessimism when you need to. The queer theorists have taught us the urgency in this matter (Lauren Berlant, Heather Love), so

51.   Go ahead and make your audience feel bad instead of good, if you want, and especially if you know your audience likes feeling bad in a naughty way, and

52.   Use "I" whenever you want, but only when you are thinking of "I" as a subjective, socially constructed, and multiple "I" that can never be known—

53.   This "I" you construct implicates them, and yes, the "them" can be an "I" because

54.   Ignore subject agreement, how normative, how boring, how unplural.

55.   Say something grammatically incomprehensible if and when the thing you are trying to say is something your language, produced also by social construction, does not want you to be able to say.

56.   "Write queertexts, not queer texts . . . do not accept the adjectival marginalization, the separation of those two words which are one" (Rhodes 2004, 388).

57. Who is "we"? Problematize this "we" *we* all use when *we* are writing, which apparently is different from when/what *they* are writing. Write a "we" that contains the possibility of common experience and contains "a strong critical sense of our radical alterity, of the critical differences that exist among different people's and different groups' experiences of the world" (Alexander and Rhodes 2014, 431).

58. Experiment. When David Bartholomae (2005) told us we "try on the peculiar ways of knowing" that belong to the university, he probably didn't mean writing is some sort of experimental drag show, but he also did mean this. And it doesn't have to belong to the university if we take it out for a drive in a fast car through neighborhoods in which it supposedly does not belong. *Language is the dress of thought,* says Cicero, so dress it up, try it on, take it off.

59. Don't summarize your argument at the end so we know where we've been and what you've done and accomplished. What you've written should not always be articulable in the tidiness of review. It should be an epic failure of a thing.

60. Don't come to conclusions. Come to other things: inquiry, questions, failures, side roads, off-road.

61. Don't take the road.

62. Never use the road or street as a metaphor.

63. Remember the scholar you were at sixteen. Remember studying the sleep rhythms of your parents so you could more easily sneak from the bedroom window out to the literal street where you'd find all the things you didn't know that might truly allow you to learn and write: cigarette smoke, heavy-metal bands whose boy singers look like girl singers, the mouths of high-schools girls who would claim you as their secret, your brother's jeans loose around your waist, your pocket watch, the ruined dark of a suburban street.

PART 2: A FAILED EXPERIMENT

Alexander and Rhodes (2011) ask, "What might it mean to 'compose queerly,' even as we recognize the potential impossibility of such?" (197). We cannot say for sure what it might mean, and even as we do say what it means, that meaning shifts and changes. Writing queer is possible in the most momentary and fleeting ways, but it is imperative—for queer scholars especially but perhaps for all scholars of writing—to resist the writing norms and assumptions that inform *how* we compose, to try to cup in our hands, however briefly and however impossibly, whatever water we can hold long enough for a small drink.

I have, for example, and for the most part, failed at writing in the ways I've outlined above, though I admit to imagining in a sort of fantasy the kind of text that might be made entirely of resistance, the kind of text composed so queerly it is neither comprehensible or recognizable as belonging to any particular area or discipline, the ultimate queertext Rhodes (2004) describes and also fails gloriously to produce in "Homo Origo." As Rhodes notes of queer pedagogy, queer writing is an impossibility even as we must, and sometimes do, write queer. But much of the writing we discuss, produce, and express is done (like anything is done) inside the bounds and constraints of institutional locations, disciplinary discourse, and normative assumptions about what it means to write inside the confines of a discipline in which you are seeking (quite likely) employment, advancement, livelihood, recognition, and stability. In other words, in order to imagine one's "livable life" (Butler 2004), one might need to imagine obeying the rules, writing the kinds of scholarship that is recognizable and conventional, producing the kind of prose that is legible in a field. This is, of course, always the trick of systemic powers of operation; we might *want* to resist but find our resistance ridden with too much risk. We find our scholarship inextricably linked to the institution, to the panopticon of tenure, the competitive capitalistic force of an impossible job market. What could be more important than behaving and writing appropriately in a time like this? And also, when would be a better time for such disobedience, for queer play, for interrogating the very rules and regulations that help the field count who counts. And saying who (or what) counts is a charge that is performative. In a 2010 video, "Your Behavior Creates Your Gender," Butler puts it this way:

> When we say gender is performed we usually mean that we've taken on a role or we're acting in some way and that our acting or our role-playing is crucial to the gender that we are and the gender that we present to the world. To say that gender is performative is a little different because for something to be performative means that it produces a series of effects. We act and walk and speak and talk in ways that consolidate an impression of being a man or being a woman. (Butler 2010)

I want to extend Butler's lucid distinction here to this discussion of writing by suggesting that "we act and walk and speak and talk in ways that consolidate an impression of being" a scholar. We produce the series of effects via our writerly decisions and our rhetorical maneuvers. We are always already, of course, doing this. But what would it mean to become aware of *how* our field is constructed *through* our normative assumptions about writing? And what would it mean to purposefully engage in acts of disruption and subversion, even knowing the possible consequences?

PART 3: WHAT NOW?

I'd tell you what to do if I could, but I don't have any queer authority. After all, this press asks for texts in Chicago style, and I've just gone through and changed the formatting to conform. After all, this essay lists itself on a curriculum vitae as a thing I did that gives me credit, worth, money, employment, purpose. Once a journal told me to "take all the narrative out" of an essay, and I did. Once I didn't. Once I told one editor to fuck off, but only after my book manuscript was accepted for publication because before that . . . *need a job, need to keep a job, need praise, need validation, need money, need house, need diapers for baby. How boring that we have a baby. Probably makes this whole essay less queer, less credible, less on the edge of what is so edgy about queerness and its own edgy norms.*

So, yeah, no one can do it.

No one can write queer.

But we should certainly do it anyway.

One way to start is to call to the surface the attitudes and assumptions we bring to the page when we write, or even think about writing. And if it's hard to start there, we can think about our "stock phrases," about the things we notice in the writing of others, the things we critique. So if, for example, you're always asking for clarity (from your students, and likely from yourself), what would it mean to ask for something else, to not be led by clarity but by something else? The assumptions we bring to writing are not the same, but so many of them are dominant inheritances we have yet to examine, or even yet to articulate.

But what now?

1. Maybe in graduate school, someone told me a dissertation had to have a lit review. And so I quoted a bunch of books but didn't "review" anything.

2. Maybe don't be afraid of the real reasons you got into writing studies in the first place. Narcissism. Survival. Invite it into an essay, an article, a book. Never write anything that doesn't contain within it the very reason you wrote it, and wrote it that way. Walk into the light of your own terror. Are you really writing a dissertation about assessment because it is an important subject of discussion in your discipline or because in the second grade Mrs. Walsh ruined your straight As by giving you a poor grade in penmanship? Why are you here?

3. Maybe you don't want to talk about what you're wearing, but maybe you should. Like right now there has been an ice storm, and I'm a bull dyke up late still wearing work boots in my living room where earlier today I made a fort out of blankets with my son, who is only three years old and so therefore I should not even call my son because the poor guy doesn't even know what gender is yet.

4.	Maybe next time someone says "yeah but you can't say that," you should.

5.	Maybe you admit in every word you ever write that academia is violently drunk on its own straightness, its whiteness, its middle-class notions of appropriateness, its norms. Its caucuses and special issues will not save it from itself.

6.	Maybe your approach is not the problem. Maybe it's the IRB.

7.	What if the next time someone asks you who is your audience?, you say you don't care. Or that it's you. Or your uncle who lives in a rehab hospital in Maine.

8.	What if you write a book about how you collected all this data and it doesn't tell you anything.

9.	What if you really admit to yourself that we have no data.

10.	What if you screw around behind the back of your discipline. Read some books about how to design bridges. Read some trash that goes against everything you believe about yourself and the world.

11.	Never write anything that doesn't scare you just a little.

12.	What if you refuse to summarize, what if, in the end, you only tell about what's left rather than what came before.

13.	What if none of this still tells you anything about what to do now?

Maybe you can't do these things. Maybe very few of us can. Maybe you need tenure; maybe you need a job; maybe you need a publication; and maybe (but only maybe) writing queer will get in the way of these material acquisitions. I'm untenured as I'm writing this, so maybe I am about to find out, or maybe I've followed just enough rules and broken none of the sacred ones. But what we can, all of us, do is become conscious of the "dominant cultural assumptions" about writing by, as Amy Winans (2006) puts it, "exploring the facets of the geography of normalization" (106). More scholars of writing studies could be writing queer. If the field, as it often claims and sometimes demonstrates, is really about revision, about the act of seeing again, we must see writing again. Anyone could (and maybe even should) write queer(er).

But wait, if any scholar can write queer, doesn't queerness lose its meaning—appropriated by all and rendered meaningless in the bad way instead of meaningless in that good-shifting-definition way we might all like it to? Sometimes I get tired of questions like these about who queerness belongs to and how it can't belong to everyone, or how it can't be moved off the queer body or away from sexuality—as if there is anything we do that moves *away* from sexuality and the body. But that worry, that worry that somehow everyone in this world will someday look at things in queer ways all the time, that worry that we will all just compose and teach in queer ways, that worry that then queerness will just be the norm, and therefore not queer anymore, that world is one I would love to see arrive—the truly impossible queer present. I would love to actually have this problem, to one day think to myself aw shucks, now everyone is writing in such queer ways, just what will we do now?

REFERENCES

Alexander, Jonathan, and Jacqueline Rhodes. 2011. "Queer: An Impossible Subject for Composition." *JAC* 31 (1): 177–206.

Alexander, Jonathan, and Jacqueline Rhodes. 2014. "Flattening Effects: Composition's Multicultural Imperative and the Problem of Narrative Coherence." *College Composition and Communication* 65 (3): 430–54.

Anzaldúa, Gloria. 1999. *Borderlands/La Frontera.* San Francisco, CA: Aunt Lute Books.

Banks, William P. 2003. "Written through the Body: Disruptions and 'Personal' Writing." *College English* 66 (1): 21–39. https://doi.org/10.2307/3594232.

Bartholomae, David. 2005. *Writing on the Margins: Essays on Composition and Teaching.* New York: Palgrave Macmillan. https://doi.org/10.1007/978-1-4039-8439-5.

Branstetter, Heather Lee. 2016. "Promiscuous Approaches to Reorienting Rhetorical Research." In *Sexual Rhetorics: Methods, Identities, Publics,* edited by Jonathan Alexander and Jacqueline Rhodes, 17–30. New York: Routledge.

Butler, Judith. 2004. *Undoing Gender.* New York: Routledge.

Butler, Judith. 2010. "Your Behavior Creates Your Gender." Big Think. http://bigthink.com/videos/your-behavior-creates-your-gender.

Dadas, Caroline, and Justin Jory. 2015. "Toward an Economy of Activist Literacies in Composition Studies: Possibilities for Political Disruption." In "The New Activism," special issue, *Literacy in Composition Studies* 3 (1): 143–55. https://doi.org/10.21623/1.3.1.12.

Elbow, Peter. 1994. "What Do We Mean When We Talk about Voice in Texts?" In *Voices on Voice: Definitions, Perspectives, Inquiry,* edited by Kathleen Blake Yancey, 1–35. Urbana, IL: NCTE.

Giovanni, Nikki. 2009. *On My Journey Now.* Somerville, MA: Candlewick.

Halberstam, Jack. 2011. *The Queer Art of Failure.* Durham, NC: Duke University Press. https://doi.org/10.1215/9780822394358.

Kipnis, Laura. 2003. *Against Love: A Polemic.* New York: Pantheon Books.

Micciche, Laura R. 2007. *Doing Emotion: Rhetoric, Writing, Teaching.* Portsmouth, NH: Boynton/Cook.

Muñoz, José Esteban. 2009. *Cruising Utopia: The Then and There of Queer Futurity.* New York: New York University Press.

Monson, Connie, and Jacqueline Rhodes. 2004. "Risking Queer: Pedagogy, Performativity, and Desire in Writing Classrooms." *JAC* 24 (1): 79–91.

Palmeri, Jason. 2012. *Remixing Composition: A History of Multimodal Writing Pedagogy.* Carbondale: Southern Illinois University Press.

Palmeri, Jason, and Jonathan Rylander. 2016. "'Intersecting Realities': Queer Assemblage as Rhetorical Methodology." In *Sexual Rhetorics: Methods, Identities, Public,* edited by Jonathan Alexander and Jacqueline Rhodes, 31–44. New York: Routledge.

Puar, Jasbir. 2007. *Terrorist Assemblages: Homonationalism in Queer Times.* Durham, NC: Duke University Press. https://doi.org/10.1215/9780822390442.

Ramsay, Steve. 2014. "The Hermeneutics of Screwing Around; Or, What You Do with a Million Books." In *Pastplay: Teaching and Learning History with Technology*, edited by Kevin Lee. Ann Arbor: University of Michigan Press. http://quod.lib.umich.edu/d/dh /12544152.0001.001/1:5/-pastplayteaching-and-learning-history-with-technology?g=dc ulture;rgn=div1;view=fulltext;xc=1#5.1.

Rhodes, Jacqueline. 2004. "Homo Origo: The Queertext Manifesto." *Computers and Composition* 21 (3): 385–90. https://doi.org/10.1016/j.compcom.2004.05.001.

Rhodes, Jacqueline. 2015. "The Failure of Queer Pedagogy." *Writing Instructor*, March. http://parlormultimedia.com/twitest/Rhodes-2015–03.

Rhodes, Jacqueline, and Jonathan Alexander. 2015. *Techne: Queer Meditations on Writing the Self*. Logan: Computers and Composition Digital Press/Utah State University Press.

Sagan, Carl. 2013. *Cosmos*. New York: Ballantine Books.

Stenberg, Shari. 2015. *Repurposing Composition: Feminist Interventions for a Neoliberal Age*. Logan: Utah State University Press. https://doi.org/10.7330/9781607323884.

Winans, Amy E. 2006. "Queering Pedagogy in the English Classroom: Engaging with the Places Where Thinking Stops." *Pedagogy* 6 (1): 103–22. https://doi.org/10.1215/1531 4200-6-1-103.

4

QUEERING AND TRANSING QUANTITATIVE RESEARCH

G Patterson

Not long ago, I sat on a panel with some of my colleagues in cultural rhetorics to talk about research methodology. During the conversation, which was geared toward graduate students, we discussed my mixed-methods study, which focused on English studies teachers' experiences navigating religion and LGBTQA issues in the classroom. When it came time to speak, I focused mainly on the qualitative portion of my project. As an aside, I mentioned that the first phase of my research included an online, quantitative survey that allowed me a bird's-eye view from which to analyze sixty-three English studies teachers' experiences navigating religion, sexuality, and gender identity in the classroom. But after the presentation, something interesting happened: the questions my audience posed focused almost exclusively on their anxieties about quantitative research. Some students wanted to know about survey software; others worried about statistics and figuring out Excel. In particular, a vocal contingent of graduate students sought me out for a follow-up conversation about how I was able to square my commitments to critical queer and trans scholarship with quantitative research. I empathize with these anxieties, and I share their suspicion toward a strain of research, rooted in positivism, that has traditionally attempted to solve problems by relying on disembodied, aggregated data. For intersectional queer and trans researchers in particular, it makes sense that we'd balk at a method that so often decontextualizes the complexity of a person's story and reduces it to numbers.

I understand these suspicions. Indeed, the reader might be interested to know I'd originally hoped to use a qualitative survey, comprised entirely of open-ended questions, to collect data for this project. However, after piloting my qualitative survey, I found it placed too much of a burden on participants. To get the data I needed and respect my participants' time commitments in the process, I shifted to a mostly quantitative survey, which relied upon closed-ended questions and

DOI: 10.7330/9781607328186.c004

produced numeric data. So, in a sense, my own journey toward quantitative research was a reluctant one.

Drawing from my own experience shifting from a qualitative to a quantitative survey design, I argue that sometimes the best way to gather data for a study might require that the researcher employ quantitative methods. And it would be a shame for a researcher to let go of a project because they've mistakenly assumed a quantitative measure will compromise their theoretical and ethical commitments. To that end, in this chapter, I argue that queer and trans researchers have no obligation to accept the positivistic terms that so often accompany quantitative research methods. Queer and trans researchers belong to a radical tradition of academic dissent, a tradition they can (and should) draw from to actively queer and trans quantitative methods. To demonstrate what this process can look like, I draw from my own experiences to demonstrate how the reluctant researcher can queer and trans survey design, recruitment, and analysis.

QUEERING RESEARCH METHODS

If there were a single conceptual umbrella for thinking about queer/ trans methodology, it wouldn't necessarily translate to a focus on LGBTQA topics so much as on a commitment to rigorously (if not deviantly) questioning our deeply held disciplinary narratives. Describing this kind of vigilance, Deborah Britzman and Jen Gilbert warn that when researchers become too complacent, our favorite disciplinary narratives can "foreclose the work of thinking about our thinking" (Britzman and Gilbert 2004, 82). Innovation requires the audacity to "consider the disjunctions, ambivalence . . . conflicts [and] 'loose ends'" of our disciplinary thinking (92).

In that vein, queer and trans of color methodologists have critiqued queer theory for creating a bodily and emotional distance from the subjects and people they claim to study. To address these failings, E. Patrick Johnson (2006) forwards a "quare" methodology, which calls on researchers to account for how their subjectivity influences their research; to acknowledge the intersections among racism, classism, and hetero/cissexism; and to attend to the ways in which oppression is experienced at emotional, embodied, and discursive levels (71–79). Similarly, Jin Haritaworn (2008) takes issue with queer theory's suspicion of empirical research and its tendency to analyze the same queer cultural texts repeatedly, moves that demonstrate a refusal to talk to actual queer and trans people (21–22).

A commitment to emotionally inhabit one's research requires both a radical honesty with regard to participants (Tierny 1994, 104–5) and a commitment to theorize with (rather than about) participants (Kumashiro 2002, 18). As an extension of this transparency, critical queer and trans methodologists also encourage researchers to claim and offer up their research failures so others might learn from them (Bowleg 2008, 317; Haritaworn 2008, 2.8). If, as Ignacio Rivera says, queerness is about exposing the underbelly of a respectable society, then by extension, critical queer and trans methodologists expose the underbelly of respectable research (Shah 2012).

QUEERING QUANTITATIVE RESEARCH METHODS

If some queer and trans theorists remain suspicious of empirical research, that suspicion only increases when quantitative research enters the frame. Not only have most surveys on queer and trans populations been created by people outside the community, but the data from this quantitative research has often been used to pathologize, surveil, and punish—particularly multiply minoritized LGBTQA people (Harrison-Quintana, Grant, and Rivera 2015, 172; Thompson and King 2015, 150). While queer and trans quantitative methodologists point out the benefits of having the numbers to demonstrate the importance of providing services to sexual and gender minorities (Browne 2008, 6.4; Reisner et al. 2015, 49), their most important interventions have been in pushing back against the violence enacted in the name of quantitative research.

Sometimes those interventions are embarrassingly straightforward, like pointing out that researchers must have a thorough understanding of the communities they study (Thompson and King 2015, 157; Zea, Reisen, and Díaz 2003, 289). This contextualized understanding of queer and trans communities, methodologists claim, should influence not only how researchers ask survey questions (Ingraham et al. 2015, 138) but also how researchers define their target population (Browne 2008, 5.1)—and whether or not it's necessary (or ethical) to count people among this population in the first place (Rohrer 2015, 176).

Similar to qualitative methodologists, some queer and trans quantitative methodologists also solicit community input in developing research measures (Harrison-Quintana, Grant, and Rivera 2015, 167–69; Knight, Flores, and Nezhad 2015, 117; Orel 2014, 55; Reisner et al. 2015, 50). When developing surveys, these methodologists recommend prioritizing the end user's experience above all else (Harrison-Quintana, Grant, and Rivera 2015, 169). Queering and transing reciprocity in survey design, for example, includes not only explaining why the researcher is asking a particular set of questions (Ingraham et al. 2015, 139; Knight, Flores, and Nezhad 2015, 117) but also ensuring the questions themselves are designed to give participants room to name their complex identities and experiences (Harrison-Quintana, Grant, and Rivera 2015, 172; Orel 2014, 70; Singer 2015, 70; Zea, Reisen, and Díaz 2003, 288). Some queer and trans researchers extend this vision of transparency by not only questioning traditional notions of validity, which hold participants at arm's length (Bowleg 2008, 320; Browne 2008, 6.4; Johnston 2003, 132) but also by inviting community members to join in the interpretation of survey data (Harrison-Quintana, Grant, and Rivera 2015, 167–69; Parrado et al. 2005, 211).

Taken together, these interventions challenge the violence of objectivity that so often inspires suspicion of quantitative methods in the first place. While much of the scholarship I reference isolates a single strategy for queering and transing quantitative research, my work considers how one might go about this process from start to finish—from survey design to participant recruitment and data interpretation.

QUEERING SURVEY DESIGN

While some considerations for designing qualitative and quantitative surveys might overlap, queering and transing *quantitative* survey design is a bit more difficult because the researcher must constantly resist the positivistic pressure to adopt an "objective" (if not clinical) stance toward their research measure. Despite this pressure, I argue that queer and trans methodologists are under no obligation to agree to these positivistic terms. Indeed, a critical queer and trans framework allows a researcher to question whether quantitative research can ever be purely objective. Drawing from queer of color and feminist methodologists (Browne 2008; E. P. Johnson 2006; Rooke 2010), I argue that quantitative research measures are always haunted by the researcher's social location and embodied/emotional funds of literacy. For example, as a queer, nonbinary, dyslexic, multiethnic person with white-skin privilege person, I can easily recall instances in which I've been required to answer closed-ended questions that erased crucial aspects of my identity—on patient-intake forms, human-resource records, government surveys, and so forth—in order to become palatable, recognizable, and convenient for institutional record keepers.

While positivistic ideology pressures quantitative researchers to disappear themselves from the survey measure so as not to "contaminate" the data, a critical queer/trans methodologist might understand quantitative data as always already contaminated. Once the queer/trans methodologist casts off the positivistic search for (allegedly) pure data, they are better positioned to self-reflexively compose a survey measure that honors the embodied/emotional realities of their participants and (as a result) captures richer data about their participants' experiences. Below, I offer two examples of how a researcher might draw from critical queer/trans theory to resist positivism in quantitative survey design.

Moving beyond Boxes and Binaries

Queer and trans people who've experienced the violence of being pinned down by discourse know firsthand how confining identity categories can be. While quantitative researchers always risk posing reductive questions because survey design doesn't allow much space for nuance, those of us committed to queer and trans justice must take extra care to honor the identifications of our participants.

One of the key ways surveys alienate participants is by forcing them to prioritize one aspect of their identity over another. For example, we see this in check-box survey questions about racial identity that ask participants to select one—and only one—option in the available drop-down menu. As a result, if a participant's identities aren't listed, they are effectively rendered invisible (Schilt and Bratter 2015, 79). Consider, also, the all-too-common check-box question that asks participants to identify their gender as either man or woman. Here, too, rigidly framed check-box questions erase the complexity of those who might identify as agender, nonbinary, two spirit, queer of color, or any of the other nuanced ways people identify themselves.

Worse still, in a failed attempt to be inclusive, some surveys ask participants to select their gender from the following options: man, woman, trans. Tremendously cissexist, such questions imply trans people always occupy a third-gender space and aren't (in the cases of binary trans people) "real" wo/men. Related, some surveys ask participants to select one—and only one—of the following categories to describe their sexuality: gay, lesbian, bisexual, transgender. These types of questions err in their inaccurate assumption that transgender counts as a sexual orientation. Consequently, the survey erases the fact that transgender people (just like cisgender people) can have any orientation—be that hetero, gay, lesbian, bisexual, pansexual, asexual, aromantic, and so on (Reisner et al. 2015, 43–47).

Table 4.1. Participant profile question

Please check _all_ identifications that apply to you:			
• Trans	• Lesbian	• Queer	• Hetero
• Bisexual	• Gay	• Questioning	• Write-In

As a corrective to these common missteps, I took care to emphasize, in bold font, that participants should select as many identities from the menu as they felt appropriate. In addition, as you can see in table 4.1, I always included a write-in option for these check-box questions to create an opportunity for participants to speak back to omissions and/or any problematic assumptions I might have made.

Note, too, my use of the term "Write-In" in the question above. Commonly, when profile questions do offer a write-in option, it tends to be labeled as *Other*. However sincere the researcher's intentions may be, question designs like these ignore the crisis they create for participants—first in not seeing their identity listed and *second* in being compelled to report themselves under the category Other. For people who walk through this world as Other, missteps like these are just one of many everyday reminders of how unintelligibility so very often translates to being disposable, if not worthy of violence and discrimination (Thompson and King 2015, 154).

Creating profile questions that allow participants to more freely embody themselves isn't just a matter of courtesy; it also allows the researcher to collect richer data. To illustrate, in response to the profile question posed in table 4.1, 50 percent of participants identified as heterosexual, 25 percent identified as queer, 17.2 percent identified as gay, 17.2 percent identified as lesbian, 12.5 percent identified as bisexual, 4.7 percent identified as trans, and 1.6 percent identified as questioning. But creating space for participants to name themselves also allowed participants to push back against traditional notions of sexuality and gender identity. Indeed, 7.8 percent of participants used the write-in option to convey the following responses:

- I have mixed feelings about categorizing myself.
- I'm not out at work/on campus.
- Mahukane, pansexual/omnisexual, genderqueer
- I identify as queer of color.
- Two spirit
- Humansexual

Other participants, still, used the check-all-that-apply feature to push back against the traditional binary logics of profile questions. For instance, a handful of participants identified as *both* heterosexual and queer, and a good many more identified as heterosexual and bisexual. Signal jamming the concept of boxes and binaries even further, one participant identified simultaneously as gay, lesbian, bisexual, and queer. In short, participants capitalized on the freedom offered them to push back against the tidy world of quantitative research, which asks survey takers to stay in their lane. While queering and transing profile questions undoubtedly complicates the process of data analysis and reporting, as I will demonstrate later on, such modifications to the traditional profile questions offer invaluable insight about each participant's context.

Proliferating Consent and Creating Dialogue

Many queer quantitative methodologists, like Jack Harrison-Quintana, Jamie Grant, and Ignacio Rivera, urge researchers to prioritize end users during survey development by considering transparency and reciprocity in their research (Harrison-Quintana, Grant, and Rivera 2015). Heeding this advice, I took care in my recruitment materials and survey consent form to communicate my research goals, acknowledge my political orientation as a queer/trans researcher, and disclose how I planned to use participants' data. This clarification becomes especially important for minoritized groups, who have often been the target of studies whose data is used to demonize and/or surveil them (Rohrer 2015; Thompson and King 2015).

Such strategies meant to foster transparency often exclusively appear in the consent form of the survey, where researchers explain the purpose of their study and advise participants of potential risks. But as quantitative researchers committed to queer and trans justice, we must find new ways to queer consent by accounting for participant risk and extending transparency *throughout the entire survey*.

There are, for example, numerous ways a survey measure might force participants to agree to terms with which they don't wish to comply. Some questionnaires count a survey incomplete unless each question is answered, strong-arming participants into answering questions they find unintelligible, irrelevant, or risky. Similarly, some surveys never allow participants an opportunity to explain their responses or interrogate the researcher's line of questioning (Zea, Reisen, and Díaz 2003, 287). Other questionnaires may provide only a single opportunity for participant feedback—often tacked onto the end of a survey. This design

feature limits organic dialogue and has the effect of silencing participants by forcing them to hold onto (and remember) their commentary
until the end of a very long survey.

In response to these flaws, I designed my survey to foster ongoing
dialogue as best as I could outside a face-to-face research scenario. To
give participants a clear indication of where they were headed, I divided
my thirty-six-question survey into four easy-to-digest sections. In each
section's introduction, I provided participants a rationale for my line
of questioning. To illustrate, in a survey section titled "Pedagogical
Situations," I explained:

> The following questions acknowledge that teachers' experiences in the
> classroom are not homogenous. Your answers will help illustrate the com-
> plexities of teachers' identities and professional circumstances, shedding
> light on how these factors influence classroom practices and pedagogies.

In each section of the survey, I also offered participants multiple
opportunities to "talk back" to quantitative questions. To illustrate what
this looks like, in table 4.2, I recount the questions I asked participants
about how their identities influence their classroom experiences.
Throughout, I periodically disrupt the flow of numeric check-box (CB)
and Likert-scale (LS) questions with the following optional, qualitative
question: "Please feel free to give any additional info that might help
explain/complicate your answer to Question(s) ____."

Finally, in both the consent form and throughout the survey, I
emphasized that participants were free to skip questions they didn't
want to answer. While one certainly empathizes with the researcher's
desire to have consistent response rates for each question, forcing participants to respond not only disrespects their time but also guarantees
that participants will answer questions poorly or haphazardly in order to
finish the survey.

When participants understand the researcher's aims and political
perspectives, and when they have regular opportunities to interact
with the survey, they are in a good position to help the researcher
should they encounter a survey question that doesn't quite make sense.
Rather than simply skipping the question or being forced into answering a question that doesn't represent their actual experiences, participants have an opportunity to offer the researcher valuable contextual
information—oftentimes highlighting issues the researcher might not
have thought to ask (Harrison-Quintana, Grant, and Rivera 2015, 172).
In short, this kind of transparency encourages participants to see themselves as coconstructing knowledge with the researcher (Sullivan and
Porter 1997, 13).

Table 4.2. Survey questions

Pedagogical Situations

1.   In what regions of the US have you taught? Select all that apply. (CB)

2.   In what types of higher education institutions have you taught? Select all that apply. (CB)

3.   With what disciplines are you affiliated? (CB)

4.   Please check all identifications that apply to you in terms of sexuality, gender-identity, gender performance, and sexual identity. (CB)

5.   Please feel free to give any additional info that might help explain/complicate your answer to Q4. (TB)

6.   Whether identifying as *LGBTQA* and/or ally, in what aspects of your career (if any) are you out? Please rate and check all that apply. (LS)

7.   Please feel free to give any additional info that might help explain/complicate your answer to Q6. (TB)

8.   Might any of the following identifications/embodiments influence your experiences in the classroom, particularly relating to addressing LGBTQA issues? (CB)

9.   Please feel free to give any additional info that might help explain/complicate your answer to Q8. (TB)

10.   In what ways might university and community attitudes/policies toward LGBTQA issues influence your classroom experience? Please answer the following questions: (LS)

11.   Please feel free to give any additional info that might help explain/complicate your answer to Q10. (TB)

Note: CB means checkbox, TB textbox, LS Likert scale, and RB radio button.

QUEERING RECRUITMENT

Queering and transing research also means critiquing normative assumptions about participant recruitment, which valorize probability sampling and devalue nonprobability sampling. Probability sampling describes a method of selecting participants in which any member of the population has "an equal or known chance of being selected" (Lewin 2009, 217). What often remains unspoken, however, is that probability sampling hinges upon the condition that both researcher and participant belong to homogeneous, privileged, and uncontroversial social groups. In contrast, nonprobability sampling, a method often used by researchers to target marginalized groups (Johnston 2003, 127), describes a method of selecting participants in a more localized, accessible manner.

Even when it is determined that nonprobability sampling is the best method for reaching a marginalized population, the researcher is often put in the position of describing their research as "taking what they can get." In short, while probability sampling is described as valid, trustworthy, and unbiased, nonprobability sampling is described as convenient, biased, and accidental. Such a hierarchy—which privileges generaliz-ability above all else—depoliticizes, disembodies, and devalues the mate-rialities of queer and trans research. Resisting such limiting frameworks, I forward a vision of *queer/trans kinship sampling*, a method of recruit-ment that unapologetically draws from embodied, intimate frameworks to reach participants. Rather than agree to hetero- and cissexist terms that would frame such specificity as a weakness, below, I articulate two examples of how alternative methods of recruitment might be under-stood as a source of strength and academic rigor.

Interrogating Disembodied Sampling

While scholars sometimes acknowledge that probability sampling works best with homogenous social groups (Lewin 2009, 217–18), I want to take this a step further and argue that the assumptions that undergird probability sampling assume not only a homogenous but also a *privi-leged* social group. Working from Allan Johnson's (2006) sociological understanding of the term, I articulate privilege as both the ability to move through social/institutional space with relative ease and, cultur-ally speaking, to get to "define reality and to have prevailing definitions of reality fit their experience" (33). Social groups aren't accidentally homogenous but rather designed to prevent heterogeneity; for that rea-son, we must consider sampling methods within frameworks of privilege, power, and difference. Below, I interrogate the privileged assumptions probability sampling makes about both participant and researcher.

To begin, marginalized social groups are often impossible to contact in using a random/probability sample—which has everything to do with a relative lack of privilege. For instance, marginalized groups may not feel safe within dominant social networks where researchers might more eas-ily solicit calls for participants. Related, because of their lack of cultural/institutional power, many marginalized groups lack the resources to cre-ate secure, robust networking infrastructures within their own communi-ties. Together, these complications limit the researcher's access to reach said marginalized group—outside of using nonprobability sampling.

In my own research, for example, I sought to understand queer, trans, and ally teachers' experiences navigating religion, sexuality, and gender identity in the English studies classroom. While I did put out a call on the largely interdisciplinary queer studies listserv, I had no systematic way of reaching LGBTQA teachers in my specific field. Similarly, while I put out a call for participants on the field-specific writing program administra-tor's listserv, this particular space isn't always friendly to queer and trans professionals. Indeed, the very week I recruited participants from the WPA-L, some listserv members engaged in a lengthy exchange that (for the most part) expressed sympathy for a conservative Christian student who was removed from a graduate counseling program for refusing to meet with gay or trans clients. While this is not to say queer and trans professionals don't belong to the WPA-L, examples such as these illustrate why some LGBTQA teachers might opt out of such hostile spaces.

I would have been in luck, of course, had the Conference on College Composition and Communication's Queer Caucus (4CQC) had access to its own listserv. Alas, it does not. Instead, the only way to recruit caucus members was through a Facebook group, set to private, because not all group members felt safe enough to identify as part of the 4CQC online. More still, because of Facebook's poor reputation for protecting its members' privacy, some 4CQC members didn't participate in this online space. While it may be tempting to read the lack of a 4CQC listserv as happenstance and some 4CQC members' decision to opt out of a private Facebook group as individual preference, it is important that we read this relative lack of access to centralized networks within the context of heterosexism and transphobia in higher education.

Related, probability sampling also assumes the process of recruiting participants will be relatively risk free for the researcher. What remains unspoken in this meritocratic vision of person-based research is the implication that the researcher occupies both a privileged social location and a noncontroversial embodiment. Such constraints make random sampling difficult (if not impossible) for multiply minoritized queer and trans researchers, who often move through social and institutional spaces as marked, controversial bodies.

For example, during the process of recruiting for my study, a white, het-cis senior faculty member cornered me during a department gathering. Incensed by the topic of my research, the faculty member pushed his finger into my chest and warned me that I had better be careful about how I represented Christians in my project. False binaries about the mutual exclusivity of LGBTQ people and Christians aside, this intimidating encounter influenced my decision—as a then graduate student and contract employee—to abstain from using the department listserv to solicit recruitment help from better-networked senior faculty members. While it may be tempting to interpret this anecdote as an aberration in an otherwise accepting field, my own research bears out that LGBTQ faculty repeatedly face physical, verbal, and professional retribution for their commitments to queer and trans justice (Patterson 2016, 136–38). Not only must we address how such risks influence the research process, but we must also challenge the ways in which disembodied recruitment narratives (shrouded in privilege) champion probability sampling as more rigorous and trustworthy while denigrating its marked cousin, nonprobability sampling, as less rigorous and less trustworthy.

Recruiting through Kinship Networks

In the previous section, I demonstrate the unsafe conditions for marginalized researchers and participants that make probability sampling a difficult, if not impossible, avenue to pursue. One of the ways marginalized researchers, who study marginalized populations, navigate around such roadblocks is to use nonprobability sampling. Unfortunately, when weighted in relation to probability sampling, nonprobability sampling is regarded as less valid, less trustworthy, and less rigorous. What I want to forward in this section is not a justification of nonprobability sampling. Rather, I want to suggest that queer and trans researchers refuse to agree to terms that entrap them and their work in a negative feedback loop, which always finds them lacking. In place of probability/nonprobability sampling, I forward an alternative vision of queer and trans kinship sampling—a method of recruitment that unapologetically draws from embodied, intimate frameworks to reach participants.

Rather than seeking to recreate a representative sample of a target group, queer and trans kinship recruitment shuns the fiction of generalizable data and instead shamelessly seeks to center marginalized voices. For example, in my own work, had I sought to recreate a representative sample of my target group—LGBTQA and ally teachers in English studies—I would have been left with a predominantly white, able-bodied, middle-class, het-cis group of participants. I had no interest in pursuing a sampling method that would simply recreate (through probability sampling) or approximate (through nonprobability sampling) an echo chamber of voices already dominant in the field. Instead, I shamelessly reached out to my queer and trans kinship networks—via e-mail, phone, social media, and in-person solicitations—asking people to share and to participate in my study. This process was unabashedly intimate; many of the colleagues who helped me recruit participants were people I knew—friends who'd been to my apartment, who'd attended parties with me, who'd helped me move, who'd shared meals, drinks, coffee with me. With my meager resources and then marginal status in the field, I can safely say I'd never have reached sixty-four participants had I stuck to traditional, purposive sampling. And while it's difficult to track how and where each of the sixty-four participants accessed the survey, I

can attest to the power of queer/trans kinship with the following anecdote: of the sixteen survey participants who elected to be contacted for
follow-up interviews for the second half of my study, the overwhelming
majority of them knew me or my friends/colleagues.

Finally, in contrast to nonprobability samples, which characterize
recruitment as "taking what one can get," queer and trans kinship sampling is a much less passive affair. A scholar who endeavors to employ
kinship sampling must be an active, visible member in queer and trans
networks long before the recruitment process takes place. In more ways
than one, queer and trans recruitment methods require intimate knowledge of one's target population. More still, because of this intimate
connection with participants, queer and trans kinship sampling holds
researchers accountable. It is not enough for the researcher to tell their
participants what they hope to find and to what ends the data will be
used. Queer and trans kinship networks will follow up, and if a researcher's work doesn't keep its promises or meet community standards, these
networks will push back. Intimacy has a cost.

QUEERING DATA INTERPRETATION

Finally, queering and transing quantitative research means pushing back
against traditional approaches to interpretation, which typically include
reading for the mean, median, and standard deviation of participants'
answers (Lewin 2009, 222). For scholars who delight in deviation and
who regard norms with a healthy suspicion, such approaches to data
interpretation seem squarely at odds with critical queer and trans commitments. Indeed, as Michael Warner (1999) observes in *The Trouble
with Normal*, queer and trans people are often left open to violence and
discrimination precisely because of the ways in which people regularly
conflate "statistical and evaluative norms" (53). As counterintuitive as it
may initially seem, quantitative researchers committed to critical queer
and trans frameworks must resist reducing participants to numbers in
write-ups of their findings.

In that spirit, I call attention to the discursive elements always at
play when researchers draw from numerical data to report findings.
As Lisa Bowleg (2008) reminds us, the data does not speak for itself;
this reminder of our active role in the interpretation process opens
up two possibilities for engaging differently with our numeric data
(320). First, queer and trans researchers might shift their perspective
of quantitative data, understanding it less as a series of Arabic numbers
on a spreadsheet and more as a narrative that, numeric or no, they can

begin to read from the margins. Second, and dovetailing with the first strategy, researchers would do well to remind themselves that a narrative (numeric or no) cannot be interpreted outside its context. Though there are a good many approaches researchers might take to resist the clinical, disembodied approach to reading quantitative data, I believe these strategies can help researchers interpret survey responses in more critical and ethical ways.

Reading for Deviation

Traditional approaches to data interpretation hinge upon the alleged neutrality and thus veracity of numbers. According to this philosophy, a researcher can average participants' aggregate answers to determine what does (and doesn't) count as an issue worthy of investigation. What sometimes gets overlooked in this process is that averages aren't just statistical norms; they're normative. Simply put, when researchers wrest participants' numeric answers from their social locations, it becomes easy to disregard how majority responses take place within a network of power, privilege, and difference. As a corrective, queer and trans researchers should consider how numbers on a spreadsheet relate to *material* sociopolitical contexts.

To illustrate this way of reading, I want to examine participants' answers to a question that asked them to describe their perception of risk—to career and to emotional/physical safety—if they were to address the intersection of sexuality, gender identity, and religious discourse in the classroom. If one were to read participants' answers only in terms of averages, it'd seem like a fairly happy picture. As evident in figure 4.1, the majority of participants didn't perceive significant risks to their career (69 percent) and physical/emotional safety (75 percent).

But focusing solely on the averages ends up consolidating socially dominant perspectives, doing a violence to people who fall outside the norm. This phenomenon struck a particular chord, given that the majority of my participants identified as heterosexual (50 percent) and cisgender (95 percent). It is for these reasons that the 25 percent of participants who perceived risks to their career and the 31 percent of participants who perceived risks to their emotional/physical safety became especially important to me. Who were these people?

In an attempt to read from the margins, I tracked participants' perceptions of risk based upon their sexual/gender identities. All of a sudden, the story about risk became a bit clearer: 31 percent of LGBTQA respondents feared that addressing the LGBTQA-religious junction

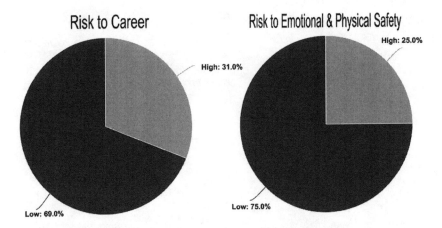

Figure 4.1. Participants' perceptions of risk to career and physical/emotional safety. Response rate: 58/64 participants answered these questions.

in their classrooms would pose a risk to their career, and a whopping 45 percent of LGBTQA respondents worried that addressing this intersection would pose risks to their physical and/or emotional safety. In contrast, 15 percent of het-cis participants perceived risks to their career and to their physical/emotional safety. Reading for perceptions of risk along the initialism, the reader can see in figure 4.2 that cisgender gay men reported such fears at significantly lower rates than their female and gender-variant counterparts.

Taking a cue from scholars like Lisa Bowleg, I resisted the urge to present these "deviations" with a politically neutral bent. Interpreting one's data queerly isn't just about embodying one's participants; it's about calling attention to how these bodies are (un)able to move through political space. With that in mind, it's important to read het-cis participants' significantly lower perceptions of risk alongside the backdrop of scholarship that shows het-cis faculty are less likely to seem "biased" when questions of sexuality and gender identity arise in the classroom (Kopelson 2003; Wood 2005).

Similarly, the comparably low risk reported by gay men alongside much higher perceptions of risk among lesbians and bisexuals cannot be separated from a body of scholarship that demonstrates that (people perceived as) women are much more likely to be harassed and/or threatened in the classroom—a phenomenon with odds that only increase if that faculty member is also a person of color, gender nonconforming, disabled, queer, or otherwise perceived as a cultural outsider (Condit 1996; Karamcheti 1996; Mitchell 2008).

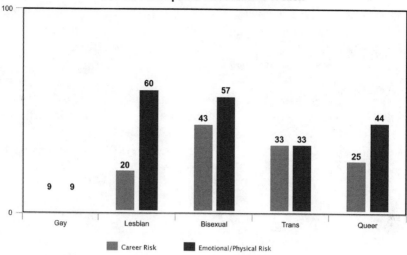

Figure 4.2. *LGBTQ participants' assessment of risk. Response rate: 58/64 participants answered these questions.*

Reading for Context

One of the ways researchers have attempted to address an interpretive process that disembodies participants is to use write-in answers to "complicate" quantitative data. While this is certainly a step in the right direction, it doesn't go far enough. Precisely because this approach still prioritizes disembodied, aggregate data, it sees little problem in uprooting individual participants' compelling write-in answers from their native context. Critical queer and trans researchers, in contrast, must shift their priorities from merely "complicating" aggregate data to embodying (or quite literally "fleshing out") participants' write-in answers. In short, the critical queer and trans researcher understands write-in answers aren't merely supplemental but are *integral* to understanding quantitative data.

To give the reader an idea of what it might mean to cling to specificity and context at all costs, I elaborate upon my previous discussion of participants' perception of risk when addressing religion, sexuality, and gender identity in the classroom. In addition to asking participants to quantify their sense of risk to career and physical/emotional safety (referenced above), I also included an optional write-in question that asked participants to further clarify their responses. Among these write-in answers, two themes surfaced: the first cluster of answers explained their perception of risk to career/safety in relation to their marginalized institutional status and/or social location. The second cluster of answers didn't address risk so much as express a preference for addressing LGBTQA issues in neutral ways—by using pro/con frameworks to discuss queer and trans issues or, for example, by sidestepping hetero- and cissexist arguments by focusing solely their "persuasiveness" (Patterson 2016, 140–45).

Certainly, even robbed of additional context, these write-in answers added depth to my already compelling numerical data. But in order to honor the complex experiences and identities that informed participants' answers, I made the decision to trace each write-in answer back to the larger context of its originating survey.

As a result of taking this extra step, I discovered that all of the participants who expressed fears about their physical safety were cis lesbians and queer transpeople. Many of these write-ins related their perception of risk to the fact that protections for LGBTQA faculty were missing, untested, or existed on paper but not in practice. For example, one participant wrote,

> For the most part, my department has been supportive. I have been threatened before by students at my present institution—and directly confronted by homophobic/transphobic faculty at another institution. But, [addressing the LGBTQA-religious juncture] is a cause worth the risk to my career and safety.

Though this write-in answer is informative even out of context, when I traced this answer back to the survey, it became clear that the participant was a queer and trans grad student of color. This participant taught at a state school in Hawai'i, where they described classroom discussions of LGBTQA issues to be volatile. This additional contextual information, gleaned from reading the participant's survey holistically, offers two insights that might otherwise have been lost had I prioritized the aggregate data: first, multiply minoritized faculty who face the most risk in addressing contentious topics are frequently graduate students and contract faculty. Second, flying in the face of common stereotypes about where faculty are most likely to experience conservative pushback, it is important to consider that such risks aren't limited to faculty teaching in the Bible Belt or at religious institutions.

Related, tracking the second cluster of write-in answers, I found that all the participants who advocated pedagogical neutrality were het-cis identified—with the exception of one cisgender lesbian who was a contingent faculty member. Among the answers from this second cluster was the following reflection, written by a white, het-cis participant:

As an instructor in composition courses—at least the ones *I teach*—has a difficult time keeping students motivated, directed, on-task, and on time. It is equally difficult to keep the writing formal, academic, and coherent. The education portion of my duties, by far, takes so much effort. Also, I have a tight schedule in terms of what must get covered and when. I try to avoid issues which, in all cases, create hard feelings in the classroom. Students come in with hard feelings toward writing. That is my first and major task to address, and the one that everyone would agree we are there for, even if most do not like that. In a public university, it is my task to show them how the rest of the university community expects them to write and how to perfect their own, individual arguments, whether I agree with them or not.

Reading this commentary out of context, what first stands out is how this particular ally articulates queer and trans issues as tangential to the field of rhetoric and writing. This write-in answer also echoes a common narrative in rhetoric and writing scholarship that characterizes LGBTQA issues as controversial topics and advocates that teachers set aside their personal beliefs to do the "real job" of teaching writing (Downs 2005; Hansen 2005; Perkins 2001; Rand 2001). In short, without tracing this write-in response back to its originating survey, it would be easy to mischaracterize this response as reactionary (if not phobic) pushback to addressing queer and trans topics in the classroom. But part of adopting a critical queer and trans lens means refusing to sensationalize decontextualized survey data.

Reading the participant's comment within the context of their survey paints a more complex (and perhaps fairer) picture. This participant is an ESL instructor who has no expertise in LGBTQA topics and whose previous discussions of queer and trans topics with students were forced and uncomfortable. Furthermore, this participant worries that some teachers' responses to LGBTQA topics might disregard the cultural and religious perspectives of international students. This is a legitimate concern—especially given how frequently mainstream LGBTQA-rights discourse portrays non-Western and non-Christian folks as somehow more phobic. And as scholars like Jasbir Puar (2007) and Dean Spade and Craig Willse (Spade and Willse 2014) argue, this picture of the Other as backwardly homo-/transphobic often serves a racist, imperialist agenda. To reiterate, had I not taken the extra step to place this participant's story within its larger context, I would have unfairly mischaracterized this participant's agenda.

Reading quantitative data queerly means putting bodies back into interpretation. This process of reading data may seem counterintuitive; it most certainly flies in the face of the notion that the best way to call attention to an issue is by demonstrating that high frequencies of people experience that problem. But by reading against the grain, we not only ensure participants aren't erased, but we also ensure researchers don't construct straw men out of participants in order to create compelling data. Moreover, by prioritizing the people behind the quantitative data, researchers can ensure that their results are not only more accessible but also that they are more urgent for readers as well. Numerical data alone won't persuade an audience to act—but the stories behind them just might.

CONCLUSION

I have submitted for the reluctant researcher a series of tactics that might be used to resist the positivistic assumptions that so often plague quantitative survey measures. Drawing from my own quantitative research, I've illustrated strategies for queering and transing survey design, participant recruitment, and data interpretation. There is, of course, no one-size-fits-all approach to queering and transing quantitative research, and I see my work here as less about offering a set of prescriptive practices and more about providing the seeds that might foment a methodological rebellion.

It would indeed be a shame for a researcher to give up on an idea for a project because it might require quantitative methods. Quantitative research describes a method, not an ideology; a researcher need not compromise their commitment to queer and trans scholarship to collect the data they need. Instead, I believe queer and trans researchers can harness their disidentification (Muñoz 1999) with quantitative methods to make productive interventions that can lead to more useful, more ethical research practices. As I mention at the beginning of this chapter, queer and trans researchers would do well to remind themselves that they belong to a radical tradition of academic dissent; aspiring scholars can (and should) employ their rigorous theoretical training—and continue to question norms and court deviance—so they can make quantitative methods their own.

REFERENCES

Bowleg, Lisa. 2008. "When Black + Lesbian + Woman ≠ Black Lesbian Woman: The Methodological Challenges of Qualitative and Quantitative Intersectionality Research." *Sex Roles* 59 (5–6): 312–25. https://doi.org/10.1007/s11199-008-9400-z.

Britzman, Deborah, and Jen Gilbert. 2004. "What Will Have Been Said about Gayness in Teacher Education?" *Teaching Education* 15 (1): 81–96. https://doi.org/10.1080/1047621042000180004.

Browne, Kath. 2008. "Selling My Queer Soul or Queerying Quantitative Research?" *Sociological Research Online* 13 (1): 1–15. https://doi.org/10.5153/sro.1635.

Condit, Celeste. 1996. "Theory, Practice, and the Battered (Woman) Teacher." In *Teaching What You're Not: Identity Politics in Higher Education,* edited by Katherine Mayberry, 155–73. New York: New York University Press.

Downs, Doug. 2005. "True Believers, Real Scholars, and Real True Believing Scholars: Discourses of Inquiry and Affirmation in the Composition Classroom." In *Negotiating Religious Faith in the Composition Classroom,* edited by Elizabeth Vander Lei and Bonnie Lenore Kyburz, 39–55. Portsmouth, NH: Boynton/Cook.

Hansen, Kristine. 2005. "Religious Freedom in the Public Square and in the Composition Classroom." In *Negotiating Religious Faith in the Composition Classroom,* edited by Elizabeth Vander Lei and Bonnie Lenore Kyburz, 39–55. Portsmouth, NH: Boynton/Cook.

Haritaworn, Jin. 2008. "Shifting Positionalities: Empirical Reflections on a Queer/Trans of Color Methodology." *Sociological Research Online* 13 (1): 1–12. https://doi.org/10.5153/sro.1631.

Harrison-Quintana, Jack, Jamie Grant, and Ignacio Rivera. 2015. "Boxes of Our Own Creation: A Trans Data Collection Wo/Manifesto." *Transgender Studies Quarterly* 2 (1): 166–74. https://doi.org/10.1215/23289252-2848949.

Ingraham, Natalie, Vanessa Pratt, and Nick Gorton. 2015. "Counting Trans* Patients: A Community Health Center Case Study." *Transgender Studies Quarterly* 2 (1): 136–147. https://doi.org/10.1215/23289252-2848922.

Johnson, Allan. 2006. *Privilege, Power, and Difference.* Boston, MA: McGraw Hill.

Johnson, E. Patrick. 2006. "'Quare' Studies or (Almost) Everything I Know about Queer Studies I Learned from My Grandmother." In *Sexualities and Communication in Everyday Life: A Reader,* edited by Karen Lovaas and Mercilee Jenkins, 69–86. Thousand Oaks, CA: SAGE.

Johnson, Jeffrey. 2015. "Information Systems and the Translation of Transgender." *Transgender Studies Quarterly* 2 (1): 160–65. https://doi.org/10.1215/23289252-2848940.

Johnston, Lynda. 2003. "Surveying Sexualities: The Possibilities and Problems of Questionnaires." In *Cultural Geography in Practice,* edited by Alison Blunt, Pyrs Gruffudd, John May, Miles Ogborn, and David Pinder, 122–38. New York: Routledge.

Karamcheti, Indira. 1996. "Caliban in the Classroom." In *Teaching What You're Not: Identity Politics in Higher Education,* edited by Katherine Mayberry, 215–37. New York: New York University Press.

Knight, Kyle, Andrew Flores, and Sheila Nezhad. 2015. "Surveying Nepal's Third Gender: Development, Implementation, and Analysis." *Transgender Studies Quarterly* 2 (1): 101–22. https://doi.org/10.1215/23289252-2848904.

Kopelson, Karen. 2003. "Rhetoric on the Edge of Cunning; Or, the Performance of Neutrality (Re)Considered as a Composition Pedagogy for Student Resistance." *College Composition and Communication* 55 (1): 115–46. https://doi.org/10.2307/3594203.

Kumashiro, Kevin. 2002. *Troubling Education: Queer Activism and Anti-Oppressive Pedagogy.* New York: Routledge Falmer.

Lewin, Cathy. 2009. "Elementary Quantitative Methods." In *Research Methods in the Social Sciences,* edited by Bridget Somekh and Cathy Lewin, 215–25. Los Angeles, CA: SAGE.

Mitchell, Danielle. 2008. "I Thought Composition Was about Commas and Quotes, Not Queers: Diversity and Campus Change at a Two-Year College." *Composition Studies* 36 (2): 23–50.

Muñoz, José Esteban. 1999. *Disidentifications: Queers of Color and the Performance of Politics.* Minneapolis: University of Minnesota Press.

Orel, Nancy. 2014. "Investigating the Needs and Concerns of Lesbian, Gay, Bisexual, and Transgender Older Adults: The Use of Qualitative and Quantitative Methodology." *Journal of Homosexuality* 61 (1): 53–78. https://doi.org/10.1080/00918369.2013.835236.

Parrado, Emilio, Chris McQuiston, and Chenoa Flippen. "Participatory Survey Research: Integrating Community Collaboration and Quantitative Methods for the Study of Gender and HIV Risks among Hispanic Migrants." *Sociological Methods & Research* 34 (2): 204–39. https://doi.org/10.1177/0049124105280202.

Patterson, G. 2016. "The Unbearable Weight of Neutrality: Religion and LGBTQ Issues in the English Studies Classroom." In *Sexual Rhetorics: Methods, Identities, Publics,* edited by Jonathan Alexander and Jackie Rhodes, 134–46. New York: Routledge.

Perkins, Priscilla. 2001. "'A Radical Conversion of the Mind': Fundamentalism, Hermeneutics, and the Metanoic Classroom." *College English* 63 (5): 585–611. https://doi.org/10.2307/379046.

Puar, Jasbir. 2007. *Terrorist Assemblages: Homonationalism in Queer Times.* Durham, NC: Duke University Press. https://doi.org/10.1215/9780822390442.

Rand, Lizbeth. 2001. "Enacting Faith: Evangelical Discourse and the Discipline of Composition Studies." *College Composition and Communication* 52 (3): 349–67. https://doi.org/10.2307/358623.

Reisner, Sari L., Kerith J. Conron, Kellan Baker, Scout, Jody L. Herman, Emilia Lombardi, Emily A. Greytak, Alison M. Gill, and Alicia K. Matthews. 2015. "'Counting' Transgender and Gender-Nonconforming Adults in Health Research: Recommendations from the Gender Identity in US Surveillance Group." *Transgender Studies Quarterly* 2 (1): 34–57. https://doi.org/10.1215/23289252-2848877.

Rohrer, Megan. 2015. "The Ethical Case for Undercounting Trans Individuals." *Transgender Studies Quarterly* 2 (1): 175–78. https://doi.org/10.1215/23289252-2848958.

Rooke, Allison. 2010. "Queer in the Field: On Emotions, Temporality, and Performativity in Ethnography." In *Queer Methods and Methodologies: Intersecting Queer Theories and Social Science Research,* edited by Kath Browne and Catherine Nash, 149–60. New York: Routledge.

Schilt, Kristen, and Jenifer Bratter. 2015. "From Multiracial to Transgender? Assessing Attitudes toward Expanding Gender Options on the US Census." *Transgender Studies Quarterly* 2 (1): 77–100. https://doi.org/10.1215/23289252-2848895.

Shah, Svati. 2012. "Sex Work and Queer Politics in Three Acts." *Scholar and Feminist Online* 10 (1). http://sfonline.barnard.edu/a-new-queer-agenda/sex-work-and-queer-politics-in-three-acts/.

Singer, T. Benjamin. 2015. "The Profusion of Things: The 'Transgender Matrix' and Demographic Imaginaries in US Public Health." *Transgender Studies Quarterly* 2 (1): 58–76. https://doi.org/10.1215/23289252-2848886.

Spade, Dean, and Craig Willse. 2014. "Sex, Gender, and War in an Age of Multicultural Imperialism." *QED: A Journal in GLBTQ Worldmaking* 1 (1): 5–29. https://doi.org/10.14321/qed.1.1.0005.

Sullivan, Pat, and Jim Porter. 1997. *Opening Spaces: Writing Technologies and Critical Research Practices.* Westport, CT: Ablex.

Thompson, Hale, and Lisa King. 2015. "Who Counts as 'Transgender'? Epidemiological Methods and a Critical Intervention." *Transgender Studies Quarterly* 2 (1): 148–59. https://doi.org/10.1215/23289252-2848913.

Tierny, William. 1994. "On Method and Hope." In *Power and Method: Political Activism and Educational Research,* edited by Andrew Gitlin, 97–115. New York: Routledge.

Warner, Michael. 1999. *The Trouble with Normal: Sex, Politics, and the Ethics of Queer Life.* Cambridge, MA: Harvard University Press.

Wood, Laurie. 2005. "Not a Hetero: Confessions of a Dangerous Homo." *Cultural Studies* 19 (4): 430–38. https://doi.org/10.1080/09502380500219449.

Zea, Maria, Carol Reisen, and Rafael Díaz. 2003. "Methodological Issues in Research on Sexual Behavior with Latino Gay and Bisexual Men." *American Journal of Community Psychology* 31 (3/4): 281–91. https://doi.org/10.1023/A:1023962805064.

5

REDRES[ING] *RHETORICA*
A Methodological Proposal for Queering Cross-Cultural Rhetorical Studies

Chanon Adsanatham

Comparative rhetoric—the cross-cultural research of undervalued/ erased communicative practices across time and space in order to transform the dominant rhetorical paradigm—has blossomed into a productive apparatus in writing studies, as evident in the growing number of works on non-Western rhetorics (Baca 2008; Lipson and Binkley 2009; Mao and Wang 2015; Schoen 2012; Stroud 2009) and, more recently, a comparative rhetoric manifesto that calls upon rhetoricians to heed historicity, specificity, and self-reflexivity in cross-cultural research. Within the manifesto, LuMing Mao (2014) has encouraged our discipline to further diversify comparative studies by attending to the facts of nonusage: rhetorical practices that have been dismissed or erased altogether as anything but rhetoric across global contexts. Toward that end, scholars of cross-cultural rhetoric have recovered a wide range of rhetorical practices and rhetors outside the West, expanding historiography beyond the Greco-Roman tradition. Yet, while these works have challenged Eurocentrism and gender bias in rhetorical theory, they have focused mainly on a gender-normative body of texts from people assigned male or female at birth or self-identified men and women. In aiming to diversify *Rhetorica*, if we fail to challenge our assumptions about gender and sexuality, we may be reifying heteronormativity in ways that run counter to the heteroglossic purpose of revisionary historiography (Rawson 2010).

Any attempt to queer rhetorical studies cross-culturally, however, raises complex issues. To begin with, studying non-Western rhetorics in the context of the West is already a complicated undertaking; it involves selecting, interpreting, and negotiating unfamiliar concepts from one culture and re-representing them to another—all of which has epistemic and ethical consequences. In addition, comparative work requires

DOI: 10.7330/9781607328186.c005

translating and redepicting ideas from one culture to another while heeding ideologies and cultural and language gaps involved in the process (Godard 2001). These already difficult undertakings become more complex when we shift our focus to unorthodox subjects and practices, those challenging the cultural logic of our tradition and, at times, their own. To research what is "nonnormative," we sometimes draw upon queer theory. As a lens, it allows us to rethink what counts as "normal" and hegemonic, but Asian scholars (Blackwood 2008; Engebretsen 2008; Sinnott 2010) have questioned the theory's universal applicability. Since queer theory was developed within an Anglo/Western sociopolitical context, uncritical application of the lens can reify Eurocentrism in ways that marginalize local uniqueness, or worse, propel power imbalance at the theoretical level. Such problematic practice can hinder the radical aim of queer theory and the reflexive mission of writing studies. Needed then is a culturally and critically sensitive methodology that fosters intercultural dialogism to challenge hetero/normativity and Eurocentric approaches in how we engage the facts of nonusage across cultures.

Interconnecting queer theory and comparative rhetoric, this chapter proposes a five-part heuristic for conducting cross-cultural rhetorical studies of nonnormative "texts": recontemplation, defamiliarization, reevaluation, the ethics of care, and seeking incongruities—or REDRES, for short. To contextualize the heuristic, I first explicate recent advances in comparative rhetoric methodologies and the major tenets of queer theory, demonstrating how their congruences have helped develop my proposed methodology. I then define the components of my fivefold approach. Specifically, to avoid drifting into the purely esoteric, I offer a set of concrete heuristic questions to help readers apply each component of REDRES. Next, I use my heuristic to read a prominent, globally worshipped Buddhist deity named Kuanyin as a queer figure to destabilize binary sexual representations of divinity and gender ideology in religious discourse, and I close by discussing the larger implications of REDRES within the global turn of writing studies.

COMPARATIVE RHETORIC AND QUEER THEORY: TOWARD A METHODOLOGICAL ALLIANCE

Integrating comparative rhetoric and queer theory to develop REDRES enhances both fields in several ways. To date, much comparative rhetoric scholarship has focused on canonical works of men and women who are rhetorical exemplars at the expense of nonnormative identities. This pattern, I fear, may limit the diversity and scope of comparative rhetoric and reify heteronormative, binary sex and gender assumptions. Specifically, comparative rhetoricians have not taken up K. J. Rawson's (2010) call for historians to move away from using a specific gender category as a starting point of recovery (see also Bessette, this volume); otherwise, Rawson cautions, the research could reify "women" or "men" as concretized staples of studies and fail to scrutinize the "naturalness" of sex and gender underpinning historical studies. Given that queer theory aims to address differences and silences that have been marginalized through binaries and to trouble monolithic understanding of identities and what is normative, integrating queer theory into cross-cultural research can offer a critical lens to expand how comparative rhetoric engages the facts of nonusage.

At the same time, comparative rhetoric can diversify queer studies and prevent an asymmetrical global flow of knowledge production and academic imperialism. Western knowledge and theories, like queer theory, are often globally exported as influential, cutting-edge epistemological frames. Judith Butler, Eve Kosofsky Sedgwick, Michel Foucault, and Jack Halberstam, for example, have become transnationally recognized figures in queer studies, while ideas and theorists from non-Western cultures continue to be lesser known and to have less impact on queer writing studies. Hence, Asian queer theorists (Jackson, Martin, and McLelland 2005) have advocated for "queerer" cross-cultural research to broaden national and cultural boundaries of queer scholarship. Even though scholars have diversified queer scholarship beyond White, middle-class contexts (Driskill et al. 2011; Eng 2010; Muñoz 1999; Pritchard 2016), much research—particularly in writing studies—still concentrates on ethnic differences *within* the West. Hence, composition theory and pedagogy, however queer, remain predominantly tied to the Western context and paradigm. To rectify these gaps in queer studies, comparative rhetoric and queer theory ought to become methodological allies. Toward that end, I would like first to outline the major tenets of comparative rhetoric and queer studies to illustrate their congruences.

Over the past decade, comparative rhetoricians (Mao and Wang 2015; Wang 2013; Wu 2002) have proposed disparate methodologies to circumvent Orientalist approaches that have harmed cross-cultural research in the past. As a whole, they advocate valuing and contextualizing non-Western rhetoric on its own terms and reaching beyond essence, borders, biases, and emic/etic views through practicing the art of recontextualization (Mao 2013a): the reflexive act of troubling our own mode of thinking through comparative analysis that critically attends to historicity, specificity, and incongruity in our own tradition and others.

Queer theory provides a useful complement to recontextualization. It allows us to challenge normative and essentialist assumptions that can hinder dialogic cross-cultural engagement; however, because *queer* is a slippery signifier with multiple meanings, I must first clarify how I am using the term. In this essay, *queer* denotes a subversive edge and critical stance against the status quo through questioning and challenging what is normative and hegemonic in culture. My definition builds upon eight key assumptions in queer studies: the imperative to

1. challenge norms in order to embrace whatever is at odds with the normal and open up new ways of knowing and being known (Halperin 1995);

2. question essentialist perspective about identities and culture (Kemp 2009);

3. overturn binary thinking and hierarchies that stem from it (Sullivan 2003);

4. scrutinize how and why some knowledge, identities, and practices are validated at the expense of others (Sedgwick 1990);

5. interrogate what politics, ethics, and epistemology are produced as a result of exclusion (Sullivan 2003);

6. expose the instability of taken-for-granted identities, knowledge, and practices produced through asymmetrical power relations (Browne and Nash 2010);

7. posit failure as desirable and productive to subvert normalization (Halberstam 2011);

8. trouble *techne* used to produce knowledge (Dadas 2016).

Based on these tenets, queer constitutes a critical position and practice toward transformative potentials. Although attunement to sex, gender, and sexuality are of central importance, queer theory invites us to challenge normativity beyond that confine. As David L. Eng, Jack Halberstam, and José Esteban Muñoz acknowledge, "Given its commitment to interrogating the social processes that not only produced and recognized but also normalized and sustained identity, the political promise of the term [queer] resided in its broad critique of multiple social antagonisms, including race, gender, class, nationality, and religion" (Eng, Halberstam, and Muñoz 2005, 1). The radical potential of queer studies ultimately lies in its refusal to be pinned down into a static, easily settled definition, allowing for endless critical reinventions and interventions, or as Kath Browne and Catherine J. Nash argue, "[Queer] is a term that should be redeployed, fucked with and used in resistant and transgressive ways, even if those ways are resisting what could, and some would argue already has, become a 'queer orthodoxy'" (Browne and Nash 2010, 9). To further "redeploy" and challenge "queer orthodoxy," comparative rhetoric and queer theory ought to become integrated.

These two disciplines share several presuppositions. They aim to contest essentialism, normativity, and power imbalance in culture; research and celebrate marginalized epistemologies, sites, values, and practices; focus on "unintelligible subjects" to challenge taken-for-granted assumptions; promote knowledge that moves away from binaries, borders, biases, and dichotomies; trouble the normative assumptions and processes involved in knowledge production. In short, queer theory and comparative rhetoric value excesses, absences, and multiplicities to promote different grids of intelligibility in order to drive epistemological and social change. Integrating comparative rhetoric and queer theory thus allows us to cultivate a productive critical lens to denormalize the purview of rhetorical studies, enriching heteroglossia in how we engage difference and *queer* theory.

A METHODOLOGY OF REDRES

In what follows, I combine insights from comparative rhetoric and queer theory to delineate a fivefold methodology consisting of recontemplation, defamiliarization, reevaluation, the ethics of care, and seeking incongruities—or REDRES. I explicate each of the five elements to demonstrate how, collectively, they provide a heuristic for queer(ing) comparative rhetorical studies.

Recontemplation

The first element of REDRES—recontemplation—calls upon rhetoric scholars to continually cultivate reflexivity by situating and resituating ourselves, by heeding how our ever-shifting subjectivities, habitus, and standpoints (SHS) are intersubjective, fluid, and contingent. Challenging the myth of fixed, stable identities, queer theory sees subjectivities as multiple, unstable, and, at times, unidentifiable (Butler 1991; Gorman-Murray, Johnston, and Waitt 2010; McDonald 2013; Sedgwick 1993). They are a negotiated product of our cultural milieu and social-epistemic interactions, which come to shape our schemas, inclinations, and practices. Hence, our SHS are never disinterested or constant. They change. They shift. They reform. Recognizing that SHS are ever shifting, we must continually resituate ourselves along the way and heed the multiple facets of our subjectivities in the research process. Thus, the act of situating one's self should remain ongoing and should take into account a spectrum of subjectivities. The prefix *re* in *recontemplation* is meant to signify the imperative of processual recursivity toward reflexivity. However, often in empirical research, scholars acknowledge their subjectivities at the beginning of the study by merely disclosing basic demographic details without reflecting more deeply about their varied status and effects. (e.g., I'm a white, middle-class lesbian with liberal political views who works at a flagship state college.) Consequently, the attempt to achieve reflexivity seems superficial; it is not deepened or dynamic in ways that align with queer assumptions about the fluidity of identities.

How, then, might we enact deeper reflexivity in queer cross-cultural rhetorical studies (or any research)? Mary Garrett (2013) has proposed the following threefold heuristic for cross-cultural rhetoricians: embodying mindfulness by observing our thoughts, feelings, and physical sensations without judgment; alternating between seeing things through concepts familiar and unfamiliar to the culture we research; and developing empathy to decenter ourselves. While helpful and important, these techniques do not explicitly address the need to account for multiple identities we (and our subject) may embody and how they may color our research, issues queer theory emphasizes (Gorman-Murray, Johnson, and Waitt 2010). Drawing upon queer insights about identities to supplement Garrett's useful techniques, I propose the following critical questions to help scholars engage recontemplation in a detailed and sustained manner:

- What are the multiple nuances of my subjectivities? How do they develop and affect how I approach my study and understand what I am studying?
- What cultural or theoretical beliefs do I hold? How might they affect my work?
- What are my preunderstanding and preconceptions of a concept, figure, or tradition I am studying? What are their genealogies/sources? What might I need to call into question as a result?
- What are my subject positions and location in relation to what I am studying?
- What is the impetus of my study? How do my subjectivities and assumptions affect how I justify my research impetus and approach?

Collectively, these questions challenge us to make ourselves an important text of study alongside the data we collect. They push us to develop a more nuanced engagement of subjectivities and move reflexivity to the fore of our research. This is particularly important given what we know about human learning from education theory: when we encounter new materials, we often draw upon existing schemas and mental maps to make sense of them (Bain 2004). These mental maps, however, often reflect hegemonic paradigms, which can initially impact our ability to interpret an unfamiliar concept from another culture on its own terms. Thus, we must be aware of their presence and potential influence through engaging reflexivity. Yet, it is important to recognize that recontemplation does not always guarantee a harmonious resolution. It may raise uneasiness and perhaps shock as a result of a more candid, accurate image of one's self (Garrett 2013). Through embracing the potential discomfort, however, we can become more critically mindful researchers in our attempt to "queer" rhetorical studies across traditions.

Defamiliarization and Reevaluation

The next two components of REDRES—defamiliarization and reevaluation—are interconnected. They involve acquiring culturally contextualized knowledge without taking it at face value for the sake of "going native" in order to overcorrect or overcompensate our interpretation, and complicating our understanding by framing and reframing it through cross-cultural thinking. These twofold praxes align with the call in queer theory and methodology to value what is disparaged and hidden through its own unique cultural logic without deferring to hegemonic or taken-for-granted assumptions in order to trouble normative paradigms (Browne and Nash 2010; Sedgwick 1990) and, at the same time, to situate our interpretation within its cultural milieu to avoid an ahistorical reading about what is normative or antinormative in a given case (Bessette 2016). In short, besides heeding context, we must make what is familiar strange and what is strange familiar without normalizing or privileging either one in order to avoid establishing a hierarchy.

Specifically, defamiliarization requires us to regard how "the other's own heterogeneity inhabits its space and how it inexorably influences the other's own multiplicity" and develop "a localized narrative and [search] for its new and broader significance within and outside its own tradition" (Mao 2013b, 47–48). We must, therefore, avoid the temptation to use the theory in one tradition as a universal barometer to interpret other perspectives and resist the temptation to search for equivalence between a concept in our tradition and another. As queer theorists posit, what often seems prevalent, universal, natural, or normal can also be exclusionary, dismissive, and oppressive (Bessette 2016; Taylor 2010; Sedgwick 1990). To enact defamiliarization, we must remain open to rethinking our knowledge and assumptions by pressing:

- What concepts or lenses am I bringing into my cross-cultural engagement that may be external to or nonexistent in the context I am researching? How do they enhance and hinder my interpretation?

- What is the local understanding of a particular concept or figure? Given what I know about the context I am studying, what must I critically be aware of as a result?

- What key terms and cognate concepts (discursive fields) must I understand to gain a contextualized understanding of what I am researching?

These questions help foster rhetorical listening (Ratcliffe 2005) by challenging us to frame our understanding of a rhetorical practice or figure within its cultural logic but, at the same time, avoid taking what we have learned without scrutiny. We are pressed to heed the ideological and material conditions influencing the culture we are examining to avoid romanticizing or totalizing it. In this process, we heed Jean Bessette's (2016) call for queer researchers to develop a queer methodology that "attends to historical specificity and examines with nuance the complexity of power relations within what seems to be normal" (161). In sum, defamiliarization promotes a comparative inquiry that moves away from reductionism and prejudice divorced from historicities and toward contextualized knowledge built upon critical curiosity and insights.

Defamiliarization fosters the third element of REDRES: a reevaluation of perspectives toward new paradigms and practices to challenge normative thinking. Specifically, reevaluation pushes us to ask:

- How might the marginalized perspective from another culture, figure, or tradition be good to think with?

- How might the insights we gained through defamiliarization denormalize the way we have thought about X? What are the affordances and limits of the new insight?

- How might our insights challenge normative assumptions and frameworks within our tradition, as well as within others?

- What new understanding, theory, and practice might be advanced as a result?

Through analyzing these issues, reevaluation compels us to question what is normative by pushing us to rethink our perspectives beyond traditional lenses, or, by reframing our perspectives in queer terms, reevaluation enables us to "make strange," "frustrate," "counteract," and "funk up" (Warner 1993) privileged knowledge to yield more varied epistemologies and multidimensional perspectives. This, in turn, allows us to circumvent epistemic violence: the erasure, silencing, and destruction of marginalized knowledge and lives from the privileging of Eurocentric knowledge and culture. Recognizing epistemic violence is particularly important in light of Asian scholars' concerns about the dominance of Anglo-US-centric works in queer studies. As Elisabeth L. Engebretsen (2008) states, "The continued primacy of Anglo-US-centrism in queer studies retains certain disciplinary effects that marginalize alternative standards of sexual subjectivity and collectivity [in cross-cultural contexts]. . . . Monolithic and hegemonic interpretations based on Western contexts as primary point and scale of reference has limited usefulness" (110–11). Reevaluation provides a critical intervention against these concern; it pushes us to recognize the limits of our knowledge through engaging the marginalized not as a corrective additive to enhance "diversity" but as a critical move to rethink the dominant paradigm and practice.

Ethics of Care

Insights gained from reevaluation must be predicated upon an ethics of care. Care, however, should not be viewed as a vague principle or value but rather situated as an ethical praxis within the queer tradition. While care is a key emphasis of feminist methodology, it is always a tacit part of queer studies because queer theory emerged out of both caring for and about the marginalized Other (Bessette 2016; Rand 2014).[1] More broadly, queer scholarship aims to subvert hegemonic norms to eradicate marginalization stemming from oppressive cultural logic. As Deepali Gokhale (1984) argues, "[Queer] requires us to honor and celebrate the wholeness of each individual. . . . It requires us to identify which parts of our community are underrepresented and to nurture those who are most wounded" (391). Similarly, Butler (2004) has urged queer researchers to recognize care as a critical part of transnational queer/gender studies. She specifically encourages the importance of interrogating "whether [our] 'representation' of the poor, the indigenous and the radically disenfranchised . . . is a patronizing and colonizing effort, or whether it seeks to avow the conditions of transformation that make it possible, avow the power and privilege of the intellectual, avow the links in history and culture that make an encounter . . . and academic writing possible" (229). Gokhale's and Bulter's arguments resonate with comparative rhetoric's commitment to promote a high degree of self-reflection and rectify the disempowerment and elision of the marginalized. They enrich how we foster accountability in queer cross-cultural work.

Enacting care as ethical praxis involves several considerations. First, we must question our own research impetus and revise it as necessary. As our research impetus functions as a compass to anchor our inquiry, we must ask *what* type of questions we are posing, *how* we are framing and asking them, and *why*? We must question our own questions, in short. Second, cross-cultural queer rhetorical studies should not be an armchair venture for us to enhance our academic capital in the ivory tower, but it should attempt to contribute to cultures we are studying in some ways, including in historical studies. Reciprocity of benefits must be considered as an important part of the research process (Lu 2015). Third, we must hold ourselves accountable to how we redepict what we are studying by recognizing the potential effects our write-up may have on the culture or people we are researching. We must realize that in doing cross-cultural work, our work is never merely a representation but rather a re-presentation that yields epistemic, social, and political consequences.

Accordingly, the ethics of care should be examined multidimensionally by considering:

- What are the impetus, potential impacts, and larger implications of our research questions and analysis to the context or culture we are studying?
- In what ways might the knowledge we have gained be useful to the culture or tradition we are investigating? If applicable, how might we involve stakeholders to help us decipher the potential contributions of our work?
- How can we make our work more meaningful and accessible to the context, culture, and stakeholders we are studying?
- How are we re-presenting the other culture or tradition in our work? What might be some potential consequences and implications?

These questions enrich care in cross-cultural research beyond matters of representation and interpretation to include a careful examination of our research aims, approach, and most notably, reciprocity of benefits. In sum, they help us guard against the impetus to speak for the Other (Alcoff 1991) without considering the fraught consequence of such an impetus and hold ourselves responsible in how we read and write about the Other. Enacting the ethics of care thus circumvents a missionary-style or imperialistic approach to researching the marginalized, deepening research accountability as we work to queer comparative studies in rhetoric and composition.

Seeking Incongruities

The last component of **REDRES** involves searching for and embracing incongruities as transformative openings. This heuristic builds upon Mao and Wang's (2015) call for comparative rhetoricians to acknowledge that all rhetorical knowledge is heterogeneous, multidimensional, and always in the process of being created through analysis, as well as queer theory's acknowledgment that all knowledge and identities are fragmented, multiple, and nonessentialist (Browne and Nash 2010; Sullivan 2003). Valuing variations, deviancies, and fissures, queer scholars (Butler 1991; Sedgwick 1993) accentuate the importance of valuing multiplicities and messy insights as a radical edge to subvert power and generate insights, or as Stacey Waite argues in her chapter in this collection, to queer research/writing is to grapple with "singular voices, conclusions, dependable narratives, and discernable data" (43). Accordingly then, the notion of a unified, singular, or homogenous tradition is a myth that elides heteroglossia, or worse, propels silencing and oppression. As cross-cultural researchers, we must seek inconsistencies—things that are messy or fail to fit the norm, the standard, or the canon—as critically productive without presupposing what is "normal" or "abnormal" through ahistorical, ethnocentric assumption (Bessette 2016). Through these practices, we are not merely challenging the normative and the hegemonic, but we are transforming the margin and multiplicities into sites of radical possibilities and transgression.

Engaging the following questions can help researchers identify incongruities to complicate heteroglossia in cross-cultural work:

- Based on what we know about the historical and cultural context, who are the major and minor players, winners and losers? How might their existence and discourse call into question what is hegemonic, normalized, well known, or accepted?

- What is failing to fit into our current narrative about what we are studying? How might the presence of what is different or unusual— "the unfit"—challenge us to rethink our insights? How might we need to reframe traditional thinking or paradigm?

- What and who are being accentuated in how we present our data and analysis? How might what we have failed to recognize generate new openings and possibilities for more nuanced recovery and analysis?

These questions motivate us to seek incongruities and what we failed to address as topoi to complicate how we analyze and understand our data. Embracing messiness (Dadas 2016), they motivate a contrapuntal reading that leads to a more multidimensional understanding of what we are researching. Thus, contrary to common expectations, incongruences are not undesirable or impertinent but rather productive and kairotic. As Sedgwick (1993) reminds us, to queer is to "open a mesh of possibilities, gaps, overlaps, dissonances and resonances, lapses and excesses of meanings" (8). As we notice that which is challenging to discern and that which does not fit into the predominant tradition, we are hereby pressed to reconsider what we are seeing/not seeing, reporting/not reporting, similar to the process of data coding. When a new code emerges in qualitative analysis, we do not simply ignore it as irrelevant but are forced to recode the data set to discover new patterns, helping us see information in a different light. Likewise, researchers seeking to denormalize comparative rhetorical studies must approach what is "unfit," what is messy, and what we failed to consider as an opportunity for in(ter)vention. In short, seeking incongruencies fosters multiplicities toward revisionary knowledge.

ILLUSTRATING REDRES: QUEERING A GLOBAL BUDDHIST ICON

Having defined the five components of REDRES, in what follows, I briefly illustrate my proposed heuristic by using it to read a widely globally worshipped Buddhist deity called Kuanyin as a queer figure. Specifically, I analyze how they have been perceived in the Mahayana and Theravada schools of Buddhism and how these insights might challenge binary gender ideology and assumptions in Thai Buddhist cultural discourse, as well as extend our thinking about religious icons beyond a binary conception. [2] In examining these questions, I focus on components of REDRES most pertinent to my study. Ultimately, I hope to complicate Kuanyin's identities and, more broadly, destabilize normative sexual categories in religious representation and discussion, the broader impetus of my illustration.

Some background about the deity is necessary: Kuanyin is a major figure in the Mahayana tradition, a branch of Buddhism popular in East Asia that emphasizes the importance of the *bodhisattva*: a being who vows to liberate all creatures from suffering and lead them to enlightenment; they devote their life toward their epiphany and freedom from karmic woes (Yifa et al. 2007). However, unlike an ordinary bodhisattva, Kuanyin is known as a celestial bodhisattva of compassion and selflessness; they have reached Nirvana or supreme enlightenment and freedom from worldly woes and rebirth but have refused Buddhahood until they can help all beings become enlightened. [3] For this reason, they are sometimes known as *the great bodhisattva of mercy*. Originally a male deity from India, Kuanyin was introduced by Buddhist missionaries to China, where he became widely worshipped in the ninth century and subsequently revered in East and Southeast Asia. Around the seventh century, Chinese artists began redepicting him as a woman, and since then, Kuanyin is typically portrayed as a female such that a male depiction is no longer as common (Paul 1985).[4] However, Buddhist sutras from 406 and 627 CE indicate that the celestial bodhisattva's sex and gender are ambiguous and unfixed. They have no definite form and can manifest as a man, woman, animal, or mythical creatures, depending on the need and disposition of the worshipper. According to the Compassion Mantra from the sixth century, a sutra about the disparate forms of Kuanyin, the bodhisattva can appear as monks, Buddhas,[5] demons, warriors, goddesses, priestesses, and so forth. Kuanyin's sex and gender are thus rhetorical manifestations that constantly evolve as a response and appeal to suit worshippers' needs. Their shifting identities provide an allegorical reminder of two major Buddhist assumptions about existence: *anicca*, the impermanence of all lives and conditions, and *anatta*, formlessness, substancelessness, or the illusion of the self. As a whole, Kuanyin's ever-shifting identities reflect a key Buddhist belief that all phenomena are insubstantial; there is no essence to matter. Accordingly, then, Kuanyin can be seen as an antiessentialist figure since they are not tied to a specific or permanent sex, gender, and physical identity. The celestial bodhisattva's constantly shifting manifestations indicate their fluidities beyond a rigid, binary sex/gender categorization and paradigm.[6]

My fascination with Kuanyin began at an early age in Thailand, my native country, where the deity is widely worshipped in the female form. They became popular among Thais through Chinese immigrants, who probably brought their statue to Thailand around the thirteenth century. Yet, Thailand is primarily a Theravada Buddhist nation. Instead of emphasizing the importance of the celestial bodhisattva, this branch of Buddhism accentuates the path to being an *arhat*, a person who works individually to reach Nirvana; it does not accentuate the bodhisattva path, and, as I will later demonstrate, has a different understanding about the bodhisattva.[7] Given the difference in emphasis between the Theravada and Mahayana traditions, some beliefs and rituals from the latter may not always be familiar to the former, and vice versa.

However, I grew up in a Thai-Chinese Mahayana-Theravada household. As a second-generation Chinese immigrant in Bangkok, my grandmother, a devout Mahayana Buddhist from China, often took me to Chinese Buddhist temples, where I learned about Kuanyin and Mahayana teachings. I have also recently been ordained as a Mahayana monk at a major Mahayana monastery in China that was built to honor Kuanyin. In addition, I have been immersed in Thai Theravada Buddhism from having been a novice, or a young monk in training, an opportunity only available to men. My male sex and masculine/cisgender, I must admit, allow me to have greater opportunities and access to worship and to interact with monks, enriching my insights about Buddhism. In Theravada Buddhism, a woman, whether ordained or not, may be prohibited from certain rites and spaces in the monastery. Moreover, she may typically be ordained as a nun, and in the Mahayana school, she can become a *bhikkhuni*, or a female monk, but only if she is committed to being one for life (whereas men may leave monkhood, though it is atypical). Within both schools of Buddhism, nuns and *bhikkhuni* are considered inferior to monks in status and seniority. Thus, from the feminist perspective, Buddhism might be considered a patriarchal religion. Altogether, my subjectivities as a male Thai-Chinese Mahayana-Theravada Buddhist have helped me gain a bicultural perspective about Kuanyin and Buddhism in general.[8] At the same time, my identity as an Asian American scholar who values feminism and liberal worldviews motivates me to question gender ideology in my native religion.[9] My reading of Kuanyin provides a case in point.

In Thai Theravada cultural discourses, Kuanyin is often portrayed as an unenlightened goddess due to a prominent cultural understanding about what a bodhisattva is. Theravada tales about the Buddha posit becoming a bodhisattva as a step to reaching Nirvana: in his previous lives, the Buddha had to undergo several reincarnations as bodhisattvas to accumulate supreme merits before he could be reborn as the Buddha, his final incarnation, in which he extinguished all temptation, desire, and passion to achieve supreme enlightenment. In these tales, the bodhisattva represents a figure who is still working to transcend desire, the cause of suffering and rebirth. Most significantly, Thai tales about the Buddha's rebirths do not distinguish between an ordinary or celestial bodhisattva, conflating the two as unenlightened. This impacts how Kuanyin is understood and represented in Thai Theravada cultural discourses: they become an inferior female deity who has yet to overcome carnal and worldly attachments. As one Thai Buddhist writes in a prominent online religious forum, "Goddess Kuanyin is a bodhisattva [in the Theravada sense]. Her energy/power is one of a bodhisattva. But the Buddha is more supreme, as he has reached Nirvana and has dissolved himself from all worldly/carnal passion." Kuanyin's inferior status is often reflected in a title Thais frequently use to refer to them: *jao mae*. These Thai words denote a celestial female spirit, angel, or lowly nymph. It is not one used to refer to Kuanyin in the Eastern Mahayana school, where they are called Kuanyin *pusa* or Bodhisattva Kuanyin instead. (Their Mahayana name here is not gender specific; it simply means the listening bodhisattva.) The inferior meaning of *jao mae* stands in contrast to *phra*, a word/title Thais use for monks, the Buddha, and other high-ranking divinities (who are often males). Thus, calling Kuanyin *jao mae* not only reinforces their lower status as an unenlightened goddess, it places them on the same level as ordinary or lowly female spirits. Most notably, they are reduced to a female form.

What's more, the relegation of Kuanyin as a *jao mae* reflects traditional Buddhist ideology about the inferiority of the female sex. According to Buddhist scholar Diana Paul (1985), women have symbolized lust, evilness, temptation, and spiritual inferiority in traditional Buddhist scriptures: "By far the most liberal portraits of women's spiritual achievements . . . are to be found in an extremely small percentage" (217). Indeed, the Buddha has always been a male; buddhahood is conflated with the male sex and masculine gender. Hence, in being recognized as a *jao mae* in Thai cultural discourse, Kuanyin's womanly image reinforces the larger religious belief about the lower status of women, but most significantly, it limits a richer understanding of the celestial bodhisattva's fluid identities, which I now examine through the Mahayana lens.

At issue here is how the complexities of Kuanyin's gender and status are overlooked in Thai Theravada discourse. Theravada's focus on the importance of *arhat* and its conception of bodhisattva hinder a productive understanding of Kuanyin as a heterogeneous figure and hir significance in the Mahayana tradition. In Mahayana scriptures, Kuanyin is associated with several cognate terms: *mercy, listener*, Buddha, *light, wisdom*, and *supreme merits*. Through these terms, they are sometimes hailed as a Buddha, leading them to be called Kuanyin Yulai or Kuanyin the Buddha. This makes them resemble a *phra* in the Theravada sense of the term, so it may be more fitting to refer to them as Phra Kuanyin in Thai. Seeing Kuanyin through the cognate terms with which they are associated allows us to redress cross-cultural misconceptions of the celestial bodhisattva as *jao mae* and, what's more, call into question misogynistic representations and assumptions about the inferiority of their sex, gender, and form. More broadly, recognizing Kuanyin's fluid identities enables us to reconceptualize our understanding of religious tradition and rhetorical representation of holy figures without an attachment to a binary male or female and patriarchal or matriarchal conceptions; we are invited to heed *anatta*, or formlessness, and *annica*, or impermanence of existence, of divine figures not as a void but as a detachment from essence in how we make sense of religious icons and depictions. Our understanding of Buddhist divinity becomes more fluid and porous—queered—as a result. The ambiguous figure of Kuanyin serves as a case in point.

However, my interpretation of Kuanyin is not without issues. Refiguring them as a queer figure may come across as heretical, as it might challenge traditional thinking and gender hierarchy and patriarchal ideology in Thai religious discourse. Yet, as Mao (2013b) argues, comparative rhetoric should not take the object of study at face value but put the object of study into critical view. Likewise, queer theory encourages us to trouble what is taken for granted and hegemonic. Toward those ends, my reading of Kuanyin through the lens of Mahayana Buddhism, a minority religion in Thailand, provides critical insights to trouble traditional assumptions about the celestial bodhisattva's image and status in Thai cultural discourse. To broaden these insights beyond academic venues as a way to enact care in REDRES, I have presented my reading of Kuanyin in a Thai Buddhist discussion forum to counter a binary and reductive understanding of the bodhisattva as *jao mae* and in concert with a Mahayana temple, which has sponsored free publications of Mahayana literature to help Thai Theravada audiences better understand the significance and functions of the bodhisattva through the Mahayana lens.

Nevertheless, Kuanyin is an enigmatic deity with incongruities. They are simultaneously a major and minor figure within Buddhism. While the celestial bodhisattva is widely worshipped in temples and households worldwide, they are typically portrayed to be lower ranking than Sakayamuni Buddha, the male figurehead and founder of Buddhism. At the same time, they are recognized and called many forms and titles, ranging from the Buddha, to the Buddha's disciple, to the future Buddha, to mother, to introspective listener, to compassionate hearer, to goddess. These titles are not mutually exclusive and are often used interchangeably, indicating that Kuanyin's genders, statuses, and positions are neither static nor consistent. Their heterogeneous manifestations and titles are not contradictions or convolutions, but rather demonstrate the fluidity and malleability of their genders and representations: Kuanyin manifests themself through a spectrum of identities beyond a singular image or binary understanding of human sex, gender, and divinity. Kuanyin may thus seem like a confusing, enigmatic figure because they do not fit traditional religious depictions of high-ranking divinities, whose sex and gender often remain static and predictable. Ultimately, however, the ambiguity and messiness of their sex, gender, and manifestations are critically productive: they denormalize our perspectives about divinity. What's more, the disparate guises of Kuanyin point to the flexible rhetorical characterizations of the bodhisattva; they could be called, evoked, or refashioned in many unique ways to respond to different unique contexts, making these characterizations rhetorical manifestations that provide fertile openings for future rhetorical studies.[10] Altogether, my reading of Kuanyin works to deconcretize "women" and "men" as the staple of historical studies (Rawson 2010). Although my analysis begins with a specific gender category as a starting point, I ultimately move beyond naturalizing or settling within these very categories to reposition Kuanyin as a queer divinity, using REDRES as a heuristic to guide my analysis.

CONCLUSION

As I hope my reading of Kuanyin has demonstrated, interconnecting comparative rhetoric and queer studies to create a methodology of REDRES allows us to develop a critical framework for cross-cultural analysis that works to challenge, twist, and question taken-for-granted assumptions and knowledge. Ultimately, to queer is to denormalize what is hegemonic; similarly, to compare is to recontextualize what is well established. Interconnecting these aims, the five components of REDRES—recontemplation, defamiliarization, reevaluation, the ethics of care, and seeking incongruities—interlock to guide critical research actions. No heuristic, however, can be a catch-all, nor can it guarantee a harmonious resolution or resolve all complexities in cross-cultural research. Indeed, it should not. As Waite argues in her chapter in this collection, queer research and writing must resist closure and celebrate messiness as radically generative and subversive in order to resist and transgress orthodoxy and straight-jacketed representations and information.[11] As we work to diversify rhetorical research through an interconnected queer and cross-cultural lens, we are not merely adding voices to rectify their absence within writing studies—we are working to redraw boundaries of rhetorical knowledge and paradigms, remapping the terrains of rhetorical studies within the global turn of rhetoric and composition with reflexive, critical, and accountable cautions. REDRES provides a compass to orient that tricky but promising expedition.

NOTES

1.   Erin Rand (2014) sees care/caring as an important historical component of queer activism, particularly during the rise of AIDS in the 1980s and 1990s. Thus, queer theory/positionality cannot be seen separately from care/caring.

2. As it is the aim of this chapter to queer normative understanding of gender and to challenge male/female dichotomy, I am deliberately using singular *they* instead of *s/he* to avoid reinforcing binary thinking. Such practice has been accepted by professional organizations such as the Modern Language Association and the Associated Press.

3. There are multiple bodhisattvas in the Mahayana tradition, and they are not accorded the same status or rank. Their merits and boons vary. Those who are of lower rank or status may still be working to attain enlightenment. Kuanyin, however, is an exception. They are a celestial bodhisattva, indicating their enlightened status.

4. Buddhist scholars have yet to offer a definitive theory for Kuanyin's sex and gender change because it is uncertain when and where the change took place. Tracing this issue is beyond the aim or scope of this article. Some monks believed that the resexing from male to female helped reinforce the image of compassion, kindness, and nurture to heighten the deity's appeal to worshippers, so Kuanyin's sexual transformation could be seen as rhetorical. Buddhist scholar Diana Paul (1985) has also suggested that the resexing of Kuanyin may have resulted from grammatical accidents when Buddhist scriptures were translated from Sanskrit into Chinese. Feminine abstract nouns are often used in Sanskrit scriptures.

5. I am pluralizing Buddhas here because in the Buddhist tradition, there is more than one Buddha. There are Buddhas of the past, present, and future. The Mahayana believes that Kuanyin can manifest as different Buddhas. For details, see the Compassion Mantra, a scripture that describes the various guises of Kuanyin.

6. For this reason, I am using *they* to refer to the bodhisattva.

7. The difference between Mahayana and Theravada Buddhism is beyond the scope of this paper. Space limitations do not allow me to examine this issue at length. Interested readers should see the *Encyclopedia of Buddhism* as a starting point.

8. My intersecting identities are in no way static. They shift and change depending upon context and through my interaction with Buddhist monasteries. For instance, as a second-generation Thai-Chinese, I am sometimes seen as not "Chinese enough" or not knowledgeable enough about rituals at traditional Chinese temples, compared to first-generation Chinese like my parents or a native Chinese citizen. At the same time, when I attend Theravada Buddhist ceremonies in rural Thailand, some see me as more Chinese than Thai. Nonetheless, my fluid and ever-shifting identities have exposed me to different branches and practices of Buddhism.

9. Women and men have different privileges in Buddhism. Although the Buddha posits that men and women are both capable of reaching Nirvana, the Buddha has always been a male. Furthermore, even when women are ordained as *bhikkhuni*, or female monastics, in Buddhism, Buddhist precepts indicate that they must remain inferior to monks and may not teach monks, regardless of their age and length of ordination.

10. There are other celestial bodhisattvas in the Mahayana tradition who possess multiple sexes and gender identities: Manjusri and Samantabhadra. In focusing on Kuanyin, I have not addressed their significance and transformations. These figures provide fertile ground for more nuanced studies through REDRES.

11. Also see Halberstam's and Dadas's works. Both scholars ask us to avoid adhering to a narrow notion of success and coherence. They advocate celebrating messiness in queer research experience, process, and discovery.

REFERENCES

Alcoff, Linda Martin. 1991. "The Problem of Speaking for Others." *Cultural Critique* 20 (20): 5–32. https://doi.org/10.2307/1354221.

Baca, Damian. 2008. *Mestiz@ Scripts, Digital Migrations, and the Territories of Writing*. New York: Palgrave. https://doi.org/10.1057/9780230612570.

Bain, Ken. 2004. *What the Best College Teachers Do*. London: Harvard University Press.

Bessette, Jean. 2016. "Queer Rhetoric *in Situ.*" *Rhetoric Review* 35 (2): 148–64. https://doi.org/10.1080/07350198.2016.1142851.

Browne, Kath, and Catherine Nash. 2010. *Queer Methods and Methodologies*. Surrey: Ashgate.

Blackwood, Evelyn. 2008. "Transnational Discourses and the Circuits of Queer Knowledge in Indonesia." *GLQ: Journal of Lesbian and Gay Studies* 14 (4): 481–507. https://doi.org/10.1215/10642684-2008-002.

Butler, Judith. 1991. *Gender Trouble*. London: Routledge.

Butler, Judith. 2004. *Undoing Gender*. London: Routledge.

Dadas, Caroline. 2016. "Messy Methods: Queer Methodological Approaches to Researching Social Media." *Computers and Composition* 40:60–72. https://doi.org/10.1016/j.compcom.2016.03.007.

Driskill, Qwo-Li, Chris Finley, Brian Joseph Gilley, and Scott Lauria Morgensen. 2011. *Queer Indigenous Studies: Critical Interventions in Theory, Politics, and Literature*. Tucson: University of Arizona Press.

Eng, David L. 2010. *The Feeling of Kinship*. Durham, NC: Duke University Press. https://doi.org/10.1215/9780822392828.

Eng, David L., Jack Halberstam, and Jose Esteban Muñoz. 2005. "What's Queer about Queer Studies Now." *Social Text* 23 (3–4): 1–17. https://doi.org/10.1215/01642472-23-3-4_84-85-1.

Engebretsen, Elisabeth L. 2008. "Queer Ethnography in Research and Practice: Reflections on Studying Sexual Globalization and Women's Queer Activism in Beijing." *Graduate Journal of Social Science* 5 (2): 88–116.

Garrett, Mary. 2013. "Tied to a Tree: Culture and Self-Reflexivity." *Rhetoric Society Quarterly* 43 (3): 243–55.

Godard, Barbara. 2001. "The Ethics of Translating: Antoine Berman and the 'Ethical Turn' in Translation." *TTR traduction, terminologie, rédaction* 14 (2): 49–82. https://doi.org/10.7202/000569ar.

Gokhale, Deepali. 1984. "The InterSEXion: a Vision for a Queer Progressive Agenda." In *Readings for Diversity and Social Justice*, edited by Mauriaane Adams, et al., 388–90. London: Routledge.

Gorman-Murray, Andrew, Lynda Johnston, and Gordan Waitt. 2010. "Queer(ing) Communication in Research Relationships: A Conversation about Subjectivities, Methodologies and Ethics." In *Queer Methods and Methodologies*, edited by Kath Browne and Catherine J. Nash, 96–112. Surrey: Ashgate.

Halberstam, Jack. 2011. *The Queer Art of Failure*. Durham, NC: Duke University Press. https://doi.org/10.1215/9780822394358.

Halperin, David. 1995. *Saint Foucault: Towards a Gay Hagiography*. New York: Oxford University Press. https://doi.org/10.1093/acprof:oso/9780195111279.001.0001.

Jackson, Peter A., Fran Martin, and Mark McLelland. 2005. "Re-Placing Queer Studies: Reflections on the Queer Matters Conference." *Inter-Asia Cultural Studies* 6 (2): 299–311. https://doi.org/10.1080/14649370500066035.

Kemp, Jonathan. 2009. "Queer Past, Queer Present, Queer Future." *Graduate Journal of Social Science* 6 (1): 1–23.

Lipson, Carol, and Roberta Binkley, eds. 2009. *Ancient Non-Greek Rhetorics*. West Lafayette, IN: Parlor.

Lu, Xing. 2015. "Comparative Rhetoric: Contemplating on Tasks and Methodologies in the Twenty-First Century." *Rhetoric Review* 34 (3): 266–69.

Mao, LuMing. 2013a. "Beyond Bias, Binary, and Border: Mapping out the Future of Comparative Rhetoric." *Rhetoric Society Quarterly* 43(3): 209–25.

Mao, LuMing. 2013b. "Writing the Other into Histories of Rhetoric: Theorizing the Art of Recontextualization." In *Theorizing Histories of Rhetoric*, edited by Michelle Ballif, 41–57. Carbondale: Southern Illinois University Press.

Mao, LuMing. 2014. "Thinking beyond Aristotle: The Turn to How in Comparative Rhetoric." *PMLA* 129 (3): 448–55. https://doi.org/10.1632/pmla.2014.129.3.448.

Mao, LuMing, and Bo Wang. 2015. "Manifesting a Future for Comparative Rhetoric." *Rhetoric Review* 34 (3): 239–74. https://doi.org/10.1080/07350198.2015.1040105.

McDonald, James. 2013. "Coming Out in the Field: A Queer Reflexive Account of Shifting Researcher Identity." *Management Learning* 44 (2): 127–43. https://doi.org/10.1177/1350507612473711.

Muñoz, Jose Esteban. 1999. *Disidentification: Queers of Color and the Performance of Politics.* Minneapolis: University of Minnesota Press.

Paul, Diana. 1985. *Women in Buddhism.* Los Angeles: University of California Press.

Pritchard, Eric Darnell. 2016. *Fashioning Lives: Black Queers and the Politics of Literacy.* Carbondale: Southern Illinois University Press.

Rand, Erin. 2014. *Reclaiming Queer: Activist and Academic Rhetorics of Resistance.* Tuscaloosa: University of Alabama Press.

Ratcliffe, Krista. 2005. *Rhetorical Listening: Identification, Gender, Whiteness.* Carbondale: Southern Illinois University Press.

Rawson, K. J. 2010. "Queering Feminist Rhetorical Canonization." In *Rhetorica in Motion*, edited by Eileen E. Schell and K. J. Rawson, 39–52. Pittsburgh, PA: University of Pittsburgh Press. https://doi.org/10.2307/j.ctt5vkff8.7.

Schoen, Megan. 2012. "Rhetoric of Thirstland: An Historical Investigation of Discourse in Botswana." *Rhetoric Review* 31 (3): 271–88. https://doi.org/10.1080/07350198.2012.683999.

Sedgwick, Eve Kosofsky. 1993. *Tendencies.* Durham, NC: Duke University Press. https://doi.org/10.1215/9780822381860.

Sedgwick, Eve Kosofsky. 1990. *Epistemology of the Closet.* Los Angeles: University of California Press.

Sedgwick, Eve Kosofsky. 1985. *Between Men: English Literature and Male Homosocial Desire.* New York: Columbia University Press.

Sinnott, Megan. 2010. "Borders, Diaspora, and Regional Connections: Trends in Asian 'Queer' Studies." *Journal of Asian Studies* 69 (1): 17–31. https://doi.org/10.1017/S0021911809991586.

Stroud, Scott. 2009. "Pragmatism and the Methodology of Comparative Rhetoric." *Rhetoric Society Quarterly* 39 (4): 353–79.

Sullivan, Nikki. 2003. *A Critical Introduction to Queer Theory.* New York: New York University Press.

Taylor, Yvette. 2010. "The 'Outness' of Queer: Class and Sexual Intersections." In *Queer Methods and Methodologies*, edited by Kath Browne and Catherine J. Nash, 69–84. Surrey: Ashgate.

Warner, Michael. 1993. *Fear of a Queer Planet.* Minneapolis: University of Minnesota Press.

Wang, Bo. 2013. "Comparative Rhetoric, Postcolonial Studies, and Transnational Feminisms: A Geopolitical Approach." *Rhetoric Society Quarterly* 43 (3): 226–42.

Wu, Hui. 2002. "Historical Studies of Rhetorical Women Here and There: Methodological Challenges to Dominant Interpretive Frameworks." *Rhetoric Society Quarterly* 32 (1): 81–97.

Yifa, Venerable, et al. 2007. *Prajnaparamita Heart Sutra.* Taiwan: BLP.

6

"LOVE IN A HALL OF MIRRORS"
Queer Historiography and the Unsettling In-Between

Jean Bessette

> *You were so much,*
> *far and nearby: where I expected*
> *my own reflection, you were, unusual,*
> *confused, your many bodies rising . . .*
> Jennifer Perrine

Historians of queerness are often invigorated by ambivalence and ambiguity. For many, this unsettling in-betweenness and multivalence are the only positions that can make (non)sense of people and pasts that defy normative desires, relations, and temporalities. As queer early-modern historian Carla Freccero (2007) explains, "Queer, in its deconstructive sense, designates a kind of Derridean différance, occupying an interstitial space between binary oppositions. . . . It is the inscription of a negativity that nevertheless may be said to have force, to act or be active in a positive sense" (18). In this definition of queerness for queer historians, it is a negative orientation with a positive force, a historiographic heuristic that deconstructs binaries by drawing their unexpected and uncanny relations—by "knocking signifiers loose, ungrounding bodies, making them strange" (Dinshaw 1995, 76). The deconstructive move to unsettle binaries has a long history in gender and queer studies.

Nonetheless, the lure of the binary can be insidious, sidling up in historiographic research questions that implicitly adjudicate whether a past person or rhetorical act is (or was) queer (enough). This question can be a binary in disguise, for despite Freccero's insistence on that "interstitial space between," queerness is often defined in opposition to normativity, a flipping of the coin that typically privileges the normal in favor of "antinormativity as the privileged figure for the political" (Jagose 2015, 27). Of course, flipping a coin binarizes our results: heads or tails, queer or normative, gay or straight, alternative possibility or

DOI: 10.7330/9781607328186.c006

coercive regulation. As Annamarie Jagose (2015) puts it, "Queer theory, for all the productive critical leverage the concept of antinormativity has given us, might not be antinormative at its definitional heart" (27)—for what can be more normal than a binary?

Yet the binary is seductive; we quite literally *desire* the revaluation of people, practices, and drives the mainstream casts out in order to prop itself up. In complex, innovative ways, queer theory has refigured and reclaimed shame from pride (Crimp 2009; Sedgwick 2003), antisociality from community (Bersani 1995; Edelman 2004), failure from success (Halberstam 2011), and regression from progress (Freeman 2010; Halberstam 2005; Love 2007; Stockton 2009). The former side of each binary represents the abjected attributes, relations, circumstances, and temporalities so often attributed to gender and sexual transgressors in various times and places, and so it is easy to understand why queer historians would desire reclamation of the antinormative when the work seeks to challenge psychic and discursive norms that have prohibited queer ways of living and loving.

Still, my goal in this project is to disrupt some of the binaries that can stubbornly infiltrate historical and archival work, particularly those that might lead historians to seek examples of queer people, rhetorics, and pedagogies and "prove" they were or were not queer. When we seek to prove queerness, we may defer the question of what precisely queerness is and does (or has done), relying instead on a binary of queerness and normativity in which the position of privilege is transferred to the formerly abjected side of the coin. By thinking dichotomously, we may limit our ability to see the ways in which normativity sidles into and under the queerness we wish to celebrate and the ways in which queerness cracks and cleaves to the normativity we wish to critique.

This unsettling in-betweenness means, methodologically, that we might ask questions other than "is this queer (enough)?" as we dig through traces of the past. As Dana Cloud (2007) argues, "To make the discussion about whether someone simply is, or is not, queer is overly simple; further, it fails to ask what someone's being queer means and does in the public sphere" (31). Instead, we could seek to learn something new *about* queer rhetoric, literacy, and pedagogy, or about how we can seek it or make it or hear it—and how when we seek, make, and hear it, we may also be engaging with insidious threads of normativity. We could seek to learn something new about queer worldmaking, how we can and have lived and loved unexpectedly and "reparatively," in Sedgwick's (2003) terms: with "multiplicity, surprise, rich divergence, consolation, creativity, and love" (Love 2010, 236). But we should also be aware that, when we have lived and loved unexpectedly and reparatively, we may also have limited the possibilities of someone or some other way of living and loving. These aims require an assiduous resistance to the lure of mutually exclusive and exhaustive frames, in which the terms we use to make sense of the past neatly classify our findings as one or the other and not both or neither.

Reconsidering the messy in-between of seemingly binary pairings is a means of finding "love in a hall of mirrors," as queer poet Jennifer Perrine writes in the epigraph. The past becomes both "far and nearby"; our subjects become "many bodies rising" where we might expect to see our own reflection; our findings become "unusual, confused" where we might have predicted certainty and contained difference (Perrine 2011, 35). In this chapter, I investigate a series of binary pairs that can tempt queer historiographers, exploring how the mutual exclusivity and dichotomy of these pairs can be illusory and limiting. Beginning with the scene of archival research, I focus on the tensions between queer and archive, silence and speech, and how these tensions manifest through the ambivalent trope of the closet. I then reconsider evidence and ephemera, truth and fiction, as a way to rethink what evidence in the archive "proves" about queerness. Finally, I investigate the messy relations between past and present, self and other, in queer historiography, moving toward a more spectral—and rhetorical—understanding of history writing.

QUEER/ARCHIVE, SILENCE/SPEECH, AND THE EPISTEMOLOGY OF CLOSETS

> The archive, much like the closet, exposes various levels of publicness and privateness—recognition, awareness, refusal, impulse, disclosure, framing, silence, cultural intelligibility—each mediated and determined through subjective insider-outside ways of knowing. These relationships strike a delicate balance between reachability and remoteness, precariousness and pleasure.
> —Amy L. Stone and Jaime Cantrell

In the 1970s and 80s, many gay and lesbian archives were created in the grassroots to rescue, uncover, preserve, and protect the eclectic mementos that traced the intimacies and activisms of queer people. As Charles Morris and K. J. Rawson explain, these "holdings register a fundamental revelation, indeed a declaration, that 'we' were here"—even as that "we" is not "given or stable or uncomplicated" (Morris and Rawson 2013, 77). As a result, queer archives are celebrated as both safe havens of rescue and as "interventions against (hetero/homo)normativity's retrospective governance and discipline" (Morris and Rawson 2013, 77) in official or institutional archives. In the process, queer archives are often defined in contrast to the institutional archives that have historically elided queer materials from their collections. But when we research queerness capaciously, those official archives may also be sources, and the binary positioning that can make queer and official archives mutually exclusive may conceal the ways in which normativity can sidle into queer archives and queerness into official ones. In this section, I explore the paradox of the queer/archive, suggesting that awareness of its unsettling in-betweenness may help historians navigate complex affective and intellectual experiences in the scene of archival research.

Queer archives are fundamentally caught up in contradiction. On the one hand, archivists rely on classification in their selection and arrangement of materials, acquiring artifacts and records they believe represent historical LGBTQ people and organizing them under subject headings that guide researchers to what they seek. However, as I suggest elsewhere, the archive's reliance on classification may "challenge the very notion of queerness, which orients against the circumscription of individuals into categories"; a queer archive, I argue, "is always at risk of collapsing under the force of one of its terms" (Bessette 2013, 43). Queer materials are difficult to classify, in other words, both because of normative elision from official archives *and* because of queerness's fundamental challenge to classification systems as such. As Marvin Taylor, a librarian at NYU, explains,

> Queer materials often stay in backlogs long after less "problematic" items have been processed. Perhaps the subject headings are too difficult to assign properly. Queer materials go beyond pointing out the problems of these library procedures—they question the structure of knowledge on which the procedures are based. In response, these materials are the most closeted of all. (quoted in Thistlewaite, *Gay Community News*, February 1995)

Institutional collections, such as the Schlesinger Library at Radcliffe College, may navigate the challenge of classifying queerness through euphemism, using subject headings like "friendship" and "single woman" to code tricky materials that suggest female same-sex desire and intimacy. At stake for Schlesinger was the risk of "outing" a writer as a lesbian without her or her family's consent or certain proof.[1] But in an article in the *Gay Community News* in February 1995, Polly Thistlewaite, a librarian and former "archivette" at the Lesbian Herstory Archives (LHA), calls these maneuvers part of a "tradition of archival cloaking and exclusion" that has precipitated "gay and lesbian invisibility in the historical record."

I suggest that Taylor's allusion to the "closet" and Thistlewaite's to "cloaking" can help us navigate the contradictions of the queer/archive if we begin to see the closet as an ambivalent trope that permeates the archival scene. According to Eve Kosofsky Sedgwick (1990), the closet (that "fundamental feature of social life" for lesbians and gays) is a "performance initiated as such by the speech act of silence" (3). To be closeted, in other words, is to *not say*, and *not saying* is itself a speech act. As Michel Foucault (1978) asserts in *The History of Sexuality*, "There is no binary division between what one says and what one does not say" (27); to not say is, finally, to say something.[2] Sedgwick (1990) calls this aspect of the closet—a silence that speaks—a "telling secret" (67), a seen hiding, an open guardedness. The closet was, and is, simultaneously protective and threatening. Historically, it could be an "embracing if temporary cocoon" or a "scary prison" for individuals with same-sex desire; likewise, for the homophobic, it could be a "place where skeletons are secluded from view so that they do not disturb household harmony, or more sinisterly, a place within the home where lurk creatures who could break out and wreak havoc" (Eskridge 1997, 706).[3] In official archives, closeting is something that happens *to* queer materials when they are discarded, distributed across the archive (unlocatable as queer materials as such), or simply hidden, unclassified, in a back room. The closeting of queer materials in official archives *says* something about the epistemology of archival classification systems as they conceal and silence nonnormative ways of living and loving.

But closeting can happen in a different way in queer archives too—even when, unlike many official archives, a queer archive like the Lesbian Herstory Archives (LHA) is deeply committed to being radically open to difference. Cofounder Joan Nestle (2015) describes her early commitment to the word *lesbian* as a "noun that stood for all possibilities of queerness, for all possibilities of deviations. . . . Not a role-model lesbian history, not an archive of safe stories, always my own undertaking of keeping in the archives the tensions of lesbian difference" (239–240). LHA's mission has resulted in eclectically diverse collections equally open to a diversity of visitors, unconstrained by "academic, political, or sexual credentials," race, or class.

Instead, the duality of the closet functions in LHA in its precarious tension between radical openness and fierce guardedness. Because the archive's exigency is in the rescue and preservation of materials discarded or hidden by official institutions and homophobic families, its collective has had to navigate legitimate fears of vulnerability and vandalism. Nestle (2015) has written often about the "uneasy terrain of invasion, diminution, and attempted erasure" that characterized queer living "let us say from 1950 until now" (235). This sense of guardedness is in tension with the radical openness the archive practices in its inclusion of people and materials. Reflecting on the growing institutional embrace of LGBT archives, Nestle (2015) says,

> I know how to live in the shifting terrain of the margin, for there we knew more than the intruders, but I move very cautiously into the new territory that is being offered. Perhaps younger women will feel more at ease, more trusting of this new place, but they will not have the same memories, the same fears of betrayal, the same sense of comrades left at the border who could not cross over. How do I remain true to Maria, the bartender from Barcelona, who protected me from police entrapment in the early 1960s, or to Rachel, the lesbian whore who lay in my arms dreaming of a kinder world, or the butch women I saw stripped by the police in front of their lovers? (235)

The place-based queer archive—replete with literal closets where boxes are stacked ten high and three deep—is imbued with this tension of radical inclusiveness and fierce protection from "intruders." Indeed, Nestle's commitment to LHA is driven by such a tension: "While I know that living in the pre-liberation Queer ghetto endangered my life, remembering it gives me life" (Nestle 2015, 235). This is the ambivalence of the closet: danger that can motivate life, silencing that bears speech.

I belabor the ambivalence of the closet, that tension between openness and guardedness, silence and speech, because it imbues the scene of research for historians of queerness. It has saturated my affect as I feel both welcomed warmly and watched at LHA. It has alerted me to the insidious closeting in official classification systems that nonetheless have revealed serendipitous findings under unexpected subject headings. It has inspired me to look for what I find when I fail to find: what is missing or misplaced, and what does its absence say? There is no space of radical openness that is not also in tension with fierce protection and there is no institutional space of erasure that does not also have the potential to reveal new and surprising glimpses of living and loving. Indeed, it is because "diverse traces of the multiple and complex representations of GLBTQ history" are also "housed in straight archives and circulated in straight collections" that Charles E. Morris (2006) urges us to become "archival queers": to harness the "tools of rhetorical criticism and theory" as we navigate queer and official archives alike. These tools shape questions like those I've asked above—questions that investigate how silences speak and how speech can silence in the archive, questions that ask how danger and protection function rhetorically to fuel invention and, paradoxically, to "give . . . life" (Nestle 2015, 235).

GOSSIP/TRUTH, FICTION/HISTORY, AND
THE EVIDENCE OF EPHEMERA

> *What is the evidence present in these traces and what is it evidence of?*
> *That is the question of any research investigation and the haunting*
> *space of the archive invites it while always promising that the answer*
> *will be incomplete.*
>
> —Rebecca Lynn Fullan

Fullan's question in this epigraph is deceptively complex. What *is* the evidence in (and outside) the archive and what is it evidence of? For "modernist historiographers," evidence is the "remains of the event, action, object, or process that once existed" and it is evidence *of* "the past thing in itself" (Munslow 2004, 9). In this "scientific model of correspondence," the historian scours the archive to prove what happened and what it means, their representation of the past collapsing into the past itself, shored up by the authority of the archive (Munslow 2004, 9). While even the most traditional historian would likely nuance this positivist understanding of archival evidence, there is something seductive about pointing to evidence. Helen Freshwater (2003) calls this seduction a "beguiling fantasy of self-effacement, which seems to promise the recovery of lost time, the possibility of being reunited with the lost past, and the fulfillment of our deepest desires for wholeness and completion" (738; also quoted in Biesecker 2006, 126). Many of us want to *prove* that queer people have lived and loved in surprising and "reparative" ways (Sedgwick 2003), that they have and can again; this is the impulse that drives what José Esteban Muñoz (2009) calls a "queer utopian hermeneutic," a "backward glance that enacts a future vision" (4). But what constitutes proof of that queer (or not queer enough) past? As Barbara Biesecker (2006) reminds, the past is not in the archive nor all of the archives combined, and "the archive as instituted trace anchors absolutely nothing" (127). The binary of evidence and ephemera is illusory; the "truth" of the past is somewhere in the middle, which makes it, as Fullan (2015) maintains, "incomplete" (207).

In search of critical glimpses of queerness and normativity, queer historiographers have turned the concept of evidence on its head. They have had to, for as Muñoz (1996) explains, leaving evidence bare has been historically perilous for queer subjects who could not afford the vulnerability of solid proof. Instead, Muñoz (1996) maintains, "queerness has . . . existed as innuendo, gossip, fleeting moments, and performances that are meant to be interacted with by those within its epistemological sphere—while evaporating at the touch of those who would eliminate queer possibility" (6). Queerness is ephemeral by necessity, he argues, and so must be its evidence. And queerness's ephemerality is not only necessary as an evasive strategy; the very *stuff* of queerness (if queerness could be said to have stuff) is slippery: it is "intimacy, sexuality, love, and activism, all areas of experience that are difficult to chronicle through the materials of a traditional archive" (Cvetkovich 2002, 110).

Feminist and queer rhetorician Pamela VanHaitsma (2016) argues that the ephemeral evidence of gossip is particularly resourceful in the historiography of disenfranchised people and pasts. Drawing on art historian Gavin Butt, VanHaitsma (2016) explains that gossip can be understood as "'non-normative' and 'deviant' evidence that, although 'unreliable' by more conventional standards of art history, does 'act as a *trace*'" (138). Gossip can serve as ephemeral evidence of how queers, women, and people of color have communicated and survived, but this evidence will always be partial and speculative, an important reminder of the "impossibilities and uncertainties inherent in attempts to know the 'truth' of sexuality, identity, and history" (VanHaitsma 2016, 139). Gossip is neither the whole Truth nor nothing but the Truth, but it is a trace that brings into relief our inability to finalize subjects' identities.

In histories of writing studies, these destabilizing traces might take the form of ambiguous euphemism purveyed secondhand. For example, in her 1999 dissertation on the leadership of Progressive-era rhetoricians Gertrude Buck and Laura Wylie, Barbara L'Eplattenier writes in a footnote that Vassar's president Henry MacCracken often described Buck as Wylie's "great friend" (86). L'Eplattenier decides, "after much consideration" of archival correspondence and papers, that she is "compelled to argue" that the euphemism is a "code word for what we today would call a domestic partner—that is, recognition of the lesbian relationship, sexual or not, that existed between Wylie and Buck" (L'Eplattenier 1999, 86). Neither L'Eplattenier's footnote nor MacCracken's "great friend" remark "proves" the women's same-sex desire and relationship, so what is it evidence of? What other questions can we ask of ephemeral evidence besides, is this true?

I suggest we can ask questions about what *relations* gossip reveals and produces. Sedgwick (1990) insists that the "precious, devalued arts of gossip, immemorially associated in European thought with servants, with effeminate and gay men, with all women" are less significant for the information those "arts" convey and more telling in what they reveal about the "refinement of necessary skills for making, testing, and using unrationalized and provisional hypotheses about what kinds of people there are to be found in one's world" (23; also quoted in

VanHaitsma 2016, 140). Gossip is a strategic practice, a way of making and understanding relations with others—with those with whom gossip is shared, with those from whom gossip is overheard, with those whom gossip is about, with those who retell it with a twist. This understanding of ephemeral evidence requires different kinds of research questions: open-ended questions that ask how evidence functions in relation to identity and difference and to create relations from identification and difference, deferring yes-or-no questions like is this true? or is this queer?

In L'Eplattenier's example, instead of seeking to prove Buck and Wylie were lovers, we might instead inquire into what relations are produced or revealed by MacCracken's "gossip" about Wylie and "her great friend." For instance, what does his remark tell us about the administration's awareness and response to Progressive-era women's sexuality? L'Eplattenier travels in this direction by maintaining that "such relationships were not unique in the Progressive Era," citing Elaine Kendall's assertion that "passionate relationships between women, particularly those with advanced political ideas and great intellectual ambitions, were usual in that era and seemed to have been accepted as a matter of course" (Kendall 1976, quoted in L'Epplattenier 1999, 86). But there are more threads to follow for a queer historiographer interested in how the normalization of same-sex passionate friendships impacted how women navigated higher education in the Progressive Era.

The incomplete evidence of ephemera is illuminating even when the figures we research *self*identify as lesbian, gay, bisexual, or queer. For example, in a study of the rhetorical-historiographic practices of the Daughters of Bilitis (DOB), a lesbian organization founded in midcentury United States, I encountered and theorized a form of ephemeral evidence I called the *anecdote*. While investigating founders Del Martin and Phyllis Lyon's influential 1972 book, *Lesbian/Woman*, I found hundreds of examples of the curious form and theorized anecdotes as

> experiences articulated second-hand and retold in absentia of the subject whose experience is divulged, with no material record to authenticate it. . . . Anecdotes in *Lesbian/Woman* are experiences temporally delayed and retroactively transformed: the experiences were endured and felt by DOB members and *Ladder* [newsletter] readers at the time they were shared with Martin, Lyon, and other DOB constituents in the 1950s and 60s; later, in 1970 as Martin and Lyon composed the archive that would become *Lesbian/Woman*, they collected these experiences and reorganized them second-hand under pseudonymic first names. (Bessette 2013, 29)

While Martin and Lyon assured readers of *Lesbian/Woman* that they had recalled the experiences from "thousands of women" they had "talked to, counseled, socialized with, and been friends with" over the previous decades, anecdotes as evidence are clearly ephemeral, temporally and interpersonally removed from the original testimony (Martin and Lyon 1972, 9).

So what can these anecdotes be said to "prove"? Following Sedgwick (1990), we can ask instead what relationships the ephemeral evidence implies and generates, what kinds of "people there are to be found in one's world" (23). I argue that the anecdotes contributed to a process of "archival consciousness raising" wherein Martin and Lyon leveraged the women's experiences to shape a middle-class lesbian identity, founded in values of femininity, hard work, and monogamy (Bessette 2013). Because ephemeral evidence can reveal relationships, I also sought how readers responded to the archive of anecdotes in *Lesbian/Woman*, studying how lesbian/women replied to Martin and Lyon in letters filled with anecdotes themselves. The ephemeral evidence of anecdotes—found both in the published book and in the letters—demonstrate that ephemeral evidence like gossip and anecdotes can both connect people and divide them; it induced different affects, including both intimate identification and painful rejection as women variously did and did not see themselves in *Lesbian/Woman*'s archive of anecdotes.

Reconsidering the evidence of ephemera—what it demonstrates, what kinds of questions it can answer (incompletely)—invites what Heather Branstetter calls a "promiscuous" rhetorical methodology, one that "intentionally seek[s] inspiration from other disciplines or art, music, public culture, and community spheres specifically in search of perspectives not limited by the terministic screens, trained incapacities, and occupational psychoses . . . of our discipline or specialty" (Branstetter 2016, 24). If historiography has traditionally understood a positivist correspondence between archival evidence and the past itself, a promiscuous historiography might look to fiction—which honors other kinds of truths than the Truth of what was—and to rhetoric—which examines how emotions, knowledge, dispositions, and relations are induced—to help us rethink what evidence is, what it does, and what it might be evidence of.

PRESENT/PAST, IDENTITY/ALTERITY, AND THE HAUNTING OF RHETORICAL FAILURE

> *I . . . invoke identification and one of its common effects, anachronism, as two intimately related and hallowed temporal processes that make up—like and along with desire—queer time. These analyses proceed oth-*

erwise than according to a presumed logic of cause and effect, anticipa-
tion and result; and otherwise than according to a presumed logic of the
"done-ness" of the past, since queer time is haunted by the persistence of
affect and ethical imperatives in and across time.
—Carla Freccero

Linear temporal models of history have been a persistent problem
for queer historiographers. On the one hand, we are drawn to them;
as Heather Love (2007) admits, "Although many queer critics take
exception to the idea of a linear, triumphalist view of history, we are in
practice deeply committed to the notion of progress; despite our reservations, we just cannot stop dreaming of a better life for queer people"
(3). It is seductive to imagine a better future than a melancholic past
and still-traumatic present, yet these same historians are also aware of
the dangers of narratives of progress for queer subjects in particular.
Historically, queerness has been caught up and contained by discourses
of backwardness. Elizabeth Freeman (2010) explains how sexology
understood "inverts" as atavistic "remnants of earlier eras" (161). If, as
Freud maintained, sexuality develops *toward* heterosexual reproduction
(this is what "progress" looks like), passing through a stage of same-sex
desire, then subjects who maintain same-sex desire are "temporally
backward" and yet "paradoxically dislocated from any specific historical
moment" (Freeman 2010, 162). In this final section, I investigate these
messy relations between progress and regress, past and present, and
identity and alterity, moving toward a "spectral" rhetoric of historiography that acknowledges queer rhetorical failures.

In discourses of displaced backwardness, temporal models that insist
on progress situate queer subjects not only as regressive themselves but
also as an impediment to the progress of society. And yet, historically,
models of progress actually *depended* upon figures of regression.

> If modernization in the late nineteenth and early twentieth century aimed
> to move humanity forward, it did so in part by perfecting techniques for
> mapping and disciplining subjects considered to be lagging behind—and
> so seriously compromised the ability of these others to ever catch up. Not
> only sexual and gender deviants but also women, colonized people, the
> nonwhite, the disabled, the poor, and criminals were marked as inferior
> by means of allegation of backwardness. (Love 2007, 5–6)

Once again, a binary (here progress and regress) positions the dominant norms in opposition to the subordinated and abjected other on
which those norms depend. This binary precluded queer history as a
possibility, for if queers were figured as always already backward, dispersed and isolated by individual pathology, then they could have no

past of their own. As Freeman (2007) explains, "Since sexual identity emerged as a concept, gays and lesbians have been figured as having . . . no childhood, no origin or precedent in nature, no family traditions or legends, and crucially, no history as a distinct people" (162). Such historical erasure has driven a desire for queer history in the twentieth century, as several scholars have cataloged (cf. Bessette 2017; Bravmann 1997; Nealon 2001).

As significant as the exigency of reclamation has been for queer history, however, it has also been imperative for queer historiographers to reconsider the modernist temporality that abjected queerness as the subordinate binary position in the first place. If we understand sexuality as complex, historically and geographically specific, and fluid, how do we trace it through time without naming and containing queer subjects of the past now in ways that mirror their containment then? If we seek (and shape) desires, acts, and individuals in the past that reflect how we understand (and feel about) ourselves now, we risk erasing their unique, complex, fluid, and contradictory subjectivity. The past may be a foreign country, but if queers *feel foreign*, it can be easy to recognize themselves in the past's (non)citizens. In this way, the binaries of past/present, regress/progress, and identity/alterity are intimately entangled.

Consequently, queer historiography has had a complicated relationship to anachronism. On the one hand, motivated by "respect for difference, particularity, and pluralism," critics of anachronism want to resist the "hasty assumption of commonalities between present and past same-sex desires" that would "project modern concepts back in time" (Rohy 2006, 65–66). This approach underpins Jack Halberstam's (1998) "perverse presentism" in *Female Masculinity*, in which Halberstam resists unearthing prototypes of present sexual identities and instead details a range of gender and sexually deviant behaviors that don't map onto contemporary categories. And yet, as Valerie Rohy (2006) suggests, despite persistent resistance to anachronism in queer historiography, "no one is ever innocent of it" (69). Indeed, the very drive to resist anachronism might have presentist motivations too. For Freccero (2007), *both* the "desire in the present to prove the persistent existence of same-sex desires and communities over time" *and* the "desire to characterize modernity's relation to same-sex desires and communities as different from or similar to the past, thereby identifying the specificity of modernity's sexual regimes" are ways to "intervene politically in the present by using the past" (64). In other words, whether we're driven to differentiate the past from the present or to map the present onto the past, we likely have political—which is to say *rhetorical*—motivations and/or effects.

This, however, is where queer historiographers of rhetoric, literacy, and pedagogy are well primed to enter the conversation. If we understand historiography—that is, the *writing of history*—as fundamentally rhetorical, a means of composing and leveraging the past for contemporary ends of politics, affect, and identity, then the exigencies, audiences, and forms of these representations of the past become ripe for investigation. Queer and feminist historiography is not the sole purview of scholars; indeed, the twentieth-century desire for queer history, instigated by historical erasure and discourses of backwardness and pathology, has motivated many activist, grassroots, and student rhetors to engage with and compose the past. These grassroots historiographic rhetors are the focus of my book, *Retroactivism in the Lesbian Archives: Composing Pasts and Futures* (Bessette 2017), which examines how lesbians in particular have turned to archives and historiography more broadly in the pursuit of shaping identity and challenging then-present social and political denigrations of same-sex desire and relations. In this study, I investigate the rhetorical strategies lesbian collectives from the 1950s to the present have invented and employed to compose and leverage the past.

The rhetoricity of such queer historiography is complicated by the muddy borders between past and present, identity and alterity.[4] As Freccero (2006; 2007) suggests, we cannot assume total agency on behalf of composers who leverage the past. Freccero theorizes a "phantasmic relation to historicity that could account for the affective force of the past in the present, of a desire issuing from another time and placing a demand on the present in the form of an ethical imperative" (2007, 184). In other words, it is not only the present that frames and influences (representations of) the past; the past also "haunts" the present with ensepulchered desires, affects, "figures and voices" (Freccero 2006, 70).

In queer historiography in rhetoric and writing studies, these mournful desires, affects, figures, and voices can reveal themselves as the traces of rhetorical failure, the attempts to express that queer "structuring and educated mode of desiring that allows us to see and feel beyond the quagmire of the present" that nonetheless do not *alter* that present (Muñoz 2009, 1). For queer and feminist rhetorics have failed more than they have succeeded, a reality never more apparent than in our contemporary political moment in which anti-PC backlash, transgender bathroom bills, and ever-bolder abortion restrictions dominate legislative priorities. As historiographers, we might come to understand past rhetorical failures as queer ghosts who haunt our present, rhetorics that failed in the past only to fail yet again. With Freccero, I believe we have an "ethical imperative" to listen to these queer ghosts, to hear rather than suppress the rhetorical failures then that haunt us now. Evidence of these failures abound in queer and official archives alike, for as Joan Nestle (2015) wrote recently,

> some of the most important collections in the LHA to me are the documents of our failures, of our own exclusions, of the complex face of gender and sexual differences. Queer archives of the future perhaps will give evidence that it is harder to live with a history than without one. (241; qtd in Bessette 2017)

Despite LHA's unparalleled influence as a queer archival, educational, community, and activist center since 1974, Nestle also seems to feel an ethical imperative to listen to its failures, those "most important documents."

The rhetoricity of listening and conversing with ghosts is abstruse indeed. Freccero (2007) calls it a "reciprocal penetrability," a queer "commingling of times as affective and erotic experience" (488–49). Such reciprocity complicates the shape of rhetorical address: are we agential and political rhetoricians and historians listening to rhetorical failures or are rhetorical failures driving our present scholarship, politics, and identity? Michelle Ballif (2013) explains that a "hauntological address addresses an indeterminable ghost"; to "speak to ghosts, then, is to speak to the 'it spooks'" (150). What happens to the rhetorical situation, Ballif asks, if an identifiable rhetor no longer speaks? This "counterrhetoric," she maintains, "is *not* reducible to an addressor/ addressee relationship in which the positions of either are clearly delineated. The 'it spooks' of the ghost renders indistinct *as such* either an addressor or an addressee" (Ballif 2013, 151). When we listen to ghosts, we are listening for unsettling, uncanny feelings, figures, and voices that don't fit our prefigured desires to see progress and perform rescue of ideal queer and feminist figures buried in the archives. We are inviting affects of restlessness, uncertainty, and discomfort; we are inviting the ghosts to "render *ourselves* unfamiliar (as scholars and as a discipline)" (140)—and, I would extend, as gendered and sexual subjects. Following Freccero and Ballif, rhetoric and writing studies can rethink the rhetorical situation of haunting and the rhetoricity of affects, desires—and failures—that call forth from the past.

POSTLUDE

In this chapter, I argue for a queer historiography of Queer and Archive and Silence and Speech and Gossip and Truth and Fiction and History and Past and Present and Identity and Alterity and Addressor and

Addressee. I have hoped for love in a hall of mirrors, where binaries, figures, voices, and ghosts become "many bodies rising," rendering us, and them, "unusual, confused," "far and nearby," queer and normative (Perrine 2011, 35). This is not a comfortable love; indeed, Perrine herself feverishly, and with regret, escaped the clutches of her "dizzying" lover, tearing out of her "endless reaching arms" into a flattened singular clarity she could "possess with one level gaze" (Perrine 2011, 35). But perhaps we can linger there in that hall of mirrors, where we might discover and create new understandings of what queer rhetoric, pedagogy, and worldmaking is and does—and hasn't done—how it cracks and cleaves normativity, how normativity sidles into and under it. More than a dream, love in a hall of mirrors may be an ethical obligation because, as I argue, mutually exclusive and exhaustive binary frames—even when we revalue the subordinated position—can depend upon the exclusion of someone or some way of living and loving. Perhaps love in a hall of mirrors is the only way we can love at all.

NOTES

1. For an astute and nuanced discussion of the politics of historical outing, see Dana Cloud (2007).
2. Cheryl Glenn's (2004) *Unspoken* offers a feminist exploration of the rhetorical art of tactical silence.
3. Now a classic metaphor for homosexual secrecy, the closet has only a relatively recent history. Legal historian William Eskridge (1997) explains that the metaphor of the closet emerged in the 1950s and came into common parlance in the 60s in response to the increased scrutiny and social control of sexuality. These decades saw a radical change in indecency, lewdness, and lewd sexual solicitation laws, which removed the requirement of a public place and made engagement in and even suggestion of consensual homosexual sex in private places a crime. The sense that the closet was being regularly and forcibly thrown ajar was pervasive.
4. A version of the following three paragraphs appears in *Retroactivism in American Lesbian Collectives: Composing Pasts and Futures* (Bessette 2017).

REFERENCES

Ballif, Michelle. 2013. "Historiography as Hauntology: Paranormal Investigations into the History of Rhetoric." In *Theorizing Histories of Rhetoric*, edited by Michelle Ballif, 139–53. Carbondale: Southern Illinois University Press.

Bersani, Leo. 1995. *Homos*. Cambridge, MA: Harvard University Press.

Bessette, Jean. 2013. "An Archive of Anecdotes: Raising Lesbian Consciousness after the Daughters of Bilitis." *Rhetoric Society Quarterly* 43 (1): 22–45. https://doi.org/10.1080/02773945.2012.740131.

Bessette, Jean. 2017. *Retroactivism in the Lesbian Archives: Composing Pasts and Futures*. Carbondale: Southern Illinois University Press.

Biesecker, Barbara A. 2006. "Of Historicity, Rhetoric: The Archive as Scene of Invention." *Rhetoric & Public Affairs* 9 (1): 124–31. https://doi.org/10.1353/rap.2006.0018.

Branstetter, Heather Lee. 2016. "Promiscuous Approaches to Reorienting Rhetorical Research." In *Sexual Rhetorics: Methods, Identities, Publics*, edited by Jonathan Alexander and Jacqueline Rhodes, 17–30. New York: Routledge.

Bravmann, Scott. 1997. *Queer Fictions of the Past: History, Culture, and Difference*. Cambridge: Cambridge University Press.

Cloud, Dana. 2007. "The First Lady's Privates: Queering Eleanor Roosevelt for Public Address Studies." In *Queering Public Address: Sexualities in American Historical Discourse*, edited by Charles E. Morris, 23–44. Columbia: University of South Carolina Press.

Crimp, Douglas. 2009. "Mario Montez, for Shame." In *Gay Shame*, edited by David M. Halperin and Valerie Traub, 63–75. Chicago, IL: University of Chicago Press.

Cvetkovich, Ann. 2002. "In the Archives of Lesbian Feelings: Documentary and Popular Culture." *Camera Obscura: Feminism, Culture, and Media Studies* 17 (149): 107–47. https://doi.org/10.1215/02705346-17-1_49–107.

Dinshaw, Carolyn. 1995. "Chaucer's Queer Touches/A Queer Touches Chaucer." *Exemplaria* 7 (1): 75–92. https://doi.org/10.1179/exm.1995.7.1.75.

Dinshaw, Carolyn. 1999. *Getting Medieval: Sexualities and Communities, Pre- and Postmodern*. Durham, NC: Duke University Press. https://doi.org/10.1215/9780822382188.

Dinshaw, Carolyn, Lee Edelman, Roderick A. Ferguson, Carla Freccero, Elizabeth Freeman, Jack Halberstam, Annamarie Jagose, Christopher Nealon, and Nguyen Tan Hoang. 2007. "THEORIZING QUEER TEMPORALITIES: A Roundtable Discussion." *GLQ: A Journal of Lesbian and Gay Studies* 13 (2–3): 177–95. https://doi.org/10.1215/10642684-2006-030.

Edelman, Lee. 2004. *No Future: Queer Theory and the Death Drive*. Durham, NC: Duke University Press. https://doi.org/10.1215/9780822385981.

Eskridge, William N. 1997. "Privacy Jurisprudence and the Apartheid of the Closet, 1946–1961." *Florida State University Law Review* 24 (703): 703–840.

Foucault, Michel. 1978. *The History of Sexuality*. New York: Pantheon Books.

Freccero, Carla. 2006. *Queer/Early/Modern*. Durham, NC: Duke University Press.

Freccero, Carla. 2007. "Queer Times." *South Atlantic Quarterly* 106 (3): 485–94. https://doi.org/10.1215/00382876-2007-007.

Freeman, Elizabeth. 2007. "Introduction." *GLQ: A Journal of Lesbian and Gay Studies* 13 (2–3): 159–176. https://doi.org/10.1215/10642684-2006-029.

Freeman, Elizabeth. 2010. *Time Binds: Queer Temporalities, Queer Histories*. Durham, NC: Duke University Press. https://doi.org/10.1215/9780822393184.

Freshwater, Helen. 2003. "The Allure of the Archive." *Poetics Today* 24 (4): 729–58. https://doi.org/10.1215/03335372-24-4-729.

Fullan, Rebecca Lynne. 2015. "Victory Celebration for Essex Charles Hemphill; Or, What Essex Saved." In *Out of the Closet, into the Archives: Researching Sexual Histories*, edited by Amy L. Stone and Jaime Cantrell, 205–32. Albany: SUNY Press.

Glenn, Cheryl. 2004. *Unspoken: A Rhetoric of Silence*. Carbondale: Southern Illinois University Press.

Halberstam, Jack. 1998. *Female Masculinity*. Durham, NC: Duke University Press.

Halberstam, Jack. 2005. *In a Queer Time and Place: Transgender Bodies, Subcultural Lives*. New York: New York University Press.

Halberstam, Jack. 2011. *The Queer Art of Failure*. Durham, NC: Duke University Press. https://doi.org/10.1215/9780822394358.

Jagose, Annamarie. 2015. "The Trouble with Antinormativity." *Differences: A Journal of Feminist Cultural Studies* 26 (1): 26–47. https://doi.org/10.1215/10407391-2880591.

Kendall, Elaine. 1976. *"Peculiar Institutions": An Informal History of the Seven Sister Colleges*. New York: Putnam.

L'Eplattenier, Barbara. 1999. "Investigating Institutional Power: Women Administrators during the Progressive Era, 1890–1920." PhD diss., Purdue University.

Love, Heather. 2007. *Feeling Backward: Loss and the Politics of Queer History.* Cambridge, MA: Harvard University Press.

Love, Heather. 2010. "Truth and Consequences: On Paranoid Reading and Reparative Reading." *Criticism* 52 (2): 235–41. https://doi.org/10.1353/crt.2010.0022.

Martin, Del, and Phyllis Lyon. 1972. *Lesbian/Woman.* San Francisco: Glide Publications.

Morris, Charles E. 2006. "Archival Queer." *Rhetoric & Public Affairs* 9 (1): 145–51. https://doi.org/10.1353/rap.2006.0028.

Morris, Charles E., and K. J. Rawson. 2013. "Queer Archives / Archival Queers." In *Theorizing Histories of Rhetoric,* edited by Michelle Ballif, 74–89. Carbondale: Southern Illinois University Press.

Muñoz, Esteban José. 2009. *Cruising Utopia: The Then and There of Queer Futurity.* New York: New York University Press.

Muñoz, Esteban José.1996. "Ephemera as Evidence: Introductory Notes to Queer Acts." *Women & Performance* 8 (2): 5–16. https://doi.org/10.1080/07407709608571228.

Munslow, Alun. 2004. "Introduction: Theory and Practice." In *Experiments in Rethinking History,* edited by Alun Munslow and Robert A. Rosenstone, 7–12. New York: Routledge.

Nealon, Christopher S. 2001. *Foundlings: Lesbian and Gay Historical Emotion before Stonewall.* Durham, NC: Duke University Press. https://doi.org/10.1215/9780822380610.

Nestle, Joan. 2015. "Who Were We to Do Such a Thing? Grassroots Necessities, Grassroots Dreaming." *Radical History Review* 2015 (122): 233–42. https://doi.org/10.1215/016 36545-2849939.

Perrine, Jennifer. 2011. "Love in a Hall of Mirrors." In *In the Human Zoo.* Salt Lake City: University of Utah Press.

Rohy, Valerie. 2006. "Ahistorical." *GLQ: A Journal of Lesbian and Gay Studies* 12 (1): 61–83. https://doi.org/10.1215/10642684-12-1-61.

Sedgwick, Eve Kosofsky. 1990. *Epistemology of the Closet.* Berkeley: University of California Press.

Sedgwick, Eve Kosofsky. 2003. *Touching Feeling: Affect, Pedagogy, Performativity.* Durham, NC: Duke University Press.

Stockton, Kathryn Bond. 2009. *The Queer Child, or Growing Sideways in the Twentieth Century.* Durham, NC: Duke University Press. https://doi.org/10.1215/9780822390268.

Stone, Amy L., and Jaime Cantrell. 2015. *Out of the Closet, into the Archives: Researching Sexual Histories.* Albany: SUNY Press.

VanHaitsma, Pamela. 2016. "Gossip as Rhetorical Methodology for Queer and Feminist Historiography." *Rhetoric Review* 35 (2): 135–47. https://doi.org/10.1080/07350198.20 16.1142845.

7

IN/FERTILITY
Assembling a Queer Counterstory Methodology for Bodies of Health and Sexuality

Maria Novotny

Writing this chapter, I sit in the room that was to be my baby's. Frequently, walking into this mauve-colored room, I remember how I imagined it as the baby's room, storing a variety of baby needs—a porta-bed, a bouncer, endless diapers, and so forth. For four years, I tried to make this the baby's room. But it never happened. Now a desk occupies the space that was reserved for a bassinet. Books are now stacked on the desk with a mirror to the right. As I write this, I find myself looking up at the mirror wondering how different my life would be if this space were actually the baby's room.

As a feminist and cultural researcher theorizing "rhetorics of infertility," an area of study that draws upon cultural and medical rhetoric to make sense of the navigational challenges institutions and systems of power impose upon the infertile body, I often find myself needing to position myself in relation to my work. As a result, I frequently find myself sharing my infertility story. Yet, in doing so, it has become more clear to me that my story is not a common infertility story. The reality that I opted against fertility treatment, that I decided not to adopt, that I did not see a need to "fix" my infertility often positions me as an outsider in my community research. Many of my oral-history participants share their stories of failed treatments, the deep desire to become a parent, the need to "beat" their infertility. As I interview these participants, we connect often with how disorienting it felt to first receive an infertility diagnosis. We share stories about how infertility impacts relationships with our bodies, our partners, our families and friends, and even with Western culture. Yet, even though I share in these experiences, I still frequently find myself feeling not quite infertile *enough.* Never undergoing treatment, never adopting, never having a miscarriage, I often feel as if I am an imposter in a secret club despite my medical chart listing infertility as a diagnosis.

DOI: 10.7330/9781607328186.c007

I was confronted about my feelings of being an imposter a few years ago while attending a national infertility event. There, we were asked to go around and share short introductions about our connections to infertility. Doing so, others began by recounting the number of years they were in treatment, the amount of money they saved and then spent to have a child, or how doctors misdiagnosed factors causing their infertility. As these experiences were shared, many stood shaking their heads in acknowledgment—they knew that story, they had heard it before, either from a fellow infertile friend or because it was similar to their own. Soon it became my turn. Standing there, I explained how I was diagnosed in my early twenties, how I started a support group in my community, and how I decided to take some time to process my infertility. And how, in taking time, I decided against fertility treatment, against adoption, against responding to this pressure I felt to *resolve* my infertility. As I shared this, a drug rep who was standing next to me whispered to her colleague, "*Well, she is going to regret that. Why not try treatment to get pregnant?*"

This comment has stuck with me, as it was a moment in which my infertility narrative became policed, became regulated. *Why is it that my story is challenged, questioned, taken as naive?* I draw upon this question as a source of inquiry to explore how narratives of the body become constructed within larger cultural norms. Such inquiry, I argue, is valuable not just to the topic of infertility but to all embodied nonnormativities, especially those that confront notions of ableism and heterosexuality. I view queer theory, and in particular queer rhetorics, as a methodological entryway into these discussions. In particular, I offer queer assemblage as a methodological ally to disrupt the limitations of contemporary narrative theory by tending to the slippages and gaps of narrative. Doing so, I argue, reorients writing studies toward more interdisciplinary spheres, such as health and medicine.

COUNTERSTORY AS METHODOLOGY

The topic of narrative is not new to the field of writing studies and rhetoric and composition. Narratives are frequently assigned in student writing courses and are also a method by which writing researchers reconstruct ethnographic inquiries. As Debra Journet (2012) notes, "One might assay that the history of composition research is, in part, the history of coming to terms with narrative" (13). Writing studies scholars, such as Victor Villanueva (1993), Malea Powell (2002), Linda Adler-Kassner (2008), and Jacqueline Jones Royster (1996), have drawn upon the field's engagement with narrative, arguing for a more critical methodology of narrative in writing studies, one that disrupts more dominant narratives of writing instruction and of student writers. Adler-Kassner (2008) advocates that one role of WPAs is to debunk institutional myths that "students simply don't know how to write anymore" by developing alternative narratives of what constitutes "good writing" in a writing classroom. This task of debunking false narratives of writing instruction and student writers demands administrators and instructors begin to expand our scope "to include the rhetorical activities of those whose voices have been neglected, silenced, or rarely heard" (Kirsch 2012, xii–xiv). Villanueva (1993), Powell (2002) and Royster (1996) offer firsthand accounts of their own narratives being dismissed and the need to disrupt the continual disciplinary repression of marginalized narratives and writers. Adopting a more critical, cultural, and dialogic view of narrative asks then for the writing instructor and writing researcher to be aware of how stories are constructed by sociocultural factors such as race, class, gender, and sexuality.

Counterstory is one such approach that engages the writer/instructor/ researcher in more critical, cultural, and dialogical discussion of narrative. As a method for critiquing stock stories, counterstory works "to strengthen traditions of social, political, and cultural survival and resistance" (Martinez 2014, 38). As such, counterstory both recognizes and is inherently attuned to stock stories, which function to "establish a shared sense of identity, reality, and naturalization of their superior position" (Martinez 2014, 38). Important to note, stock stories are "powerful because they are often repeated until canonized or normalized" (Martinez 2014, 38). Because stock stories function as representations of mainstream norms, alternative stories or narrative forms are "deemed biased, self-interested, and ultimately not credible" (Martinez 2014, 38). Stock stories then not only dictate normative narratives but also work methodologically to create and construct the continued repetition and power of these narratives. Counterstories serve to deconstruct the normalizing narratives of whiteness, ableism, and heterosexuality central to stock stories.

Scholars such as Aja Y. Martinez (2014) and Lee Anne Bell (2010) propose counterstory as a methodological framework useful to confronting stock stories around race. In particular, Martinez's (2014) model offers a critical race theory (CRT) counterstory framework that "recognizes the experiential and embodied knowledge of people of color . . . that is often well disguised in the rhetoric of normalized structural values and practices" (37). As methodology and narrative form then, CRT counterstory provides a moment to juxtapose narrative realities of inequality in the academy against institutional and ideological norms, often theorized by scholars yet rarely translated into a tangible narrative. Such a juxtaposition is made possible in a CRT counterstory framework by "critically examining theoretical concepts and humanizing empirical data while also deriving material for counterstory's discourse, setting, and characters from sources" (Martinez 2014, 37). While Martinez offers CRT as a framework to disrupt racialized narratives, Bell (2010) provides a framework for analytically interacting with, in attempts to dismantle, such racialized narratives. For Bell (2010), narrative typology centers upon the following four narrative moments:

- the stock story—which represents "the tales told by the dominant group" (23)
- the concealed story—which "critique[s] or 'talk[s] back' to mainstream narratives" (23)
- the resistance story—which "demonstrate[s] how people have resisted racism, [and] challenged the stock stories" (25), and
- the emerging/transforming story—which represents "new stories deliberately constructed to challenge the stock stories" (25)

According to Bell (2010), these "four story types provide language and a framework for making sense of race and racism through exploring the genealogy of racism and the social stories that generate and reproduce it through the stock stories that keep it in place" (22). Engaging in a counterstory methodology to confront racism requires instructors to create a scaffolded space in which individuals first come to understand stock stories, and upon doing so, move into concealed stories and ultimately toward moments of acknowledging how stories may resist dominant narratives so as to begin building a more socially just story at the emerging stage. Counterstory in these two examples, Martinez and Bell, demonstrates how attending to critiques of power and race embedded in narratives represents allied methods of more socially just writing instruction.

And while Martinez's and Bell's lines of inquiry focus on making more apparent the racialized injustices embedded in stock stories, I suggest other institutional and ideological spaces may benefit from a similar examination, including, but not limited to, narratives related to nonnormative identities (e.g., queer and trans identities). Thus, this chapter concerns itself with pondering the following question, *how might other embodied orientations, in addition to race, benefit from a counterstory methodology?* In posing such a question, I turn my attention to queer theory—particularly queer assemblage—as a methodology to reorient counterstory, to queer it. In doing so, I offer a less uniform account of narrative theory, one that may better attune ourselves as instructors, students, administrators, and researchers to the narratives of other non-normative bodies.

QUEERING COUNTERSTORY

Queering counterstory, through Jasbir K. Puar's (2013) concept of queer assemblage, offers one methodological option for attending to other embodied, and often marginalized, nonnormative subjectivities in narrative. Theorized within the context of the United States' post-9/11 "war on terror," Puar's (2013) queer assemblage serves as a methodology for examining the multiple modalities, identities, and discourses intertwined around nationalist and assumed normative constructions of terrorists as "racialized perverse sexualities" (515). Concerned then with "intersectional and identitarian paradigms" and "in favor of spatial, temporal, and corporal convergences, implosions, and rearrangements" (Puar 2013, 516), I find queer assemblage a well-suited methodology for queering counterstory for three reasons.

First, a queer assemblage works to disrupt the binary positioning of stock versus counterstory. Puar (2013) describes queer assemblage as a disruption to binary positioning, explaining that "queerness as an assemblage moves away from excavation work, deprivileges a binary opposition between queer and not-queer subjects, and, instead of retaining queerness exclusively as dissenting, resistant, and alternative . . . it underscores contingency and complicity with dominant formations" (516). Second, a queer assemblage works to capture non-normative identities, positionalities, and the moments of being and becoming often unseen in counterstory. Queer assemblage works, then, to move beyond representation of identity. This distinction is key to understanding how assemblage differs from intersectionality. Notably, Puar (2013) distinguishes assemblage from intersectionality, explaining that "intersectionality privileges naming, visuality, epistemology, representation, and meaning" whereas assemblage "underscores feeling, tactility, ontology, affect, and information" (520). Intersectionality, for Puar (2013) then, operates around a concern over epistemological truth while assemblage concerns itself with ontological knowing—attending to "what cannot be known, seen, or heard, or has yet to be known, seen, or heard," which thus "allows for becoming/s beyond being/s" (520). And third, queer assemblage destabilizes narrative itself by calling out notions of coherence and unity, thus rendering narrative even more slippery than usual. In those spaces of slippage and wiggle, queer assemblage finds agency and purpose by embracing multiple, and at times contradictory, moments of becoming. Assembling a queer counterstory allows for the gaps, the reorientations, the spaces between systems of power that influence identity making and knowledge making, while a CRT counterstory focuses upon the actual narratives produced by those knowledge-making practices. Queer assemblage yields a layered methodology for unpacking identity constructions, situating narratives among each other in various scenes and moments in contrast to counternarrative's orientation toward linearity and cohesion.

THREE NARRATIVE ASSEMBLAGES: COLE, ROB AND SCOTTY, MARIA

In what follows, I construct a queer narrative assemblage. Taken together, infertility serves as a thread winding among all three. Yet, each offers layered and, at times, nonunified experiences of infertility. Further, while some of the characters in each narrative identify as queer, it is not only just their sexuality that queers this assemblage. Rather, it is also the lack of a unified narrative arc that resists a dominant stock story of infertility and supports the queering of infertility as counterstory.

My focus on infertility is intentional, aiming to highlight that infertility as discourse operates as a type of counterstory to dominant stock stories of fertility. It is in in/fertility that a binary is always, already apparent, and it is subconsciously reinforced in the genre of birth and/or family-building stories. An assemblage of these vignettes provides a layered and more complex narrative to infertility than each story would alone, even as each shares various elements of Bell's narrative typology. These vignettes presented as an assemblage, however, highlight the always becomingness of identity formation, inventing new spaces for and pointing to the slippages of narratives that make space for agency in an always-changing identity construction like infertility. Understanding narrative less as an epistemological form and more as an ontological genre suggests how narrative is never stable, always orienting bodies to a sense of continual becoming. The three vignettes that follow attempt to demonstrate how a queering of counterstory may begin to unfold the multiple moments of ontological transformations, particularly when the subject contains topics of health, sexuality, and gender.

Cole

In July 2015, I was introduced to Cole by his fertility doctor. At this time, Cole was an eighteen-year-old trans teen who was in the process of transitioning from Nicole to Cole. Cole had just undergone an egg retrieval before starting testosterone to complete his transition. Wanting to advocate for trans kids to think about their future fertility, I met Cole at his house for the interview. There, I asked him to share with me how he made the decision to freeze his eggs before transitioning. In response, he shared with me that on the day he was to self-administer his first injection of testosterone, he was sitting in the doctor's office when he was casually handed a fertility preservation brochure. Cole took one look at the info given to him and passed it to his mom. *I told my mom and, if it was something I wanted to do and I thought about it and considered it, she supported it. But, financially, there was a conversation about how we'd pay for it because transitioning costs a lot too. As far as the support, she said, if this is what you really want to do, we'll do our best to make it happen for you.* Cole's parents had undergone their own struggles with infertility, which led them to eventually adopting Cole. Understanding the importance of not taking advantage of one's fertility, Cole's parents supported him in undergoing fertility-preservation treatment.

As our conversation continued, Cole recounted that initially he was relieved that he was handed the brochure. He thought it was odd a conversation hadn't been started earlier in his transition process about the need to consider fertility preservation. But he also shared how frustrating it was to postpone his transition. For Cole, taking the time to undergo hormone treatments and transvaginal ultrasounds served as more explicit reminders of the female body he occupied but did not identify with. At one moment during the interview, he recounted how his body morphed right before his egg retrieval. Standing in front of the mirror, Cole's body resembled that of pregnant body—his ovaries bloated by the overproduction of eggs and follicles. *I was in a lot of discomfort, not just physically but emotionally, you know? Like I wanted to transition so bad but I knew that this discomfort would be worth it for a child that I can later bring into the world.*

Rob and Scotty

I met Rob and Scotty through the same fertility doctor who had introduced me to Cole. For two years, the couple had been working with a gestational surrogate to try and conceive a child, and their doctor thought they might be interested in sharing their story for the project.

She reached out to them, and they soon wrote me an e-mail explaining that while they were more than happy to participate in the project, they worried that they were "unfit" to share an infertility story. They don't identify as being infertile. Rather, they simply find themselves in the infertility scene because of their desire to have a biological child. Understanding their unease, I wrote back and explained how the oral-history project collects a range of infertility stories. This range is important to the project, as it attempts to disrupt ideas of what it means to "beat infertility" and to "succeed" with family building. So, the project believes there is not "one" type of infertility story; there are multiple stories, but they are not always shared. After I communicated this via an e-mail, Rob and Scotty became more interested and agreed to speak with me. A few days later, we met in a hotel bar near their home, where they spoke to me for nearly two hours about their journey.

Sharing their story, Scotty explained how surprised he was with the surrogacy process. *I don't wanna say we were time sensitive, but it was an eye opener for me to see how long it is to actually get in touch with a donor. In my mind, not knowing how anything worked, it was like okay find a donor, you whip up a contract, you get paid, you get the eggs, but there is just so much time in between all of that that it's a big shock for me.* There was also a desire to opt for fertility treatment, as opposed to adoption. Scotty desired a biological connection to the child. *When we were dating, Rob was doing that process, and in our relationship I didn't feel that the kid was going to be mine if it did actually become successful; it would just be, I'm dating this person and that's their kid. So I spoke out and I was like, "Hey! I want kids too, don't know when, eventually. Let's have our own journey together." I mean obviously because of school, I can't prioritize that at the time, but obviously we had a conversation of it and I pitched the idea and he liked it that we should both donate and have the same donor, the egg donor is both related. Half-siblings. Biologically.* But the couple also realized surrogacy does not always guarantee a successful pregnancy. They explained to me how their first transfer failed, which came as a bit of a shock to the couple, who thought the biggest challenge was figuring out a donor and a surrogate. They shared that because the failure of the first transfer made them realize the challenge of sustaining a pregnancy, they had just completed a second transfer, but that this time they were *keeping things close until it's further along where the risks are lower.*

As we wrapped up the interview, we started talking about all the sacrifices and surprises they have had to encounter: not only paying for eggs, but paying for a surrogate, which led them to paying for a fertility doctor and paying lawyers and paying for psychological evaluation and paying for medications and paying for the surrogate's insurance. As they stopped listing off the numerous fertility-related costs as well as fertility communities they'd had to interact with, they noted with surprise, *Hey, I guess we do know a thing or two about infertility, huh?*

Maria

It's a Wednesday evening and I am sitting around a table in a private room at a local brewery with my husband and several other couples who range in age from their early twenties to late forties. Glancing at my phone, I note that it's 7:30. Time to get started. As a support-group leader, I welcome everyone to the meeting, explain the agenda, and then start the meeting by sharing my own infertility story. As I share my story, I keep thinking to myself how disjointed it sounds and am keenly aware of how different it is from every other story in that room. Thinking this, I hear myself sharing out loud,

> *Kevin and I got married about four years ago and decided to start trying immediately. After six months of nothing, we knew something was up, but it took us about one year to actually make an appointment to see an OBGYN. We saw the doctor; he did an exam and ordered some blood work. Everything came back normal for me. Kevin had a semen analysis and everything was ruled generally all right. Not being able to figure out the exact diagnosis for our infertility, the OBGYN directed us to the Fertility Center. So we attended an initial consultation meeting and both of us left feeling totally overwhelmed. At that time, we were only twenty-four years old, and we weren't ready to come to terms with the fact that we may actually never get pregnant naturally. And so we decided to just give it some time. Four years later, we are still giving ourselves time. Never doing any treatment. Never pursuing adoption. Instead we both decided to work on our marriage, to work on our careers. I started by returning to graduate school for my MA and now PhD. Kevin is now getting his MS. And you know, we are still under the age of thirty and perhaps things will change and we will decide to create a family. But right now, we are actually very seriously considering living without children.*

I look around the room after sharing this. Many of the returning folks, whom I now consider my dear friends, exchange a slight smile or head nod. They've heard this story before. The new folks seem a bit perplexed and puzzled. One person even asks, *So you've never done any treatment?*

REORIENTING COUNTERSTORY VIA QUEER ASSEMBLAGE

These three vignettes, taken together, offer a queer assemblage of infertility narratives. Embedding these narratives within a queer assemblage methodology invites readers to reflect on how the stories work together to produce an alternative reality, a counterstory. In this section, I offer an analysis of this particular queer assemblage to demonstrate how counterstories function to reorient readers toward more complex, layered understandings of infertility narratives. Infertility assemblages, I argue, extend how we think of narratives of nonnormative bodies by offering critical insight on issues of sexuality and ableism embedded within narratives of health and medicine. Queered assemblages of health and medicine, then, rather than counterstories of health and medicine, make space to question biomedical practices and discourses that construct bodies of health within paradigms of "normalcy." To support such claims, I begin by discussing how the three narratives above create a narrative assemblage reorienting readers beyond infertility as counter to the stock story of fertility. These narratives suggest a need to disrupt narratives of infertility, which perpetuate cultural ideals of normalcy in the contexts of both ableism and sexuality. I argue then that a queer narrative assemblage of nonnormative bodies has implications beyond writing studies, drawing connections to more interdisciplinary spheres such as health and medicine. In particular, I ponder what queer narrative assemblage as a methodology may offer patients and practitioners.

Disrupting In/Fertility, Constructing Assemblages

To understand how the assemblage above begins to disrupt binary narrative representations of identity construction, allow me to first unpack the relationship between infertility (as counterstory) and fertility (as stock story). To begin with, *infertility* as a diagnostic term connotes a direct juxtaposition between being fertile and being not fertile. Embedded within such a presumption, and perpetuated through biomedical models of fertility (Walks 2007), is the understanding that fertility is equated with normalcy and infertility is equated with an inability to conform to able-bodied functions. Further, gender constructions around what it means to be female frequently become correlated with notions of fertility. That is, to be female is to be fertile, enforced by cultural practices positioning motherhood as a need-to-be-sought-out identity for many who identify as female (De Hertogh 2015; Greil 2002; Greil, Slauson-Blevins, and McQuillan 2010; Walks 2007; Whiteford and Gonzalez 1995). As a result, fertility narratives (often appearing via the genre of birth stories) frequently become positioned as stock stories, while infertility is positioned as an indirect result of failing to conform to fertility. In this way, infertility becomes positioned as a counterstory to fertility.

Infertility, then, as counterstory takes on a particular narrative arch, beginning often with a woman's desire to become fertile, often through biomedical intervention, in order to have a biological child. In this way, infertility as an embodied counterstory almost always connotes beliefs that an infertility story is a story about a woman trying to conceive. Yet, as the assemblages above contest, such a presumption is false. The experience of infertility told as an embodied narrative impacts many—beyond those who identify as female and heterosexual. Further, the assemblage above offers an additional critique of Western culture's impulse to norm gender expectations through biomedical interventions like in vitro fertilization. In this way, in vitro fertilization often sustains normative ideals of ableism, removing space to embrace bodily failure. Thus, the assemblage reorients readers toward more critical insights on whom infertility impacts, as well as the instability and continued identity formation attached to infertility experiences. Queering counterstory, then, by assembling narratives of experience reveals more layered and complex narratives of infertility, disrupting the discursive binary embedded within in/fertility narratives. In this way, queering counterstory through an assemblage of narratives allows readers more complex understandings of the spaces of becoming. And this, I argue, is what is important and valued in assemblage narratives. Narratives work together to construct less unified narratives, allowing readers to see the slippages and gaps with identity narrative, allowing, as Puar (2013) explains, readers "to attune to intensities, emotions, energies, affectivities, textures as they inhabit events, spatiality, and corporealities" (520). Queer assemblage then becomes concerned with the phenomenological, with "diverse intellectual and political histories that cannot be stabilized as objects" (Ahmed 2006, 5). As such, queer assemblage disrupts narratives of coherency, and in doing so, allows for the following:

First, a queer assemblage allows the disruption of binary positioning, that is, stock story versus counterstory.

It is the construction itself of an assemblage of narratives that begins to break down infertility (as counter) and fertility (as stock) stories. Readers of an infertility assemblage learn from the vignettes above how queered counterstory complicates infertility as a counterstory. All three vignettes, taken together as an assemblage, construct infertility narratives that fail to counter fertility as a stock story. The vignettes are stratified, pointing to the various subjectivities impacted by infertility, as well as how those diverse subjectivities create a range of infertility experiences. From these stories, readers learn how there is not one dominate infertility story. Embodied subjectivities matter and influence the types of infertility experiences one will encounter, as elaborated in the second point.

Second, a queer assemblage captures nonnormative identities, positionalities, and the moments of being and becoming often unseen in counterstory.

Embodied subjectivities matter to and influence the types of infertility experiences one encounters. Experiences of infertility then, we see from this assemblage, are mediated by individual subjectivities. Cole, Rob and Scotty, and Maria tell incongruent infertility narratives: Cole, whose subjectivity as a trans teen, forces him to encounter infertility experiences prior to even having immediate intent to start a family; Rob and Scotty, who, as a gay couple wanting biological children, are forced into infertility experiences; and Maria, who, as a heterosexual infertile woman, grapples with the decision to reject certain infertility experiences like IVF. Embodying these distinct subjectivities, a more layered narrative of infertility emerges for readers, one that challenges more dominant understandings of infertility.

Third, queer assemblage destabilizes narrative itself by calling out notions of coherence and unity, thus rendering narrative even more slippery than usual. In those spaces of slippage and wiggle, queer assemblage finds agency and purpose by embracing multiple, and at times contradictory, moments of becoming.

From the narratives of Cole, Rob and Scotty, and Maria, readers can see how queer assemblage operationalizes Sara Ahmed's concept of queer phenomenology—reorienting narrators and readers to queer experiences of "how bodies become orientated by how they take up time and space" (Ahmed 2006, 5). In the context of infertility then, the assemblage provided above allows for stratification for the layering of narratives—continually shifting as a mode to capture their phenomenological orientation to cultural expectations and desires of normalcy and heteronormativity. Stratification opens the gaps binaries often seek to dismiss. It is through queer assemblage then that in accounting for phenomenological shifts of becoming, of resisting, and of revising bodily experiences in tension with cultural norms, more complex and embodied understandings of fertility and reproduction are formed. In operation, a queer assemblage of counterstory allows then for not only the ability to include embodied orientations often not included in dominant stock-story narratives. Methodologically, though, queering counterstory situates assemblage as a tool to locate diverging and contesting stories that are not cohesive narratives. As a methodology, queering counterstory serves to open up more moments of slippage for readers to grasp the multitude of complexities that embodied orientations encounter. A queer assemblage of these narratives thereby disrupts the counterstory of infertility, which perpetuates cultural ideals of normalcy, and reorients readers to more layered lived experiences of infertility.

IMPLICATIONS AND CONCLUSION

As a rhetorician interested in queering the fields of health and medicine, I see that queer assemblage can assist both the field of writing studies and the practice of medicine in advancing more complex representations of how embodied orientations (like infertility) reorient individuals toward more nuanced identities. Such is important whether one identifies as a writing instructor or reproductive endocrynologist. Much of the rhetoric of health and medicine scholarship concerns itself with advocating on behalf of those whose agency is removed due to unethical situations in order to promote better practices of communication and greater rhetorical inquiry into the labeling of subjects as well as into the topic of risk. Some queered methodological approaches to health and medical rhetorics have entered these inquiries, yet almost always a queer methodology is only applied to queer subjects or queer topics, such as HIV/AIDS (see Scott 2003). If queer arguably "focuses on the mismatches between sex, gender and desire; locates and exploits the incoherencies in those three terms which stabilize heterosexuality (and homosexuality); ruptures traditional models; and finds pleasure in radical politics and unsettlings" (Rallin 2008), then queer embodies the methodological potential for intervention, a pinnacle point of importance to rhetoricians of health and medicine. And given biomedicine's continued reinforcement of normativity, queer's embodied resistance to normativity furthers the potential of methodological intervention among subjects of health.

Further motivating this chapter is accounting for how stories of infertility are constructed within a heteronormative lens. I ground this theory by exploring medical trends toward biomedical models of health intervention—which label the infertile body as a body of risk and assigns fertility treatment, and thereby the conception of a child, as a method to resolve infertility. In fact, Lee Edelman's (2004) scholarship suggests that the child serves as a rhetorical trope symbolizing "the universal value attributed to political futurity" (19). Rhetorically then, the child becomes a political signifier of nation-building practices, as the child suggests a future lineage for both the family and the greater nation. Thus the creation of the family is not only a constructed individual pursuit but also one linked directly to larger heteronormative projects. Establishing how infertility is constantly in tension with heteronormative desires, I turn to counterstory as a methodological musing. In/fertility and counter/story operate along binaries—infertility in tension with fertility and counterstory in tension with stock story.

Yet these binaries fail to attune to the counter-counterstories operating within these tensions. Applying a queered methodology to counterstory, I find my own resistance to fixing my fertility as a site of not only challenging dominant heteronormative reality but also of embracing a queered, liminal reality. A queered counterstory then thrives on resistance to the norm, to the stock story, always reinventing itself against cultural norms as a site of invention by residing in a nonlinear, non-normative, nonresolved space. It embraces notions of queering failure (Halberstam 2011) and promotes infertility stories that may not align with success—allowing for a more queer construction of infertility and the narratives attached to an infertility story. A queer assemblage counterstory thus becomes a methodological approach to better surface these stories but further to call a more queered rhetorical inquiry into the medical stories and practices we are called to listen and orient ourselves to. By calling for such inquiry, my hope is to raise issues with how rhetoricians—and physicians and those in medical settings who listen to patient stories—may better advance the ways in which we care for those whose stories we are simply not trained to hear.

> I am back in my writing room, the room that was to be my baby's. Feelings of sadness, frustration, and grief have frequented this space. Now, as I look up and take a break from writing the stories of other infertile people, I feel traces of their stories in my body, noting how their stories have undoubtedly shaped my own. Taken together, they work as an assemblage constructing an embodied orientation to my own infertility story.

REFERENCES

Adler-Kassner, Linda. 2008. *The Activist WPA: Changing Stories about Writing and Writers.* Boulder: University Press of Colorado. https://doi.org/10.2307/j.ctt4cgqss.

Ahmed, Sara. 2006. *Queer Phenomenology: Orientations, Objects, Others.* Durham, NC: Duke University Press. https://doi.org/10.1215/9780822388074.

Bell, Lee Anne. 2010. *Storytelling for Social Justice: Connecting Narrative and the Arts in Antiracist Teaching.* New York: Routledge.

De Hertogh, Lori Beth. 2015. "Reinscribing a New Normal: Pregnancy, Disability, and Health 2.0 in the Online Natural Birthing Community, Birth without Fear." *Ada: A Journal of Gender, New Media, and Technology* 7.

Edelman, Lee. 2004. *No Future: Queer Theory and the Death Drive.* Durham, NC: Duke University Press. https://doi.org/10.1215/9780822385981.

Greil, Arthur L. 2002. "Infertile Bodies: Mediclization, Metaphor, and Agency." In *Infertility around the Globe: New Thinking on Childlessness, Gender, and Reproductive Technologies,* edited by Marcia Inhorn and Frank van Balen, 101–18. Berkeley: University of California Press.

Greil, Arthur L., Kathleen Slauson-Blevins, and Julia McQuillan. 2010. "The Experience of Infertility: A Review of Recent Literature." *Sociology of Health & Illness* 32 (1): 140–62. https://doi.org/10.1111/j.1467-9566.2009.01213.x.

Halberstam, Jack. 2011. *The Queer Art of Failure*. Durham, NC: Duke University Press. https://doi.org/10.1215/9780822394358.

Journet, Debra. 2012. "Narrative Turns in Writing Studies Research." In *Writing Studies Research in Practice: Methods and Methodologies*, edited by Lee Nickoson and Mary P. Sheridan, 13–24. Carbondale: Southern Illinois University Press.

Kirsch, Gesa E. 2012. *Writing Studies Research in Practice: Methods and Methodologies*. In *Writing Studies Research in Practice: Methods and Methodologies*, edited by Lee Nickoson and Mary P. Sheridan. Carbondale: Southern Illinois University Press.

Martinez, Aja Y. 2014. "A Plea for Critical Race Theory Counterstory: Stock Story versus Counterstory Dialogues Concerning Alejandra's 'Fit' in the Academy." *Composition Studies* 42 (2): 33–55.

Powell, Malea. 2002. "Rhetorics of Survivance: How American Indians Use Writing." *College Composition and Communication* 53 (3): 396–434. https://doi.org/10.2307/1512132.

Puar, Jasbir K. 2013. "Queer Times, Queer Assemblages." In *The Routledge Queer Studies Reader 2013*, edited by Donald E. Hall and Annamarie Jagose, 515–28. New York: Routledge.

Rallin, Aneil. 2008. "A Provocation: Queer Is Not a Substitute for Gay/Lesbian." *Harlot: A Revealing Look at the Arts of Persuasion* 1(1). http://harlotofthearts.org/index.php/harlot/article/view/5/3.

Royster, Jacqueline Jones. 1996. "When the First Voice You Hear Is Not Your Own." *College Composition and Communication* 47 (1): 29–40. https://doi.org/10.2307/358272.

Scott, J. Blake. 2003. *Risky Rhetoric: AIDS and the Cultural Practices of HIV Testing*. Carbondale: Southern Illinois University Press.

Villanueva, Victor Jr. 1993. *Bootstraps: From an American Academic of Color*. Urbana, IL: NCTE.

Walks, Michelle. 2007. "Breaking the Silence: Infertility, Motherhood, and Queer Culture." *Journal of the Motherhood Initiative for Research and Community Involvement* 9 (2): 130–43.

Whiteford, Linda M., and Lois Gonzalez. 1995. "Stigma: The Hidden Burden of Infertility." *Social Science & Medicine* 40 (1): 27–36. https://doi.org/10.1016/0277-9536(94)00124-C.

8

QUEERING NETWORKED WRITING
A Sensory Autoethnography of Desire and Sensation on Grindr

Michael J. Faris

There is an open secret about sex: rhetoric and writing scholars don't like it.[1] And queer rhetoricians don't seem to like it very much either. One might think that in the normative space of rhetoric and writing scholarship—where historically the field has been most interested in students creating "composed" essays in composition and in studying "proper" public discourse outside education—that the "queer turn" (Alexander and Wallace 2009, W302) in rhetoric and writing might have involved a turn to desire and *eros* to challenge these norms.[2] But, alas, queer rhetoric and writing studies has remained firmly attached to identity and identification, to the composed, and to the epistemic turn in rhetorical studies.

In this chapter I raise the question, what might turning to the materiality of sexual bodies afford us in rhetoric and writing studies broadly and in queer rhetorical studies specifically? For something so integral to human life, for something some of us just can't get enough of, for something so repulsive to so many, one might think queer rhetoric and writing studies might explore questions of how, in its various instantiations, sex is related to rhetoric. But despite the "corporeal turn" (Dolmage 2012, 115) in rhetoric and writing, we have been pretty resistant to the study of the corporeality of sex. Perhaps sex is so distant from the "good man speaking well" that the field can't imagine what we would do with bodies thwacking against each other in a bedroom, back alley, back seat of a car, bathhouse, or even a dorm room on a college campus. Perhaps, as Christine Harold (2000) suggests, we have been averse to bodies and desires because of our attachment to "moral norms," which "obscures or denies a particular site of rhetorical forces that threaten the assumptions of the critic: the physical body" (865).

Rhetoric and writing isn't alone in the humanities for its aversion to sex. Even queer theory has been tragically averse to actual sex. In

DOI: 10.7330/9781607328186.c008

his critique of queer theory's "critical squeamishness about sex," Tim Dean (2015) explains, "When attached to the dignity of personhood, sex merits research inasmuch as those it marks are deemed worthy of legal and institutional protection. When detached from the dignity of personhood, however, it becomes much sketchier. The recurring anxiety is that sex will demean personhood; it is assumed to need strong identity formations to redeem and render it safe" (615). That is, when sex is attached to personhood and identity, it's worth our scholarly attention because it has been tamed, made safe. However, as Dean makes clear, "Sex is not primarily an expression of identity but its undoing" (616). In short, "*sex undermines identity*" (619). Dean suggests that this insight—that sex undermines identity—has been "germinal for queer theory" (619), but it's an insight largely ignored by rhetoric and writing scholars. If we understand identity as a primarily discursive understanding and representation of the self, and corporeality as always excessive or rupturing of the symbolic order, then sex and desire (and indeed bodily pleasure and pain) exceed, disrupt, and rupture—or undermine—our senses of the self as coherent and discrete identities.

As Dean (2015) charges queer theory, I too charge queer rhetoric and writing: it exhibits a "genteel reluctance to engage sexuality save through the domesticating lenses of identity" (623). I argue that by incorporating sex into the study of rhetoric, we can push the boundaries of rhetoric and writing studies, and I suggest that perhaps we need an anti-identitarian, impersonal approach to rhetoric. By *sex*, I want to be clear: I don't mean the category of one's biological sex (male, female, intersex) but rather actual, embodied sexual desires and practices—those moments and practices that, as Leo Bersani (1987) argues, challenge our subjectivity and bodily coherence. That is, as much as we like to think otherwise, we are not fully in control of desires and sexual experiences. Sex and desire are, as Bersani claims, masochistic: about losing control of oneself, about exploding limits of the body, about—in its most powerful moments of *jouissance*—the shattering of the self.

In order to explore potential implications of turning to sex, this chapter provides an autoethnographic account of my experiences using Grindr, a mobile application that allows men to find other men for sex, romance, friends, and/or flirting. Exploring my experiences with Grindr offers an opportunity to move away from an epistemic focus on identity and toward a queer study of desire, affect, and sensations. As Frederick Corey and Thomas Nakayama write, "Grindr connects men, haphazardly, deliriously. . . . With little attention to social categories,

Grindr has the potential to disrupt social institutions such as marriages, gay or straight, but offers no institution in its place other than free flowing desire" (Corey and Nakayama 2012, 21). It is this "free flowing desire" that I wish to explore, both theoretically and through a brief autoethnographic account.

Before turning to my autoethnographic account, however, I first explore how queer rhetoric and writing scholarship has largely focused on identity, identification, and representation and thus has failed to attend to desire's and sexuality's free-flowing natures detached from subjectivity. Following queer thinkers like Sasho Alexander Lambevski (2004), I suggest we need to move beyond "the idea of sexuality as a subject position . . . and develop instead a vocabulary about affective intensity, flux, and the sensual assembling of human and nonhuman elements into a pleasure machine" (305). I then sketch out queer theory's anti-identitarian and posthumanist impulses and explain new materialist turns in rhetoric and writing that attempt to trace objects, affects, and sensations. These developments suggest we turn away from the centrality of hermeneutics, identification, and representation in rhetoric and turn instead to affect and sensations. I then briefly overview insights from ethnographic and autoethnographic approaches before turning to my discussion of Grindr, where I suggest that the interface encourages an anti-identitarian, sensual openness to others. As I conclude, I call for rhetoric and writing scholars to attend to how sensation, desire, and affect may precede persuasion (instead of Burkean identification) and to attend to rhetoric's "perverse movement" (Morrison 1992, 20).

QUEER RHETORIC AND WRITING'S ATTACHMENT TO IDENTITY AND REPRESENTATION

Rhetoric and writing has not seriously taken up one of the central insights of queer theory: its antihumanist and anti-identitarian understanding of sexuality. Queer theory certainly means many different things to different scholars, but I prefer Annamarie Jagose's (2013) succinct gloss of the field: "those posthumanist and anti-identitarian critical approaches that are engaged by thinking against the practices, temporalities, and modes of being through which sexuality has been normatively thought" (1).

With few exceptions, queer rhetoric and writing studies has largely ignored the bodily indignities of sex, focusing instead on representation, identity, and identification.[3] This identitarian focus is readily apparent in how rhetoric and writing scholars have understood queer theory. David Wallace (2011) introduces queer theory in *Compelled to Write*, only to limit it to a theory of intersectionality and opacity—that is, that identities are intersectional and that complete self-knowledge is not possible. Jonathan Alexander (2008) stresses that "queer theory is designed to provoke consideration of the construction of *all* sexualities in our culture as sites of identity, knowledge, and power" (14). Elsewhere, Alexander and Michelle Gibson provide a list of "tenets" of queer theory, which are fundamentally identitarian: "Identities are constructed and performed"; "We negotiate multiple identities"; "Understanding the construction and negotiation of these identities allows us to resist *normalizing* identity"; "Queer theory . . . moves us *toward* the more difficult process of understanding how identity, even the most intimate perceptions of self, arise out of a complex matrix of shifting social power" (Alexander and Gibson 2004, 3). None of their six tenets of queer theory speaks to the anti-identitarian or antihumanistic potentialities of queer theory. Just a sampling of other scholarship reveals a similar focus on identity and representation: Mary Elliott's (1996) discussion of coming out to students; Alexander and Elizabeth Losh's analysis of coming-out videos (Alexander and Losh 2010); Serkan Görkemli's (2014) analysis of the literate activities of LGBT organizations in Turkey; Scott Lloyd DeWitt's (1997) discussion of coming out online; Marc Ouellette's (2014) critique of queer representation in video games; Randal Woodland's (2000) analysis of how digital spaces shape LGBT identities; and Jan Cooper's (2004) argument that the metaphor of the contact zone ignores how fluid and performative identities are.

I want to be clear that I am not necessarily critiquing any of these approaches as singular projects. Certainly, these works are quite generative, have been influential on many in the field, and have shaped my own thinking. Further, I think much of this work has been and continues to be necessary. Indeed, I follow Cindy Patton (1993) in valuing identities "as strategic systems with pragmatic purposes and unintended effects" (175). That is, identity is a real and important aspect of our social and political lives and warrants rhetorical study (Anderson 2007). Rather, my concern is just how central identity has been to queer rhetoric and writing: when queer rhetorical approaches consistently attend to identity, we may be missing out on the affective, on desires, and on pleasures that might come before identity. Further, we continue to value the human as the focus of our rhetorical inquiry, failing to see how sex and desire are impersonal, even antihumanistic, in nature.

QUEER THEORY'S ANTI-INDENTITARIANISM

While rhetoric and writing scholars have drawn from queer theory to explore how identities are social constructions and implicated in power relations, we as a field have largely ignored the anti-identitarian impulses of queer theory. By anti-identitarian impulses, I do not mean the deconstruction of identity recognizable in queer rhetoric and writing scholarship. As Bersani (1995) argues, the deconstruction of identities is usually accompanied by a desexing of gayness: "Gay critiques of homosexual identity have generally been *desexualizing* discourses" (5). Further, these deconstruction projects, as a hermeneutics of suspicion or paranoid reading, too often create a queer/normative dichotomy and, as Eve Kosofsky Sedgwick (2003) explains, never really surprise us. Such readings are determined from the outset, anticipatory: "It can't help or can't stop or can't do anything other than prove the very same assumptions with which it began" (Sedgwick 2003, 135). While the hermeneutics of suspicion places its faith in exposure and demystification, what Sedgwick calls "reparative reading"—or, in Isaac West's (2013) terms, "generous readings"—instead traces affects and effects and starts from curiosity rather than suspicion. As West encourages rhetorical critics, we should "understand how rhetors are themselves theorizing genders, corporealities, sexualities, desires, and other embodiments in ways that exceed our extant explanatory frames" (540). These theorizations do not necessarily need to be explicitly laid out linguistically: they can be kinesthetic, embodied theories, as Patton (1992) shows in her analysis of voguing: those queers who vogue in nightclubs are kinesthetically learning and enacting critiques of gender. Most recently, Jean Bessette (2016) makes similar critiques of queer rhetoric and writing's hermeneutics, arguing for a contextual and contingent understanding of norms and queerness not as something prefigured in advance.

Instead of an anti-identitarian impulse based on paranoid readings, the anti-identitarian impulses I have in mind question the centrality of subjectivity and identity to stranger sociability. In his 1981 interview with *Le Gai Pied*, Michel Foucault (1997) suggests that the radical potential of homosexuality doesn't lie in gay identities but rather in the ways noninstitutional intimacies can lead to new relationalities: "What makes homosexuality 'disturbing'" is its potential to create new ways of relating to each other (136). Foucault continues, "Homosexuality is a historic occasion to reopen affective and relational virtualities, not so much through the intrinsic qualities of the homosexual but because the 'slantwise' position of the latter, as it were, the diagonal lines he can lay out in the social fabric[,] allow these virtualities to come to life" (138).

Following Foucault's thinking and Lacanian psychoanalysis, Bersani (1987) claims that the radical potential of sex lies in how sex destroys the ego: sex is disturbing, socially abrasive, violent, disrespectful, and we should not pastoralize it or try to redeem it as romantic. This understanding of sex as destructive of the ego counters both commonsense understandings of sex and some feminist and gay theories of sex. Many have argued that sex is about power—often violent toward others—and attempt to recuperate it by attaching it to love or community building. Bersani flips this understanding around: sex *is* violent, but this violence is toward the self, toward the ego, because sex is about becoming powerless, about losing control of the self. This is the very reason sex should be explored and cherished: we should value sex for its "anticommunal, antiegalitarian, antinurturing, antiloving" nature (215). The self, he argues, is a practical convenience, it's been promoted to an ethical ideal, and it's used to sanction violence. For Bersani, we should celebrate an obsession with sex, not because it's subversive, not because it builds community, not for diversity, but because it makes visible "self-dismissal": "Male homosexuality advertises the risk of the sexual itself as the risk of self-dismissal, of *losing sight* of the self, and in so doing it proposes and dangerously represents *jouissance* as a model of ascesis" (222). There is, Bersani (1995) writes, "a potentially revolutionary inaptitude—perhaps inherent in gay desire—for sociality as it is known" (76). Here, Bersani is not claiming gay men *qua* gay men are inept at being social but rather that queer desire encourages reformulations of relationality because it can reject, or perhaps just ignore, how intimacy is privatized and sex pastoralized (see Berlant and Warner 1998 on the privatization of intimacy). For instance, Bersani (2010) also finds potential in gay cruising in new relationality because it calls attention to how intimacy is impersonal.

Similarly, in his study of barebacking subcultures, Dean (2009) argues that "cruising entails a remarkably hospitable disposition toward strangers" because it is marked by an impersonal openness to the radical alterity of strangers (176). Following Samuel Delany (1999) in *Times Square Red, Times Square Blue*, Dean argues that cruising is a form of *contact* that involves crossing class boundaries in public, as opposed to networking, which involves a more stratified stranger sociability (e.g., meeting other professional gays in an expensive martini bar). Notably, for cruising to function as contact, it must involve a "risking [of] the self by opening it to alterity" (210); thus, cruising must be aimless, with "a centrifugal openness," rather than "a single-minded quest [that] insulates the self from alterity" (211). Dean's argument rests on the idea that such an ethical stance of openness to radical otherness requires that we don't domesticate the other, which means we do not need to know or identify with a stranger. That is, ethical contact with strangers involves an impersonal intimacy rather than one of identification: we cruise without aim, are open to the alterity of others, and are hospitable to them without needing to know or identify with them; in fact, identification annihilates alterity. For Dean, then, "Identities of whatever sort remain incompatible with openness to alterity, and thus identity may be understood as not merely illusory but also, in this sense, as unethical" (212). That is, if identity works through identification with others, then identity is a domestication not just of the self but of the other: reducing the strangeness of strangers to something knowable, identifiable, rather than being open to their alterity.

Central to Dean's (2009) understanding of cruising is that intimacy, desire, and fantasy are impersonal and not attached to identity. Humans have, he explains, "an antihumanist inability to respect the inviolable integrity of personhood in the sphere of sexuality" (160). Lambevski (2004) follows this sort of understanding of desire when he critiques queer theory's focus on identity. We have traditionally seen identity "as a relatively stable position" inscribed by "prefabricated social discourses" (305). What if, instead, we were to explore sensual, affective, and desirous bodies not as discursive constructions but rather as "an erogenous composite body that is an unpredictable collection" (305)? Rather than seeing sexuality as a subject position or "firmly wedded to identity" (306), we might see it as something unpredictable, something than can be "aroused by anything under the sun, given certain conditions" (307).

NEW MATERIALISM AND THE TURN AWAY
FROM EPISTEMIC RHETORIC

My thoughts in this chapter are further animated by a broad theoretical shift over the last few decades in the humanities that many shorthand as *new materialism*. New materialism covers a broad theoretical space that responds to the linguistic turn in the humanities by variously investigating the ontologies of objects, rejecting the subject-object binary, exploring the materiality of affects and sensations, and challenging the primacy of language toward understanding phenomena in the world. As John Muckelbauer (2007) describes the linguistic turn, it is often understood as "an intellectual trajectory wherein the signifying movement of language becomes the paradigm for analyzing a whole host of diverse phenomena," usually attending to the production of meanings or the interpretations of meanings (238). New materialism doesn't necessarily reject the insights of studying representation, but it does recognize "the limits of knowledge production inherent in research focused principally on representation, mediation, signification, and subjectivity," turning instead to "the intersection of sensation, intensity, and materiality" (Paasonen, Hillis, and Petit 2015, 4).

In rhetoric and writing, new materialist scholars have questioned the centrality of epistemic rhetoric in which "rhetoricians sometimes count only the human, symbolic, and discursive," turning instead to ways we can "account for the nonhuman, the nonsymbolic, and the nondiscursive" (Lynch and Rivers 2015, 4). Such a turn conceives of rhetoric as "not reducible solely to questions of meaning, intersubjective negotiation, and propriety" (Lundberg 2015, 173). In *Ambient Rhetoric*, for example, Thomas Rickert (2013) proposes we challenge the subject-object dichotomy that has been so central to rhetorical studies, abandon theories of representation, and turn instead to "the incorporation of the material world as integral to human action and interaction, including the rhetorical arts" (xii). Debra Hawhee (2015) challenges us to attend to "connective, participatory dimensions of sensing" (5). As she writes, "The epistemic approach to rhetoric has run its course; rhetoric is not, or not only, a means of knowing and needn't be so attached to meaning" (13).[4]

In particular, turns to sensation and affect are influential in my thinking in this chapter, as scholars have attended to phenomena that might not be so wrapped up in subjectivity and representation. Scholars like political theorist Davide Panagia (2009) argue that sensation is central to political life. By sensation, Panagia means "an experience of unrepresentability in that a sensation occurs without having to rely on a recognizable shape, outline, or identity to determine its value" (2). That is, before we can make sense of something, we are interrupted by it, in a way. Whereas rhetorical studies has understood identification as central to political life (following Burke 1969), Panagia suggests instead the primacy of aesthetics: "The first political act is also an aesthetic one, a partitioning of sensation that divides the body and its organs of sense perception and assigns to them corresponding capacities for making of sense" (9). Whereas identification requires a stable subject who identifies with an other, focusing on sensation takes another approach: "a relinquishing and a reconfiguring of our selves" (11). As Panagia explains, "The experience of sensation disarticulates received forms of subjectivity and regimes of perception, and . . . the event of disarticulation precedes the productive role of figuration or presentation" (16). What I am suggesting, then, is to set aside representation, identity, subjectivity, and identification and to think through what it might mean to focus instead on desire, sensation, and affect. For, as Panagia argues, "The experience of sensation does not rely on a preconstituted composition of individual subjectivity or consciousness" (23).

SENSORY AUTOETHNOGRAPHY: CRUISING ETHNOGRAPHIES

In order to explore the potentialities for attending to sex, desire, and affect in digital environments, I provide an autoethnography of my experiences using Grindr. Ethnography has been a staple of rhetoric and writing research (e.g., Chiseri-Strater 2012; Sheridan 2012) and has become one of the most useful approaches for studying digital practices, as ethnographers typically participate in those online environments (Hine 2015; Smith 2007). While my autoethnography differs from traditional ethnography in that I did not set out to study Grindr and design a study as I was using the app, I follow Mary Sheridan (2012) in understanding ethnography as a set of flexible "orientations that help us examine situated practices through a variety of methods" rather than a "seemingly static ethnographic tradition" (82). Autoethnography is one such approach that has been flexibly applied to various sites of study, providing an "insider perspective" that fuses the roles of researcher and research subject (Canagarajah 2012, 114). As Christine Hine (2015) explains, digital autoethnography involves "attend[ing] to the generalized tropes and commonly available discourses that inform actions and shape expectations" (83). Such an approach "emphasizes the embodied and emotional experiences of engagement with diverse media" (83).

In the sensory autoethnographic account that follows, I attend to these particularities on Grindr, with special attention to sensations, affect, and desire. Sara Pink (2015) uses the term "sensory ethnography" to describe the increasing attention in ethnographic accounts to sensory experiences. As she explains, sensory ethnography "demands a form of reflexivity that goes beyond the interrogation of how culture is 'written' to examine the sites of embodied knowing" (13). While ethnographic studies have traditionally been interested in the semiotic or linguistic construction of culture and cultural practices, a sensory ethnographic approach attends to sensorial aspects of the relationships among bodies, materials, and places, understanding the bodies as emplaced in particular contexts.

While postmodern revisions to ethnographic practices have challenged the idea of the distant, disembodied researcher by admitting to and being reflexive about "the embodied experiences of the researcher"

(Hine 2015, 19), most ethnographic accounts ignore the researcher's sexual body. However, some ethnographic accounts of homosexual cruising have attempted to attend to the sexual experiences of both the participants and the researcher while further challenging the subject-object dichotomy and the propriety of traditional ethnography. As John Edward Campbell (2004) writes of his ethnography of homosexuality in online chats, "I am less an academic gone native than a native gone academic" (25). And in his controversial *Tearoom Trade: Impersonal Sex in Public Places*, Laud Humphreys (1975) similarly challenges the propriety of doing sociological research by "standing around in public lavatories making mental notes on the art of fellatio" (168). In response to claims that his work might harm the integrity of sociology, he scoffs, "Concern about 'professional integrity,' it seems to me, is symptomatic of a dying discipline. Let the clergy worry about keeping their cassocks clean" (168) (see Ashford 2009 for a comprehensive overview of ethnographies of cruising both online and offline).

From accounts of queer cruising in both digital and nondigital spaces, we can learn quite a bit about sex, desire, and sociality. But I'll just focus on the fact that these sorts of spaces and activities are not identitarian in their organization. That is, participants in gay cruising are not necessarily gay: they are often heterosexual and possibly married and come from a variety of racial and class backgrounds. Indeed, as Humphreys (1975) shows, those engaged in tearoom trade (sex in public bathrooms) are not necessarily gay (indeed, many are not) and are a diverse population. In the following autoethnographic account, I particularly attend to issues of impersonal desire and sensations instead of issues of representation, identity, and identification.

AN AUTOETHNOGRAPHY OF GRINDR:
OBJECTS, DESIRES, SENSATIONS

Grindr is a free mobile app that geolocates users and maps them on a cascading grid, arranged by distance from the user, for easy scanning and messaging. A free account allows a user to see the one hundred closest users who have opened the app recently. Users can see the details of a profile by tapping on a profile's image, and they can message users individually by then tapping on a dialogue box on a profile page. Since its launch in 2009, Grindr has gained immense popularity, with two million active users opening the app every day in 196 countries (Grindr 2015a). Its success has influenced the development of many other apps for men attracted to men, like Jack'd, Hornet, and Scruff, and apps for straight folks, like Tinder and Blendr. I first joined Grindr in 2009, mere months after Grindr first became available in the Apple App Store. In the six years since, I have chatted with perhaps thousands of other men on the app and met hundreds of men for coffee, drinks, dates, or sex.

Interfaces, of course, have politics (Selfe and Selfe 1994), and in this autoethnographic account, I explore some (though certainly not all) of the political implications of Grindr by attending to affect, desire, and sensations. First, I want to suggest that Grindr eschews identitarian politics: while the majority of users are probably gay-identified cisgender men, many users are on the down low, straight identified, bisexual, or representative of a host of other potential identities. In addition, cisgender women, transwomen, transmen, and genderqueer folk often use the app. One reason Grindr is so open to a variety of users is its ease of entry: Grindr can be downloaded easily for free from Google Play or the Apple App Store and, until recently, did not require an account to log in.[5] Fill out a profile and possibly upload a picture, and a user is set. There are many reasons users turn to and keep using Grindr: sex, flirting, meeting new friends, seeking romantic relationships, learning about new locations after a move, developing friendships, and killing time or alleviating boredom (Gudelunas 2012; Van De Wiele and Tong 2014).

A user doesn't expect that their profile is an authentic representation of their identity. Unlike other dating sites, where authenticity is central to one's profile building (e.g., Almjeld 2014), Grindr profiles are minimalist and not expected to represent one's subjectivity. This is most evident in profiles that are left blank: no image and no profile data. But it is also true of profiles that use part of the body: I am not trying to convey who I am, I am trying to arouse others' desire or be open to encounters. In my experiences, most Grindr profile pictures are blank, a picture of one's face, an artistic or landscape image, or a photo of one's body parts—sometimes legs, biceps, or backs, but most often torsos.[6] In addition, Grindr's interface encourages a limited textual profile: users can mark their age, height, weight, ethnicity, relationship status, what they're "looking for" (chat, dates, friends, networking, relationship, or "right now"), and their "Grindr Tribe"—a series of quasi identity markers like Bear, Clean-Cut, Jock, Poz, Trans, Twink. They can also provide a profile "name," a 70-character "headline," and a 255-character "About Me" description. Many, if not most, Grindr users leave much of this blank, leaving their profile mostly a picture with little contextual clues. My most recent profile, shown in figure 8.1, provides an example.

This isn't to say authenticity doesn't play a role: once a conversation starts, users often ask for authentication measures, especially face pics

(Blackwell, Birnholtz, and Abbott 2015). But I want to suggest that the initial encounter with a profile picture isn't necessarily one of interpretation but rather one of interruption. This is especially true when I receive a message from a blank profile—"Hey"—and their next message is a picture of their body. As Laurie Gries (2015) notes, rhetorical studies has a "longstanding tradition of representationalism" that casts visual artifacts as akin to symbolic texts (18). Jeff Rice (2013) also critiques this "hermeneutics focus on textual interpretation (what does the digital artifact mean) in order to reveal what is hidden from immediate perception" (360). Both Gries and Rice suggest we might attend to how visuals suggest, intrigue, wound, strike, or assemble network associations. These profile images on Grindr function as things, as Gries suggests visuals do: a hot torso that intrigues, a cute face that delights, a gaping asshole that disgusts or attracts, a huge cock that raises my body temperature. The image, as Panagia (2009) suggests, interrupts, producing desires (or even disgust) not related to the identity of the image's source.

The "reduction" of other humans to objects and the simplicity of Grindr's interface design allow for the production of desire and thus the potential for contact. Many argue Grindr's visual design encourages objectification that leads to antisocial behavior. For example, Jaime Woo (2014) argues such privileging of "visuals above everything else" makes personality nearly meaningless on the app and suggests that more text or providing common interests would help make the app more personal and less likely to support normative beauty standards (67). And artist Tom Penney (2014) describes Grindr profile pictures as "non-visceral, gaze-oriented visual bodies, for consumption, as objects" (108).

While these concerns have warrants, here I follow Gilles Deleuze and Félix Guattari's understanding of desire to help explain how Grindr might encourage an opening up of desire (Deleuze and Guattari 1983). I suggest Grindr's interface makes possible an openness to strangers through how it *produces desires* and these desires *produce new relations*. Indeed, Grindr provides opportunities to challenge the tyranny of the sovereign subject who believes in their already-known fixed desires. Commonsense notions of desire are that they are inherent or related to identity (e.g., "I'm gay, so I like men"); desires are conceptualized in terms of "lack," in things or objects we don't yet have or are missing. The only thing standing in our way of happiness, in this commonsense logic, is repression of these preexisting desires, and it is only when we can speak freely our desires and act on them that we will be liberated or happy (a view also critiqued by Foucault [1990] in *The History of Sexuality*). But for Deleuze and Guattari (1983), "The traditional logic of desire is all wrong

Figure 8.1. The author's profile on Grindr

from the very outset" (25). Such a model leads to identification with a restricted set of others; that is, one identifies with others of the same race or gender (Holland 1999, 39). Deleuze and Guattari (1983) instead propose that desire is produced in new and unexpected ways, and that desire is productive of new ways of being and doing in the world. As Eugene Holland (1999) glosses their work, "Desire, they insist, does not lack anything, does not aim at what it does not have or what is 'missing'; it does not construct a fantasy-world containing objects of desire apart and different from the real world. On the contrary, desire is first and foremost a productive force" (22). Attachments to subjectivity encourage us to territorialize our desire, but Deleuze and Guattari encourage us to seek out "'deterritorialized' flows of desire" (Seem 1983, xvii). To deterritorialize desire is to see it as a productive force that generates and is generated in fragmentary ways not based in subjectivity. For Deleuze and Guattari (1983), desire leads to questions of production and effects, not to questions of meaning or subjectivity (109).

For instance, I open Grindr not because I'm horny or "looking" but because I am killing time, or frustrated with my writing project in a coffee shop, or experiencing a lull in the conversation at a bar (although I do often open Grindr because I'm horny as well). My phone blurps, a sensory experience that raises my interest, and I look. A profile I have seen hundreds of time and generally thought nothing of has sent me a message, "Horny?" This may be a terse, intrusive message for some, but it can also be a desire-producing message, changing my sensory experiences of my environment, my stance toward this object-image, my affective experiences. Following is not a face pic—and even though I write in my profile that I prefer to see a face picture, I set aside that prefigured condition and focus instead on the torso, the fine V of his pelvic muscle leading down to a tuft of hair above his cock.[7] "Yeah," I reply. I was not horny, but I feel urges that weren't there a moment ago.

I've experienced countless conversations like this, with many men of various ages and body types. Life interrupted by a blurp and a new image, a sonic interruption that isn't necessarily felt by the ear only but by the full body as well. Tapping on the messages center leads to either a textual greeting or an image. And these can lead to flirtatious experiences that arouse new desires without even meeting, like when I've sat in my hotel and talked to a young twink about sharing his two hung daddies and their toys. And it can lead to meeting folks who just turn out to be fleeting friends, like a wonderful time I had over drinks in Oklahoma City with a public-school teacher. Or experiences that border on sexual encounters but don't lead anywhere, such as when I met a young man, dressed as a woman, at a (nearly empty) dance club, where we chatted and grinded against each other on the dance floor before I grew tired and headed home.

Many of these conversations go nowhere: guys come and go, fail to respond, fall asleep late at night, are only driving through town, or I get busy or fall asleep. Some result in hours of flirtation over a period of days and we never meet up. Others are quick conversations, and we meet at his place, or my place, or a hotel room. These are impersonal, intimate encounters that don't depend upon identification but are fostered through aesthetic and erotic rhetorical actions. And these are often men who, to come clean, I probably would not have talked to at a bar—because they are much older, or much younger, or because I would have judged them too quickly for some other reason. This sensuous experience is a desire-producing experience that creates intimacy with objects and with others—but not the traditional notion of intimacy understood as personal intimacy between full humans. Rather, this impersonal intimacy potentially allows for the alterity of others without having to domesticate them and identify with them.

Grindr is greatly disappointing to many, but I believe one of the reasons Grindr is so disappointing to so many users (including myself at times) is that users come to Grindr with expectations—I want a date,

I want to be fucked now, I want a soul mate—attached to preconceived desires attached to their subjectivity. If instead we cruise aimlessly, as Dean (2009) suggests, then Grindr can be a quite pleasurable experience of being open to alterity without domesticating others. Penney's (2014) complaints that Grindr is disappointing are perhaps related to his attachment to interpretation: he "reads" faces; profile pictures that are landscapes "are not at all 'readable' and do not communicate affect" (110); pictures of penises "can stand in for an identity" (111). Perhaps, instead, a cock pic is just a cock pic that, rather than representing someone, piques curiosity, produces desire, makes me want to get on my knees and get fucked. Penney looks for identification, wherein users "project their own desires" onto other profile images (111). I suggest instead that, when users cruise aimlessly on Grindr, new desires are created in potentially free-flowing ways, not attached to subjectivity or identification.

Again, I am not arguing for a wholesale move away from representation, identity, and identification in this chapter. It is well documented that users on Grindr and other mobile apps can be quite exclusionary based on race, ability, body size, age, gender performance, and HIV status. In what has become shorthanded as the "no fats, no femmes, no Asians" phenomenon, users—particularly normatively attractive white men—write in their profiles that they are not interested in "fat" or older men or "queens," specifically list races they are not attracted to, and look for "clean" others—equating HIV status and other infections with "dirty." And significantly, these users usually privatize their desire by claiming it is a "preference" rather than a territorialization of their desire through socialization. These instances are so well known that a popular blog called *Douchebags of Grindr* shares screenshots of profiles with such discriminatory statements, and many activists and scholars have written about the problem (see, for example, Abbas 2012; Callander, Holt, and Newman 2012; Faris and Sugie 2012; Miller 2015; Raj 2011; Riggs 2013).

But I attribute these instances not to Grindr's interface but to a sociopolitical climate that privatizes and territorializes desire, making it seem that desire is something attached to who you are rather than something constantly produced and productive of new relations and scenarios. Indeed, I think even if a guy on Grindr doesn't believe he's attracted to black men, for example, he might be open to such an encounter on Grindr, given the right moment—given he hasn't publicly announced in his profile that he's not interested in black men. Because profiles don't go away on Grindr (unless you block them)—unlike on Tinder or other apps where users reject profiles and might never see them again—profiles in the same area of a city can be visible to a user for months, ignored, until they message you at a moment you may actually be open to.

CONCLUSION: RHETORIC'S PERVERSE MOVEMENTS

By turning to desire, affect, and sensation, and by questioning our commitment to identity, identification, and subjectivity, I suggest rhetoric and writing scholars might better attend to the queer potentialities of rhetorical action. Exploring sexual desire and sexual activity in digital spaces affords us two important moves: first, it is another contribution to shifts in rhetorical studies away from epistemic-centric conceptions of rhetoric that have focused on representation, identity, and identification. Second, as interest in queer thinking in rhetoric and writing studies grows, turning toward the materiality of sex provides more radical thinking about how rhetorical action might provide possibilities for new relationalities and ways of being in the world.

Attending to sex provides an opportunity to further question the centrality of representation and identification to our understanding of rhetoric. Identification, of course, has been a central figure to rhetorical studies since Kenneth Burke's (1969) famous argument that identification precedes persuasion. One of the influential scholars who focuses on identification, Krista Ratcliffe (2005), expands on identification in her book *Rhetorical Listening: Identification, Gender, Whiteness*, in which she argues that perhaps rhetorical listening precedes conscious identification. Ratcliffe proposes rhetorical listening as "a trope for interpretive invention and more particularly as a code of cross-cultural conduct" (17). As an interpretive act, rhetorical listening involves the analysis of cultural logics, those unstated logics that inform others' assumptions and claims. Thus, rhetorical listening becomes just another hermeneutic: while Ratcliffe denies that listening is mere reading, it is an enterprise in *logos* that disappears sensorial and bodily engagement, becoming an epistemological activity that seeks to "*hear* things we cannot *see*" (25).

Should identification and hermeneutics be so central to our understanding of persuasion? Is identification necessary to *be moved*? I want to suggest identification is a liberal understanding of rhetoric that places primacy on epistemology, identity, and textuality. Perhaps such an understanding of rhetoric as based in identification depends on a belief that we need to see others as full persons. Thinking queerly about sex,

I propose, helps us explore the potential for how humans are ontologically objects. Here I align myself with Dean (2009), who argues, "There is something about sex that troubles identification, rendering a politics of identification malapropos when it comes to sexual matters" (22). Dean proposes that, instead, "It is possible to care about something without recognizing oneself (or an aspect of oneself) in it" (24–25). In other words, can we not be moved by things or objects that we *do not identify with?* Perhaps we should understand rhetorical action as impersonal. Dean calls for "an impersonal ethics in which one cares about others even when one *cannot* see anything of oneself in them" (25). By *impersonal*, Dean means that, instead of demanding we see others as full persons, we might fail to identify them as full persons and thus see them as something more. This "ethics of alterity" (25) and impersonal understanding of rhetoric suggests that perhaps persuasion is not necessarily preceded by identification but rather by the force of objects, desires, sensations, and affect. While the specifics of sociality and sexuality on Grindr I've discussed are perhaps limited to this particular site, I want to suggest that the sensuality of images and text does not have to be interpreted, is not necessarily epistemic, and can be understood rhetorically outside the frameworks of identity, identification, and subjectivity. This does not just have import for male homosexual sociality: I believe, following Robert Caserio (2006), that the implications for the antisociality of eros are not relevant to queers alone but instead allow for "undeclared straight-gay alliance, founded in agreement about the inaptitude of all eros for sociality" (820).

Queer rhetoric and writing studies can contribute to investigating how alliances, relationships, and collective life assemble in new and unpredictable ways through attending to desires, sensations, and affects. While this chapter has drawn on autoethnography as a method to explore digitally mediated desire and sexual practices, I do not intend to advocate for autoethnographic approaches specifically for studying digital rhetoric. That is, I am not suggesting scholars in the field cruise for sex on their mobile phones, participate in online user-generated pornography communities, or seek out some rough trade on Craigslist (though I'm cool with that too). Instead, through the interventions I am advocating in this chapter, I hope digital rhetoric and writing scholars attend more specifically to affects, desires, and sensual life by queering a variety of methods and methodologies in the field. I think the potentials here are numerous, but I'll suggest just a few. Rhetoric and writing scholars have been investigating how identities are constructed and represented online for decades now, but a queer turn might explore instead how relations are created through affective intensities and the circulation of desires online. Or other recent materialist methods might be queered. For example, actor-network theory has been useful in refusing to essentialize actors, tracing nonhuman actors in assemblages and exploring distributed agency, but it "tends to neutralize the intensity of events" (Sampson 2012, 43): what might a queer attention to desire do for an ANT study? In another instance, Gries's (2015) methodology of iconographic tracking seems quite amenable to queer alliances that seek to trace affect, sensations, and desire online. In digital ethnographies, we might attend more to bodies and the effects of digital rhetoric on bodies in potentially creating new ways of being and relating in the world (and see those bodies as rhetorically engaged in digital environments). Or, we might consider how rhetorical listening might be queered (and cripped) by attending to the whole bodiedness of sonic experiences (as Ceraso [2014] suggests we do). My goal here in this brief list has been to be suggestive—not comprehensive or prescriptive—of potential interventions made possible by a queer turn to desire, sex, and affect.

Turning to queer theory's antihumanist impulses, I suggest, is useful for queering rhetoric and writing scholarship and exploring rhetoric's material potential for new ways of being in the world. These queer potentialities were recognized in the early 1990s as rhetoric scholars began thinking queerly. In her introduction to the 1992 special issue of *Pre/Text* on queer rhetorics, Margaret Morrison (1992) calls for a queer rhetorics that places bodies, desire, and language in conjunction with each other. Morrison asks readers to consider how identities "territorialize or map their bodies in extraordinarily constraining ways" (15) but "finally fail to contain profuse desire" (17). Rather than looking toward the stability of identity, Morrison's queer thinking encourages us to look to movement: "This 'queer rhetoric,' therefore, suggests not inertness but perverse movement" (20). What, then, if we take the god terms of rhetoric and writing—*text, representation, identity, identification, interpretation, hermeneutics, meaning, epistemic*—and set them aside? What if instead we turn to *desire, affect, sensation, bodies, aesthetics, eros, objectifications, ontology*? Perhaps instead of a personal rhetoric, we conceive of rhetoric impersonally. Perhaps we would do well to attend to rhetoric's perverse movements.

NOTES

1.   This opening line is a nod to Leo Bersani (1987), who famously opened "Is the Rectum a Grave?" by writing, "There is a big secret about sex: most people don't

like it" (197). More recently, Tim Dean (2015) opened a review essay that scathingly critiqued queer theory for its aversion to sex: "There is an open secret about sex: most queer theorists don't like it" (614).

2.   See Robert McRuer's (2006) argument that composition studies is firmly attached to creating composed bodies who create composed texts (146–70).

3.   Jonathan Alexander and Jacqueline Rhodes's work is perhaps the best example of queer rhetoric and writing scholars who have challenged us to consider the relationships between bodies, sex, desire, and writing. They challenge rhetoric and writing studies to see queerness as incommensurable with college composition because of queerness's "excess" (Alexander and Rhodes 2011, 186) and suggest queerness resists representation and being known (Alexander and Rhodes 2012).

4.   Though I have aligned recent turns away from epistemic rhetoric with new materialism, I don't want to imply that focus on the asygnifying nature of rhetoric is altogether new. As Debra Hawhee (2015) shows, there is a long history of attending to senses in rhetorical studies, and John Muckelbauer (2007) suggests that what makes rhetoric distinctive from other fields is that "rhetoric seems inclined toward what we might call an 'asignifying' dimension of language, focusing on forces, actions, and effects" rather than solely on signification (239).

5.   Grindr began encouraging users to create accounts in 2013 so users could have the same account across devices (e.g., on their iPhone and iPad) and to prevent spam on the app. In summer 2016, Grindr released a new version of its app that now requires having an account. Grindr also has a premium version with a monthly fee that allows users to see more profiles.

6.   Grindr, following Apple App Store terms and conditions, does not allow profile photos of genitals or photos that reveal the outline of genitals through underwear or swimwear (see Grindr 2015b). Users are able to (and often do) send these photos through private messaging, but Grindr's policy was initially designed to get the app approved by Apple for inclusion in the App Store. To enforce this policy, Grindr profile photos must be approved before becoming public. In his analysis of these profile policies and related practices on Grindr, Scruff, and Manhunt, Yoel Roth (2015) observes that this approval is anything but transparent. I have had the same photo approved at one point in time and not approved at another. As Roth argues, these policies are not neutral, and Grindr is promoting a certain type of "inclusive" (in developer Joel Simkhai's words) politics often at odds with the desires of users (426). While circumventing or resisting the photo policy is difficult, users have turned to using emoji and coded language—such as emoji of up and down arrows to signify topping and bottoming, or terms like *sk8ing* to reference drug use—in the profile descriptions to circumvent Grindr's policies against drug references or describing sex too explicitly (Roth 2015).

7.   Readers might be curious: if I am arguing against the primacy of representation, identity, and epistemic approaches in rhetorical action, why would I be concerned about seeing a face picture on Grindr? After all, isn't a face a representation of identity? Am I not looking for someone who is *identifiable?* To a degree, I think these are valid questions. But providing a face picture is also a *trust* mechanism that, while not guaranteeing any sort of trustworthiness, exhibits a possibility of goodwill that this conversation will continue (see Baron 2009 on trust mechanisms we develop for new media). Further, a face isn't simply a representation of someone's identity. While it can be, it is also an aesthetic object, one that can produce desires and invite response. I have in mind here Diane Davis's (2010) *Inessential Solidarity*, in which she argues that rhetoricity is dependent upon "a fundamental structure of exposure" (3).

REFERENCES

Abbas, Ali. 2012. "Death by Masculinity." In *Why Are Faggots So Afraid of Faggots? Flaming Challenges to Masculinity, Objectification, and the Desire to Conform*, edited by Mattilda Bernstein Sycamore, 33–38. Oakland, CA: AK.

Alexander, Jonathan. 2008. *Literacy, Sexuality, Pedagogy: Theory and Practice for Composition Studies*. Logan: Utah State University Press. https://doi.org/10.2307/j.ctt4cgqkw.

Alexander, Jonathan, and Michelle Gibson. 2004. "Queer Composition(s): Queer Theory in the Writing Classroom." *JAC* 24 (1): 1–21.

Alexander, Jonathan, and Elizabeth Losh. 2010. "'A YouTube of One's Own?': 'Coming Out' Videos as Rhetorical Action." In *LGBT Identity and Online New Media*, edited by Christopher Pullen and Margaret Cooper, 37–50. New York: Routledge.

Alexander, Jonathan, and Jacqueline Rhodes. 2011. "Queer: An Impossible Subject for Composition." *JAC* 31 (1–2): 177–206.

Alexander, Jonathan, and Jacqueline Rhodes. 2012. "Queerness, Multimodality, and the Possibilities of Re/Orientation." In *Composing (Media) = Composing (Embodiment): Bodies, Technologies, Writing, the Teaching of Writing*, edited by Kristin L. Arola and Anne Frances Wysocki, 188–212. Logan: Utah State University Press. https://doi.org/10.2307/j.ctt4cgnxt.16.

Alexander, Jonathan, and David Wallace. 2009. "The Queer Turn in Composition Studies: Reviewing and Assessing an Emerging Scholarship." College Composition and Communication 61 (1): W300–W320. http://www.ncte.org/library/nctefiles/resources/journals/ccc/0611-sep09/ccc0611queer.pdf.

Almjeld, Jen. 2014. "A Rhetorician's Guide to Love: Online Dating Profiles as Remediated Commonplace Books." *Computers and Composition* 32:71–83. https://doi.org/10.1016/j.compcom.2014.04.004.

Anderson, Dana. 2007. *Identity's Strategy: Rhetorical Selves in Conversion*. Columbia: University of South Carolina Press.

Ashford, Chris. 2009. "Queer Theory, Cyber-Ethnographies and Researching Online Sex Environments." *Information & Communications Technology Law* 18 (3): 297–314. https://doi.org/10.1080/13600830903424734.

Baron, Dennis. 2009. *A Better Pencil: Readers, Writers, and the Digital Revolution*. Oxford: Oxford University Press.

Berlant, Lauren, and Michael Warner. 1998. "Sex in Public." *Critical Inquiry* 24 (2): 547–66. https://doi.org/10.1086/448884.

Bersani, Leo. 1987. "Is the Rectum a Grave?" *October* 43:197–222. https://doi.org/10.2307/3397574.

Bersani, Leo. 1995. *Homos*. Cambridge, MA: Harvard University Press.

Bersani, Leo. 2010. "Sociability and Cruising." In *Is the Rectum a Grave? and Other Essays*, 45–62. Chicago, IL: University of Chicago Press.

Bessette, Jean. 2016. "Queer Rhetoric in Situ." *Rhetoric Review* 35 (2): 148–64. https://doi.org/10.1080/07350198.2016.1142851.

Blackwell, Courtney, Jeremy Birnholtz, and Charles Abbott. 2015. "Seeing and Being Seen: Co-situation and Impression Formation Using Grindr, a Location-Aware Gay Dating App." *New Media & Society* 17 (7): 1117–36. https://doi.org/10.1177/1461444814521595.

Burke, Kenneth. 1969. *A Rhetoric of Motives*. Berkeley: University of California Press.

Callander, Denton, Martin Holt, and Christy E. Newman. 2012. "Just a Preference: Racialised Language in the Sex-Seeking Profiles of Gay and Bisexual Men." *Culture, Health & Sexuality* 14 (9): 1049–63. https://doi.org/10.1080/13691058.2012.714799.

Campbell, John Edward. 2004. *Getting It On Online: Cyberspace, Gay Male Sexuality, and Embodied Identity*. New York: Harrington Park.

Canagarajah, A. Suresh. 2012. "Autoethnography in the Study of Multilingual Writers." In *Writing Studies Research in Practice: Methods and Methodologies*, edited by Lee Nickoson and Mary P. Sheridan, 113–24. Carbondale: Southern Illinois University Press.

Caserio, Robert L. 2006. "The Antisocial Thesis in Queer Theory." *PMLA* 121 (3): 819–21. https://doi.org/10.1632/pmla.2006.121.3.819.

Ceraso, Steph. 2014. "(Re)Educating the Senses: Multimodal Listening, Bodily Learning, and the Composition of Sonic Experiences." *College English* 77 (2): 102–23.

Chiseri-Strater, Elizabeth. 2012. "'What Goes On Here?': The Uses of Ethnography in Composition Studies." In *Exploring Composition Studies: Sites, Issues, and Perspectives*, edited by Kelly Ritter and Paul Kei Matsuda, 199–210. Logan: Utah State University Press. https://doi.org/10.2307/j.ctt4cgjsj.15.

Cooper, Jan. 2004. "Queering the Contact Zone." *JAC* 24 (1): 23–45.

Corey, Frederick C., and Thomas K. Nakayama. 2012. "deathTEXT." *Western Journal of Communication* 76 (1): 17–23. https://doi.org/10.1080/10570314.2012.637542.

Davis, Diane. 2010. *Inessential Solidarity: Rhetoric and Foreigner Relations*. Pittsburgh, PA: University of Pittsburgh Press. https://doi.org/10.2307/j.ctt5vkfx1.

Dean, Tim. 2009. *Unlimited Intimacy: Reflections on the Subculture of Barebacking*. Chicago, IL: University of Chicago Press. https://doi.org/10.7208/chicago/9780226139401.001.0001.

Dean, Tim. 2015. "No Sex Please, We're American." *American Literary History* 27 (3): 614–24. https://doi.org/10.1093/alh/ajv030.

Delany, Samuel R. 1999. *Times Square Red, Times Square Blue*. New York: New York University Press.

Deleuze, Gilles, and Félix Guattari. 1983. *Anti-Oedipus: Capitalism and Schizophrenia*. Translated by Robert Hurley Mark Seem and Helen R. Lane. Minneapolis: University of Minnesota Press.

DeWitt, Scott Lloyd. 1997. "Out There on the Web: Pedagogy and Identity in Face of Opposition." *Computers and Composition* 14 (2): 229–43. https://doi.org/10.1016/S8755-4615(97)90024-4.

Dolmage, Jay. 2012. "Writing against Normal: Navigating a Corporeal Turn." In *Composing (Media) = Composing (Embodiment): Bodies, Technologies, Writing, the Teaching of Writing*, edited by Kristin L. Arola and Anne Frances Wysocki, 110–26. Logan: Utah State University Press. https://doi.org/10.2307/j.ctt4cgnxt.11.

Elliott, Mary. 1996. "Coming Out in the Classroom: A Return to the Hard Place." *College English* 58 (6): 693–708. https://doi.org/10.2307/378394.

Faris, Michael J., and M. L. Sugie. 2012. "Fucking with Fucking Online: Advocating for Indiscriminate Promiscuity." In *Why Are Faggots So Afraid of Faggots? Flaming Challenges to Masculinity, Objectification, and the Desire to Conform*, edited by Mattilda Bernstein Sycamore, 45–51. Oakland, CA: AK.

Foucault, Michel. 1990. *The History of Sexuality*, Volume 1: *An Introduction*. Translated by Robert Hurley. New York: Vintage.

Foucault, Michel. 1997. "Friendship as a Way of Life." Translated by John Johnson. In *Ethics: Subjectivity and Truth*. Edited by Paul Rabinow, 135–40. New York: The New Press.

Görkemli, Serkan. 2014. *Grassroots Literacies: Lesbian and Gay Activism and the Internet in Turkey*. Albany: SUNY Press.

Gries, Laurie. 2015. *Still Life with Rhetoric: A New Materialist Approach for Visual Rhetorics*. Logan: Utah State University Press.

Grindr. 2015a. "Grindr Fact Sheet." https://www.grindr.com/press/.

Grindr. 2015b. "Grindr Profile Guidelines." https://www.grindr.com/profile-guidelines/.

Gudelunas, David. 2012. "There's an App for That: The Uses and Gratifications of Online Social Networks for Gay Men." *Sexuality & Culture* 16 (4): 347–65. https://doi.org/10.1007/s12119-012-9127-4.

Harold, Christine L. 2000. "The Rhetorical Function of the Abject Body: Transgressive Corporeality in *Trainspotting*." *JAC* 20 (4): 865–87.

Hawhee, Debra. 2015. "Rhetoric's Sensorium." *Quarterly Journal of Speech* 101 (1): 2–17. https://doi.org/10.1080/00335630.2015.995925.

Hine, Christine. 2015. *Ethnography for the Internet: Embedded, Embodied and Everyday*. London: Bloomsbury.

Holland, Eugene W. 1999. *Deleuze and Guattari's* Anti-Oedipus*: Introduction to Schizoanalysis*. London: Routledge.

Humphreys, Laud. 1975. *Tearoom Trade: Impersonal Sex in Public Places*. Enlarged ed. Chicago, IL: Aldine.

Jagose, Annamarie. 2013. *Orgasmology*. Durham, NC: Duke University Press.

Lambevski, Sasho Alexander. 2004. "Movement and Desire: On the Need to Fluidify Academic Discourse on Sexuality." *GLQ: A Journal of Lesbian and Gay Studies* 10 (2): 304–8. https://doi.org/10.1215/10642684-10-2-304.

Lundberg, Christian O. 2015. "Revisiting the Future of Meaning." *Quarterly Journal of Speech* 101 (1): 173–85. https://doi.org/10.1080/00335630.2015.994907.

Lynch, Paul, and Nathaniel Rivers. 2015. "Introduction: Do You Believe in Rhetoric and Composition?" In *Thinking with Bruno Latour in Rhetoric and Composition*, edited by Paul Lynch and Nathaniel Rivers, 1–19. Carbondale: Southern Illinois University Press.

McRuer, Robert. 2006. *Crip Theory: Cultural Signs of Queerness and Disability*. New York: University of New York Press.

Miller, Brandon. 2015. "'Dude, Where's Your Face?' Self-Presentation, Self-Description, and Partner Preferences on a Social Networking Application for Men Who Have Sex with Men: A Content Analysis." *Sexuality & Culture* 19 (4): 637–58. https://doi.org/10.1007/s12119-015-9283-4.

Morrison, Margaret. 1992. "Laughing with Queers in My Eyes: Proposing 'Queer Rhetoric(s)' and Introducing a Queer Issue." *Pre/Text: A Journal of Rhetorical Theory* 13 (3–4): 11–36.

Muckelbauer, John. 2007. "Rhetoric, Asignfication, and the Other: A Response to Diane Davis." *Philosophy & Rhetoric* 40 (2): 238–47. https://doi.org/10.1353/par.2007.0023.

Ouellette, Marc. 2014. "Come Out Playing: Computer Games and the Discursive Practices of Gender, Sex, and Sexuality." In *Computer Games and Technical Communication: Critical Methods and Applications at the Intersection*, edited by Jennifer deWinter and Ryan M. Moeller, 35–51. Routledge Series in Technical Communication, Rhetoric, and Culture. Burlington, VT: Ashgate.

Panagia, Davide. 2009. *The Political Life of Sensation*. Durham, NC: Duke University Press.

Paasonen, Susanna, Ken Hillis, and Michael Petit. 2015. "Introduction: Networks of Transmission: Intensity, Sensation, Value." In *Networked Affect*, edited by Ken Hillis, Susanna Paasonen, and Michael Petit, 1–24. Cambridge, MA: MIT Press.

Patton, Cindy. 1992. "In Vogue: The 'Place' of 'Gay Theory.'" *Pre/Text: A Journal of Rhetorical Theory* 13 (3–4): 151–57.

Patton, Cindy. 1993. "Tremble, Hetero Swine!" In *Fear of a Queer Planet: Queer Politics and Social Theory*, edited by Michael Warner, 143–77. Minneapolis: University of Minnesota Press.

Penney, Tom. 2014. "Bodies under Glass: Gay Dating Apps and the Affect-Image." *Media International Australia, Incorporating Culture & Policy* 153 (1): 107–17. https://doi.org/10.1177/1329878X1415300113.

Pink, Sarah. 2015. *Doing Sensory Ethnography*. 2nd ed. Los Angeles, CA: SAGE.

Raj, Senthorun. 2011. "Grindring Bodies: Racial and Affective Economies of Online Queer Desire." *Critical Race and Whiteness Studies* 7 (2): 1–12. http://www.acrawsa.org.au/files/ejournalfiles/171V7.2_3.pdf.

Ratcliffe, Krista. 2005. *Rhetorical Listening: Identification, Gender, Whiteness*. Carbondale: Southern Illinois University Press.

Rice, Jeff. 2013. "Occupying the Digital Humanities." *College English* 75 (4): 360–78.

Rickert, Thomas. 2013. *Ambient Rhetoric: The Attunements of Rhetorical Being.* Pittsburgh, PA: University of Pittsburgh Press. https://doi.org/10.2307/j.ctt5hjqwx.

Riggs, Damien W. 2013. "Anti-Asian Sentiment amongst a Sample of White Australian Men on Gaydar." *Sex Roles* 68 (11–12): 768–78. https://doi.org/10.1007/s11199-012-0119-5.

Roth, Yoel. 2015. "'No Overly Suggestive Photos of Any Kind': Content Management and the Policing of Self in Gay Digital Communities." *Communication, Critique and Culture* 8 (3): 414–32. https://doi.org/10.1111/cccr.12096.

Sampson, Tony D. 2012. *Virality: Contagion Theory in the Age of Networks.* Minneapolis: University of Minnesota Press. https://doi.org/10.5749/minnesota/9780816670048.001 .0001.

Sedgwick, Eve Kosofsky. 2003. "Paranoid Reading and Reparative Reading, or, You're So Paranoid, You Probably Think This Essay Is about You." In *Touching Feeling: Affect, Pedagogy, Performativity*, 123–51. Durham, NC: Duke University Press.

Seem, Mark. 1983. Introduction to *Anti-Oedipus: Capitalism and Schizophrenia*, by Gilles Deleuze and Félix Guattari, xvii–xxvii. Minneapolis: University of Minnesota Press. https://doi.org/10.1520/STP29497S.

Selfe, Cynthia L., and Richard J. Selfe Jr. 1994. "The Politics of the Interface: Power and Its Exercise in Electronic Contact Zones." *College Composition and Communication* 45 (4): 480–504. https://doi.org/10.2307/358761.

Sheridan, Mary P. 2012. "Making Ethnography Our Own: Why and How Writing Studies Must Redefine Core Research Practices." In *Writing Studies Research in Practice: Methods and Methodologies*, edited by Lee Nickoson and Mary P. Sheridan, 73–85. Carbondale: Southern Illinois University Press.

Smith, Beatrice. 2007. "Researching Hybrid Literacies: Methodological Explorations of 'Ethnography' and the Practices of the *Cybertariat*." In *Digital Writing Research: Technologies, Methodologies, and Ethical Issues*, edited by Heidi A. McKee and Dànielle Nicole DeVoss, 127–49. Cresskill, NJ: Hampton.

Van De Wiele, Chad, and Stephanie Tom Tong. 2014. "Breaking Boundaries: The Uses and Gratifications of Grindr." In *Proceedings of the 2014 ACM International Joint Conference on Pervasive and Ubiquitous Computing*, 619–30. New York: Association for Computing Machinery. https://doi.org/10.1145/2632048.2636070.

Wallace, David L. 2011. *Compelled to Write: Alternative Rhetoric in Theory and Practice.* Logan: Utah State University Press. https://doi.org/10.2307/j.ctt4cgnrd.

West, Isaac. 2013. "Queer Generosities." *Western Journal of Communication* 77 (5): 538–41. https://doi.org/10.1080/10570314.2013.784351.

Woo, Jaime. 2014. "Grindr: Part of a Complete Breakfast." *QED: A Journal in GLBTQ Worldmaking* 2 (1): 61–72. https://doi.org/10.14321/qed.2.1.0061.

Woodland, Randal. 2000. "Queer Spaces, Modem Boys and Pagan Statues: Gay/Lesbian Identity and the Construction of Cyberspace." In *The Cybercultures Reader*, edited by David Bell and Barbara M. Kennedy, 416–31. London: Routledge.

9

QUEER/ING COMPOSITION, THE DIGITAL ARCHIVE OF LITERACY NARRATIVES, AND WAYS OF KNOWING

Deborah Kuzawa

The moment you say "queer" . . . you are necessarily calling into question exactly what you mean when you say it. Queer includes within it a necessarily expansive impulse that allows us to think about potential differences within that rubric.

> Phillip Brian Harper, E. Francis White,
> and Margaret Cerullo

In general, "queer" may be seen as partially deconstructing our own discourse and creating a greater openness in the way we think through our categories.

> Ken Plummer

Queerness at its core embraces ambiguity, excess, and instability, whereas methods represent logics that provide structure for inquiry. So when we discuss a *queer method*, we are discussing a contradiction in terms: unstable and ambiguous logics and ways of knowing. In this chapter, I examine one queer way of knowing and in the process follow queerness's "expansive impulse" (Harper, White, and Cerullo 1990) to better understand how queer method/ologies might help us understand phenomena and texts not exclusively by or about LGBTQ people. Teresa de Lauretis (1991) argues that queer theory—and I extend her definition to encompass queer method/ology—provides space for instructors, students, and researchers to examine "the conceptual and speculative work involved in discourse production, and . . . the necessary critical work of deconstructing our own discourses and their constructed silences" (de Lauretis 1991, iv). In other words, we can use a queer framework or method to develop a differently nuanced understanding of a topic, context, or issue the way we might use a feminist

DOI: 10.7330/9781607328186.c009

framework or method to understand a socially conservative political campaign: to provide a more complex and differently nuanced understanding and to deconstruct the silences and discourses surrounding the subject at hand whether gender related or not. So, how might queerness, as a framework of analysis, help us better understand sociocultural institutions such as archives[1] and the ways in which hierarchies of power and meaning might be inscribed, perpetuated, and normalized by these institutions?

I argue that queerness and queer values may be used heuristically for understanding dominant sociocultural spaces and relationships, regardless of sexuality, gender, or political orientation of the subjects or topics. This chapter has two major components: (1) defining my use of *queer* in order to establish a basis for a queer method/ology; and (2) exploring how a literacy-focused resource, the Digital Archive of Literacy Narratives, might be used in writing classrooms to demonstrate and practice queer methods and analyses. The Digital Archive of Literacy Narratives, established in 2007 and currently maintained by The Ohio State University and Georgia State University, is "a publicly available archive of personal literacy narratives in a variety of formats (text, video, audio) that together provide a historical record of the literacy practices and values of contributors, as those practices and values change" (Digital Archive of Literacy Narratives Blog n.d.). The DALN is one of the few publicly available repositories of stories focused on literacy practices and values (Selfe and DALN Consortium 2013), and I have chosen to examine the DALN because of its openness and malleability as a resource. I contend that using the DALN can be productive for writing classrooms because its subject is literacy (broadly interpreted), and literacy is the core of writing courses no matter how literacy or a writing course is defined. First, literacy is defined not by the DALN nor by its representatives but by the contributors to the DALN, which means there is a broad range of ways of understanding what literacy is, does, and looks like, many of which contradict or push against each other and against standard school- and expert-based definitions. Second, the DALN is self-archiving, which means narrators can submit to the DALN without permission or assistance from a gatekeeper. And finally, unlike most archival spaces, DALN narrators control copyright and determine what metadata to include (or not include) with their narratives. The openness of the DALN, including its structures, processes, and foci, provides a unique space for teachers, students, and researchers to explore not only literacy, adding their own experiences to the archive, but also the value of queerness and a queer method for understanding the world.

DEFINING QUEER METHOD/OLOGY

In his article "Queer Techne: Two Theses on Methodology and Queer Studies," Tom Boellstorff (2010) asks, "What does it mean to say a method is *queer?*" (Boellstorff 2010, 215). There is not a straightforward answer to this question, in part because queerness thrives on ambiguity, openness, and the spaces among different ideas, communities, concepts, identities, and processes. In particular, queer theory's initial focus involved critiquing the legitimacy of heteronormativity and the associated binaries of male/female, masculine/feminine, hetero/homo, as well as the ways in which queerness challenges, dismantles, disrupts, or opens up these hierarchical norms (Alexander 1999a; 1999b; Boellstorff 2010; Browne and Nash 2010; Rhodes and Alexander 2012; Rhodes 2004; Sedgwick 1990; Warner 1993; Wiegman 2015). However, queer theory and queer inquiry provide the basis for better understanding not only heteronormativity (*and* homonormativity) but the whole range of binaries that shape Western modes of thinking, acting, and engaging with the world. Susanna Luhmann (1998) claims, "Both queer theory and pedagogy argue that the process of making (sense) of selves relies on binaries such as homo-hetero, ignorance-knowledge, learner-teacher, reader-writer, and so on. Queer theory and pedagogy place at stake the desire to deconstruct binaries central to Western modes of meaning making, learning, teaching, and doing politics" (Luhmann 1998, 50–51). In other words, binaries shape the classroom (including literacy) and the world at large, and a queer method provides a way of interrogating those binaries. The focus on binaristic norms makes sense, as Boellstorff (2010) contends that "binarisms are ubiquitous in all languages; no human analytic can avoid them" (Boellstorff 2010, 222). Despite the ubiquity of binaries, according to both Robyn Wiegman (2015) and Boellstorff (2010), queer studies' emphasis on dismantling and disrupting sociocultural binaries erroneously assumes two things: (1) norms are stable, and (2) it is possible to disrupt or dismantle normative binaries and exist outside of them. The antinormative stance of queer studies falsely stabilizes norms—and queerness—ignoring the evolutions and complexities of sociocultural binaries; ultimately, "norms are more dynamic and more politically engaging than queer critique has usually allowed" (Cohen 1997; Morris 1998; Wiegman 2015, 2). However, following Boellstorff, I also argue that interrogation of sociocultural binaries and queerness can be fruitful for research and knowledge making, including research and knowledge making about literacy.

Boellstorff's (2010) concept of "surfing the binaries" offers one way to better envision and understand the relationship between binaries and queerness. Boellstorff writes,

> To surf is to move freely upon a wave that constrains choice (you cannot make it move in the opposite direction), but does not wholly determine one's destination. *A wave in a sense does not exist, for it is but a temporary disturbance in the ocean, yet waves are consequential:* they not only move surfers but can destroy buildings in tsunamis, or erode coastlines of the hardest rock. While any analogy is imperfect, what I mean to underscore with this notion of surfing binarisms is that a queer method could recognize the emic social efficacy and heuristic power of binarisms without thereby ontologizing them into ahistoric, omnipresent Prime Movers of the social. (Boellstorff 2010, 223; my emphasis)

Sociocultural binaries, similar to waves, "do not exist": they are socially constructed, based on a specific context, time, and space. But at the same time, these binaries are also consequential in that they shape our cultural psychology and impact how our culture identifies and defines individuals and groups (Butler 1990; 2004; Worthen and Dirks 2015). Surfing allows us to acknowledge and explore the binaries that shape our sociocultural worlds while at the same time acknowledging that all binaries are historically and culturally situated and fluctuating. This approach allows us to acknowledge what Cathy J. Cohen (1997) argues is the "radical potential of queer"—the possibility to develop "a more nuanced understanding of power" by embracing the complexities of identities and categories while exposing the ways a "dominant power [structure] . . . normalizes, legitimizes, and privileges" certain identities and categories over others (Cohen 1997, 458).

Moving between the nodes of a binary—that is, drawing attention to the constructed and false nature of binary structures by demonstrating possibilities beyond either/or—provides openings to push against or expand upon how we understand or conceptualize the nodes and the binary itself. Important to note, Boellstorff (2010) claims, "Characterizing this movement [between and across binary nodes] in terms of 'blurring' is . . . misleading, because it is through the perduring presence of the binarism that the 'movement' can have cultural consequences. . . . The realization that one must surf binarisms [has] pivotal *methodological* implications" (Boellstorff 2010, 228). I argue that surfing binaries is one hallmark of queer/ness (whether methodology, analysis, life), and this concept provides a way to not only better understand the binaries that shape different contexts or communities or subjects but also to also expand upon the associations or signifiers of those binaries. I argue this is the primary purpose and benefit of a queer method: exposing the dominant sociocultural binaries and discourses and providing openings to questions that reshape those binaries, discourses, and the broader culture in the process.

SURFING PRONOUNS: AN ILLUSTRATION

Now for an illustration of what surfing binaries can look like: personal pronouns. In mainstream (i.e., hetero- and cisdominant) communities, personal pronouns for individuals are gendered, based on assumed genetics and associated gendered behavior: *he, him,* or *his* is for male humans and *she, her,* or *hers* is for female humans. *It* or *its* is used for nonhuman individuals or objects, and *they, their,* or *theirs* is used for more than one human or object, though increasingly *they* is used as a gender-neutral, singular pronoun. However, dating back to at least the 1850s, there have been numerous attempts to introduce gender-neutral pronouns to English, primarily to be used when the gender of the referent is unknown (Baron n.d.). More recently, in some queer communities, the gender-neutral pronouns *ze, hir,* and *zirs* are an attempt to provide a gender-neutral option for those who do not identify as male or female or do not identify with the various behaviors and expectations associated with binary gender[2] (see Baron n.d.; Bornstein 1994, 1998; Harper 2012; Hartman 2000; Wilchins 1997). Unfortunately, these alternative pronouns are neither in wide use nor indeed even widely understood by the public outside some alternative or queer communities. A community may be able to create a new term outside the binaries, but the success of the term and idea relies upon others (i.e., the larger hetero/cisnormative sociocultural context) to recognize and use the terms. Surfing the *he/she* binary—alternating gendered pronouns in reference to an individual—is one potential response to the restrictive nature of the pronoun binary. However, in practical terms, others may simply favor one pronoun or the other consistently, negating any surfing that may be the intention of the individual using the terms and inadvertently misgendering that person.

Some universities have begun providing alternative pronouns on their applications, such as *e, ze,* and *they* ("More Universities" 2015), and more college instructors are beginning their courses by asking students not only their names but also their preferred pronouns, whether *he, she, ze, they,* or something else. However, when the Office for Diversity and Inclusion (ODI) at the University of Tennessee (UT) at Knoxville provided a guide to alternative pronouns, there was backlash, and the

ODI was ordered by the head of the UT system to take down the guide (Jaschik 2015). At the center of the concerns is the binary of *he/she*: few complaints about alternative pronoun guides are about singular *they* but instead focus on *ze/xe, zir/hir*, and the other more recently invented pronouns. Some of the loudest criticisms focus on two erroneous assumptions: that faculty, staff, and students would be "forced" to use language they do not approve of or recognize and that the recognition and use of the alternative pronouns means the elimination of *he* and *she*. Other critics focus more on the suitability of the alternatives and argue that pronouns such as *ze/xe* do not follow standard phonology and orthography for the English language and are too far removed from standard English pronouns to be useful.

The alternative pronouns attempt to sidestep the gender binary, and as a result the public's concern seems to be twofold: (1) the overall intelligibility of alternative pronouns, and (2) fear that traditional gendered pronouns (and perhaps traditionally gendered people) will be eliminated. This is where singular *they* comes in. *They* exists within already-established and powerful pronoun binaries, which means it is recognizable, but as a third-person-singular pronoun, it represents a nonstandard, modern use. I argue that singular *they* has been gaining ground and acceptance partially because *they* is already recognized and understood as a (plural) personal pronoun.[3] Further, the pronouns *ze* and *hir* attempt to move beyond the dominant binary of male/female and may blur or dismantle that binary. However, shifting the meaning of the pronoun *they* from meaning only plural to meaning plural or singular based on the context is an example of surfing binaries: it recognizes both the enduring value and the power of established binaries and simultaneously pushes against those binaries and uses them in unexpected ways.

Singular *they*, then, is an example of how we may exist within powerful, world-shaping binaristic norms and simultaneously surf among the various definitions, understandings, and uses of the norms. *They* does not dismantle pronoun binaries, but it does expand the ways in which we use and understand those binary concepts. As Jacqueline Rhodes (2004), in "*Homo Origo*: The Queertext Manifesto," argues, "To identify or come out as [queer] is to resist the connection between" signifier and signified (Rhodes 2004, 388). Key here is that resistance does not mean dismantling or blurring binaries but instead acknowledging the enduring value, social significance, and institutional entrenchment of the binaries and related knowledges and associations while simultaneously pushing against the established meanings and associations. Though

Audre Lorde is correct that "the master's tools will not dismantle the master's house," the master's tools can be used to renovate that house until it is no longer recognizable as the master's house (Lorde 2007). The case of singular *they*, I argue, is an example of using the master's tools for categorizing individuals and groups (i.e., gendered pronoun binaries) and reconfiguring and recasting them until the meanings and associations shift and expand. Juana Maria Rodriguez (2003) argues, "This breaking down of categories, questioning definitions and giving them new meaning, moving through spaces of understanding and dissention, working through the critical practice of refusing 'explication' is precisely what queer entails" (Rodriguez 2003, 24). I contend that singular *they* is an example of queerness-in-action not only because of the gender (and related sexual) ambiguity it produces but also because the modern journey of singular *they*'s usage rests on understanding, dissention, and movement across a range of binary nodes.

I argue queer methods in general, and surfing binaries in particular, provide a way to tackle some of the concerns of the modern university and composition studies, particularly the nature and power dynamics of knowledge production. In the following section I explore how we might surf binaries to better understand literacy, archives, research, and power in our writing classrooms by examining the Digital Archive of Literacy Narratives and its possible role in and impact on writing classrooms.

QUEER AND QUEERING: THE DIGITAL
ARCHIVE OF LITERACY NARRATIVES

Though I am interested in what queerness and queer methodology offer to a range of fields and subjects, I am most interested in how a queer method, such as surfing binaries, might be used to better understand the powerful (and often invisible) binaries that shape the writing classroom, including binaries associated with literacy, knowledge, and power. I suggest that writing instructors turn to the Digital Archive of Literacy Narratives, a repository of personal literacy narratives, to begin discussing the ways *queer* can be a useful heuristic for understanding objects and productions not explicitly or solely related to LGBTQ people and cultures. Eve Kosofsky Sedgwick (1990) claims, "'Queer' can refer to . . . the open mesh of possibilities, gaps, overlaps, dissonances and resonances, lapses and excesses of meaning. . . . [Queer occurs] when the constituent elements of anyone's gender, of anyone's sexuality aren't made (or *can't be* made) to signify monolithically" (Sedgwick 1990, 8). Sedgwick's definition of queer is applicable beyond an individual's gender or sexuality, and I argue that the DALN is queer partially because, taken as a whole, it demonstrates that literacy, research, and archives are not and cannot be made to "signify monolithically."

The DALN's implicit structures and values, including the ways the public interacts and contributes to the DALN, the values implied through those structures, and the DALN's mission, may be understood as queer because they move between dominant discourses and binaries that shape archives, literacy, and knowledge making, such as *academic/ personal, restriction/ openness,* and *expert/ novice.* Further, the DALN's structures and processes, metadata, and the narratives themselves may be *queering* or used to draw attention to and question dominant sociocultural binaries shaping not only literacy and education but also personal and cultural identities, institutions, and so forth. In other words, the DALN can be used to demonstrate queerness and to provide a queer lens for approaching a variety of contexts and institutions. The DALN's literacy narratives often expose the hidden work of literacy or the "work involved in discourse production" (de Lauretis 1991, iv) both related and unrelated to literacy, and working with personal narratives from the DALN may help instructors and students (and researchers) begin the process of deconstructing both society's and their "own discourses and their constructed silences" (de Lauretis 1991, iv) around literacy and its intersections with sociocultural identities and knowledges.

The DALN's queerness as an archives and academic resource begins from its very subject: literacy. Though the DALN does provide texts and resources discussing how one might define or understand literacy, the DALN does not require contributors or users to understand literacy in a specific way in order to contribute or use the archive. The DALN is maintained by experts, but each contributor, rather than the experts, defines literacy and literacy narratives for themselves. This openness marks the DALN as queer. For Jack Halberstam (2011), "*Open* . . . means questioning, open to unpredictable outcomes, not fixed on a telos, unsure, adaptable, shifting, flexible, and adjustable" (Halberstam 2011, 16). The structure of the DALN, with its lack of controlled vocabularies and bare-minimum requirements for narrative submission, encourages "unpredictable outcomes," from the interpretation of what literacy and literacy narratives are to the topics a contribution might cover (see Hearts 2010; Swither 2009) to how the narratives might be used by others, both experts and nonexperts alike.

The openness of the processes for collection and description of narratives and accessing the DALN's contents is unique; nearly all archives restrict who and what are preserved, based on perceived value, interest, and uniqueness, and almost no other archives allow individuals other than archivists (or other institutional stewards) to add materials to archives. However, the DALN allows anyone with an Internet connection (and knowledge of the DALN) to access and contribute to it, without any connection to or help from DALN representatives. All solicited information, from demographic information (such as gender, race, ethnicity, socioeconomic class, and so on) and keywords to copyright permissions, are open ended so narrators can choose how their narratives are labeled in the archives and how open or accessible (and useable) their stories are to the public.

Ideally, each narrative would include detailed demographics about the narrator and at least five keywords because the metadata is how users find different narratives related to their interests. However, the DALN does not provide a master list of terms or require that keywords are provided in order to submit to the DALN. This openness results in both excess and scarcity in meaning and terms.[4] Rather than specific check boxes or specific options for possible class or gender identifications, the DALN instead asks, "Do you want to self-identify with regard to your class background (ex.: working class, middle class, wealthy)?" and "Do you want to self-identify with regard to gender (for example: female, transgender male) and/or sexual orientation (for example: gay, bisexual, heterosexual)?" As of September 2012, there was a wide range of class identifications (including "artist class"), and there were thirty-nine distinct genders provided by DALN contributors, as well as many narrators who chose not to identify their gender at all (Ulman 2013). Of course there is no way to know how many, if any, alternative terms would have been provided if the gender question included check boxes for *male, female, trans,* and *other* (with a text box), but the diversity in gender responses (from "sure. Why not?" to "transgender, non op mtf") points to the affordances of providing an open-ended question. Gender, sexuality, and class develop from personal experiences, so leaving the questions open allows contributors to reflect on these concepts and determine (and provide or not provide) the language and concepts that have the most meaning for them.

Of course this openness means some narrators may choose to have virtually invisible narratives by not including any keywords or demographic information (including name), making the narrative difficult to find unless one knows the date it was submitted. At the 2010 TransOhio Symposium, a woman wanted to share her story, but she did not want any information tied to it except what was required (the date of submission). Her reasons for submitting and desiring no descriptions are unknown, and ultimately, her narrative is unknown to most who use the DALN because it is virtually impossible to find. Despite this, her narrative was accepted to the DALN because it meets the requirement of being personal and about literacy, and her self-determination overrules any archival or research impulses for description. Her narrative may be difficult to locate, but it is still possible for users to stumble across, and ultimately, we can assume the narrator submitted it in the way she did for her own reasons.[5] The broad goal of the DALN is to provide a record of literacy practices and values as they change over time, but at the same time, this overarching goal does not preclude additional purposes and foci for individual stories.

In the first six months of 2016 alone, 430 narratives were submitted, ranging from formal written narratives about early memories of reading (e.g., Mocilnikar 2016) and songs about literacy and finding the right language for the context (e.g., Anonymous Male 2016) to navigating literacy, deafness, and family (e.g., Anonymous and Villinski 2016). Each of these narrators interprets what a literacy narrative should be and what literacy is, and each plays with a variety of binaries that shape personal and social identities and knowledges. At the same time, each of these narrators works from relatively straightforward and conventional definitions or understandings of literacy, focused on reading, writing, and communicating with alphanumeric text (even if signed instead of spoken). Other DALN narratives touch on conventional reading and writing but also take a broader approach to understanding literacy. For example, Calvin Hairston's 2016 narrative about Poindexter Village on the Near East Side of Columbus, Ohio, centers on how one can read, interpret, and respond to changing neighborhoods, communities, and politics (Hairston 2016), and Erin Spencer Upchurch's 2016 narrative, "Helping Others Understand," discusses the literacy of personal identities, sexuality, and gender at the personal and community levels. Both Hairston and Upchurch interpret literacy more broadly than reading and writing alphanumeric text and instead think about different types of literacy within particular sociocultural, political, and community contexts.

Queer archives exist extralinearly, collapsing historical, geographical, ideological, and topical differences and distances, and in the process push against conventional archival structures and values, including time (cf. Eichhorn 2013; Halberstam 2011). The DALN in particular is a living resource that is relational and in flux; it is not the same archive each time one returns to it. Part of the difference stems from the continual and unpredictable growth of the DALN, but part of the difference lies in the queerness of the time and space of the archives. Just as no surfer can ride the exact same wave twice because waves are inherently ephemeral or "temporary disturbance[s]" in the ocean (Boellstorff 2010, 223), no researcher can surf the same exact thread themselves or surf the exact thread of another researcher. The constant shifts in the contents of the DALN and our own changing desires and affective investments we bring with us to the archives each time impact the waves we see and surf. As people engage with the DALN and bring their own experiences and purposes to the experience, as new definitions and experiences of literacy are added, as research projects about the DALN, and narratives from the DALN, are circulated publicly, the DALN becomes more and more complex and heterogeneous. This heterogeneity provides room for researchers, students, and instructors (and any others who turn to the DALN) to identify dominant binaries, themes, and narratives most relevant, interesting, and appropriate for the tasks at hand. The DALN's openness and queerness as an archives provide space to explore where thinking about literacy and other topics stops or diverges. Amy Winans (2006) argues, "A queer pedagogy draws attention to the parameters of questioning, thus highlighting the process of normalization as it draws attention to the places where thinking stops" (Winans 2006, 113). I argue that instructors could use the DALN and the method of surfing binaries to draw attention to the edges of our (i.e., society's, specific social groups') thinking and questioning about literacy broadly and about literacy narratives and the DALN in particular. The following section begins to explore the DALN as a classroom resource and the usefulness of using a queer framework for understanding and analyzing the DALN and its narratives.

INTO THE CLASSROOM

Exploring and analyzing the DALN, its narratives, and associated binaries using a queer method provides space within the classroom to re/produce and de/construct discourses and silences, particularly as they relate to the issues of literacy, expertise, and education. The relative openness of the writing classroom lends itself to queer methods and resources such as surfing binaries and the DALN. As Kelly Ritter and Paul K. Matsuda have argued, "Due to its inherently interdisciplinary nature, composition studies draws its students and prospective scholars from many areas inside and outside English studies," and these people bring with them a variety of ways of understanding and using composition and literacy (Ritter and Matsuda 2012, 1). As a field, composition is dynamic and open because it draws on different disciplines for its content and

methods and, in the twenty-first century, includes multimodal composi-
tions, which has meant a shift and openness in the pedagogy, research,
and expectations for composition (see Bloom, Daiker, and White 1997;
Reid 2009; Ritter and Matsuda 2012; Selfe and Hawisher 2004; Yancey
2004). Such openness is central to surfing binaries because the act of
surfing requires flexibility to embrace contradictions and ambiguities.
To talk about literacy in the composition classroom is to highlight the
tension—and ultimately surf—the binary of *literacy/illiteracy*, whether
explicitly or implicitly. Illiteracy is always in the background of literacy
narratives and literacy-focused classrooms, whether articulated or not,
and therefore the DALN is always already moving between binaries (cf.
Branch 2007; Cushman et al. 2001; Stuckey 1991). Surfing this binary
and the range of binaries that appear in literacy narratives is a way to
expand and complicate our understandings of both literacy knowledges
and practices.

In addition, in the DALN, the voices of the marginalized and the
underrepresented are placed side by side with dominant, hegemonic
voices, which calls attention to sociocultural binaries that characterize
many personal literacy narratives. Instructors may use the DALN and
these binaristic oppositions and tensions to highlight the overlaps and
gulfs among dominant and marginalized ways of thinking, knowing,
and existing in a literate world. As a result, students may be exposed
to ways of knowing and ways of being literate they have not previously
encountered or taken seriously. This process provides the space for
students to reflect on their own literacy experiences and expectations,
as well as the explicit and implicit messages and expectations about literacy and knowledge making they have encountered in their schooling,
families, and even popular culture.

One way to use DALN narratives in the classroom is to pair or group
DALN narratives and explore different dominant binaries and how
they shape experiences, uses, and beliefs about literacy. For example,
Abdi's (2009) narrative "My Mom's Struggle to Read" explores his
mother's journey from illiterate to literate as she learns to read the
Quran in Arabic for herself. The narrative highlights what I argue is
the most basic binary related to literacy—*literate/illiterate*—as well as
the binaries of *male/female, public/private, expert/novice (or self)*, and
restriction/openness. The central narrative focus moves from a place of
restriction (unable to read the Quran for herself) to *openness* (able to
read and interpret the Quran and other Arabic writings on her own)
but is disconnected from classroom and academic literacies.[6] Relatedly,
in "The CCCC Virtual Underground: Making Sense of My First Cs" by

Kathryn Trauth Taylor (2010), the voices and experiences of multiple first-time attendees of the Conference on College Composition and Communication are woven together. The people included in the narrative are all graduate students in English and related fields, and therefore, they are all invested to a certain degree in academic understandings and uses of literacies (even if they may critique the workings of those understandings and literacies). Unlike Abdi's narrative, *illiteracy* is not explicitly part of Taylor's narrative, but similar to Abdi's narrative, the binaries of *expert/novice* and *restriction/openness* are central. Side by side, these narratives show how a Somali woman learning to read Arabic and the Quran and graduate students learning to navigate a professional and academic space share similarities in relation to literacy: in their own particular contexts, they are defined by their status as novices who are restricted in their knowledge and (intellectual) movements and have moved or are moving toward expertise. When taken together, these two narratives provide different understandings and foci on what literacy narratives can be; what expertise is and how it relates to the self and nonexpertise or being a novice; and the role of restriction and openness in literacy-based experiences. When examined together in a classroom context, these narratives provide a richer understanding of how literacy and associated binaries might impact different types of people in different contexts. In a classroom context, this understanding provides an opportunity to discuss what a queer method such as surfing the binaries might offer us in terms of knowledge and understanding.

The idea of examining and comparing narratives from graduate students and a narrative about a recently literate Somali woman may seem a little unusual—or a little queer, as I contend—but the DALN's structure encourages this type of work. Narratives are placed side by side in the archive without any explicit hierarchy or external categorization of value, and this openness and freedom of movement and association are strengths of the DALN as a resource. Surfing binaries helps students, instructors, and researchers question "normative constructions of socially constructed binaries such as male/female, teacher/learner, leader/follower, research/practice . . . [and as such,] queer theory might contribute to addressing larger questions in higher education" (Renn 2010, 132). In other words, instructors may use queer methodologies to scaffold examinations of literacy, as well as a wide, almost unlimited range of issues and topics, by drawing attention to the overlaps, gaps, and artificial boundaries among topics, values, communities, and literacies.

Further, the openness of both the DALN and queer methods provides an opportunity for instructors to shift classroom power dynamics in two main ways: by having students determine what narratives, binaries, or topics are most relevant or important for their particular project or purposes and by having students contribute their own narratives to the DALN, demonstrating their expertise and adding new knowledge to the DALN. First, students can take charge of their educational experiences by spearheading a collection effort, focusing on communities important or unfamiliar to them. This process provides students with a variety of academic and leadership experiences including interviewing and oral history collection, project management, using digital media equipment and software, and more. Second and perhaps more important, students may compose and publish their own narratives and knowledges in the DALN. Providing a public space for students to contribute their experiences may help students shift from relatively passive (literate) consumers of knowledge to active producers of knowledge, with their contributions potentially becoming part of someone else's research into literacy or a particular topic. Students adding their own narratives to the DALN emphasizes they have expertise that might help others better understand (or understand differently) literacy and its impacts and influences.

Instructors may use the DALN in the classroom to demonstrate the ways queerness is not only about sexuality or gender but also about particular worldviews and values that refuse either/or approaches to life, whether they involve sexuality, gender, literacy, or education.

CONCLUDING TO BEGIN

I opened this chapter with a quotation from Phillip Brian Harper, E. Francis White, and Margaret Cerullo: "Queer includes within it a necessarily expansive impulse that allows us to think about potential differences within that rubric" (Harper, White, and Cerullo 1990, 30). I recognize others will understand and use queer methods in different ways, and some may feel strongly that queerness and queer methods should be used only to better understand LGBTQ subjects and artifacts and issues of sexuality. Because queer methods grow out of real, live queer communities with a range of values, desires, and goals, there can be an impulse to retain ownership of queerness and queer methods. However, restricting queer methods to obviously queer subjects is a disservice to queerness and to the broader culture that could use the insight queerness can provide. To limit queer methods to only LGBTQ subjects and artifacts is a narrow approach to analysis and a limited understanding of queerness and the value of queer worldviews. To return to an example used early in this chapter, most people would not argue to limit feminist methodologies to only feminist, woman-focused, or even gender-focused subjects and topics, so it seems unnecessary to limit queer methods to only queer subjects and topics. Both feminism and queerness provide unique perspectives on how meaning and knowledge are created, disseminated, and valued.

Writing instructors could use queerness and queer method/ologies to expose dominant sociocultural binaries and their roles in shaping larger worldviews and power dynamics in our broader culture, as well as within writing classrooms and related spaces. This means using resources easily recognized or identified as queer (such as QZAP—The Queer Zine Archive Project or the Lesbian Herstory Archives 2013) but, more important, also using resources not obviously queer or identified as queer (such as the Digital Archive of Literacy Narratives). The latter move—exploring resources not explicitly or solely about or by LGBTQ people or communities, as I do in this chapter—may more directly and easily provide the intellectual and cultural space to understand queerness as a set of values, worldview, and method for analysis and understanding rather than something forever owned by particular communities.

Though the DALN is not a perfect or unproblematic resource, I contend writing instructors can use the DALN and its content to demonstrate what queerness can look like when it is untethered from individuals and sexuality and to show the ways a queer method might provide useful for understanding a range of social and cultural phenomena. Further, instructors may use the DALN to show what queer method might have to offer not only areas like writing, research, and critical analysis but also how a queer framework may provide us with tactics for understanding and engaging in a sociocultural context marked more and more by stark binaries of *us/them*. William Pinar is correct: "*Queer* is not a neutral term" (Pinar 1998, 3; emphasis in original), and I argue that in our highly polarized historical moment, we cannot afford to be neutral. Critical engagement and critical thinking—the basis for higher education as a whole, really—are not about being neutral but about pushing to the edges of our knowledge and abilities. Queerness, in its open, complex, and contradictory glory, is one method for not only making sense of the classroom and the world but also for pushing our thinking and creating new ways of knowing and being in the world.

NOTES

1. According to the Society of American Archivists' glossary (Pearce-Moses 2005), *archives*, as a noun, functions as both singular and plural; *archive* (without the *s*) is the verb form (Pearce-Moses 2005).
2. Alternative spellings of *ze* include *xe, zie,* and *sie,* and sometimes *hirs* is used instead of *zirs.*
3. As many have pointed out, singular *they* has a historical basis: "You can find the singular *they* back into at least Middle English" (Curzan 2009) and in canonical literature (Curzan 2009; Nunberg 2016; Zimmer, *Wall Street Journal,* April 10, 2015). Further, 2015 seemed to signal a turning point for singular *they* within public discourse, particularly within journalism and academic spaces. For example, the stylistically conservative *Washington Post* determined in late 2015 that the time has come to use singular *they*. Bill Walsh, "the keeper, more or less, of Post's style manual," determined singular *they* is necessary and useful in a world where there's "increasing visibility of gender-neutral people" (*Washington Post,* December 4, 2015). So the *Post*'s decision is not simply based on situations in which gender may be ambiguous or unclear to the speaker or writer but in which individuals have indicated *they* is their preferred pronoun. Additionally, the American Dialect Society named singular *they* as the 2015 Word of the Year ("2015 Word of the Year" 2016), and numerous publications from NPR to the *Wall Street Journal* ran stories about singular *they* during late 2015 and into 2016.
4. The scarcity in terms also signals a degree of restriction. If there are no keywords or demographic information, a narrative is far more difficult to find. Further, though the DALN is marked by openness, there is a degree of restriction as well. If one is not technologically literate or does not have Internet access, the DALN is a restricted resource difficult or impossible to access.
5. K. J. Rawson (2012) argues that "archiving is not always a desirable venture because material traces can betray a person's carefully constructed identity" (246) and we must be aware that we do not "violate a person's right to self-identification" simply because it makes our research stronger or more interesting or helps us in some way (Rawson 2012, 247). In this case, the contributor wanted her story archived, but at the same time, it seems she did not necessarily want her contribution to be easily traceable back to her.
6. Though study of the Quran can be and is an academic pursuit, in this particular case, the purpose of Quranic study is personal and religious enrichment rather than academic analysis or understanding.

REFERENCES

Abdi. 2009. "My Mom's Struggle to Read." Digital Archive of Literacy Narratives. http://daln.osu.edu/handle/2374.DALN/783.

Alexander, Jonathan. 1999a. "Introduction to the Special Issue—Queer Values, Beyond Identity." In "Queer Values, Beyond Identity," special issue, *Journal of Gay, Lesbian, and Bisexual Identity* 4 (4): 287–92.

Alexander, Jonathan. 1999b. "Beyond Identity: Queer Values and Community," in "Queer Values, Beyond Identity," special issue, *Journal of Gay, Lesbian, and Bisexual Identity* 4 (4): 293–314. doi: 1083–8t47/99/1000–0293.

Anonymous and Tracy Villinski (American Sign Language interpreter). 2016. "Biliteracy and Visual Literacy." Digital Archive of Literacy Narratives. http://www.thedaln.org/#/detail/392607da-62c9–492f-adff-668232e40970.

Anonymous Male. 2016. "What Do They Mean?" Digital Archive of Literacy Narratives. http://www.thedaln.org/#/detail/c9a785b6-1250-4505-a345-1afcd7e526e7.

Baron, Dennis. n.d. "The Words that Failed: A Chronology of Early Nonbinary Pronouns." http://www.english.illinois.edu/-people-/faculty/debaron/essays/epicene.htm.

Boellstorff, Tom. 2010. "Queer Techne: Two Theses on Methodology and Queer Studies." In *Queer Methods and Methodologies: Intersecting Queer Theories and Social Science Research*, edited by Kath Browne and Catherine J. Nash, 215–30. Farnham: Ashgate.

Bornstein, Kate. 1994. *Gender Outlaw: On Men, Women, and the Rest of Us*. New York: Routledge.

Bornstein, Kate. 1998. *My Gender Workbook: How to Become a Real Man, a Real Woman, the Real You, or Something Else Entirely*. New York: Routledge.

Bloom, Lynn Z., Donald A. Daiker, and Edward M. White, eds. 1997. *Composition in the 21st Century: Crisis and Change*. Carbondale: Southern Illinois University Press.

Branch, Kirk. 2007. *"Eyes on the Ought to Be": What We Teach about When We Teach about Literacy*. Cresskill, NJ: Hampton.

Browne, Kath, and Catherine J. Nash. 2010. "Queer Methods and Methodologies, an Introduction." In *Queer Methods and Methodologies: Intersecting Queer Theories and Social Science Research*, edited by Kath Browne and Catherine J. Nash, 1–24. Farnham: Ashgate.

Butler, Judith. 1990. *Gender Trouble: Feminism and the Subversion of Identity*. New York: Routledge.

Cohen, Cathy J. 1997. "Punks, Bulldaggers, and Welfare Queens: The Radical Potential of Queer Politics?" *GLQ: Journal of Lesbian and Gay Studies* 3 (4): 437–65. https://doi.org/10.1215/10642684-3-4-437.

Curzan, Anne. 2009. "Spelling, Usage, and the Singular 'They': Behind the Dictionary." https://www.visualthesaurus.com/cm/dictionary/spelling-usage-and-the-singular-they/.

Cushman, Ellen, Eugene R. Kintgen, Barry M. Kroll, and Mike Rose, eds. 2001. *Literacy: A Critical Sourcebook*. Bedford, MA: St. Martin's.

de Lauretis, Teresa. 1991. "Queer Theory: Lesbian and Gay Sexualities." *Differences: A Journal of Feminist Cultural Studies* 3 (2): iii–xviii.

Digital Archive of Literacy Narratives Blog. n.d. "About." https://thedaln.wordpress.com/about/.

Eichhorn, Kate. 2013. *The Archival Turn in Feminism: Outrage in Order*. Philadelphia, PA: Temple University Press.

Halberstam, Jack. 2011. *The Queer Art of Failure*. Durham, NC: Duke University Press. https://doi.org/10.1215/9780822394358.

Harper, Martin. 2012. "Gender-Free Pronouns (edited entry A770960)." https://h2g2.com/edited_entry/A770960.

Harper, Phillip Brian, E. Francis White, and Margaret Cerullo. 1990. "Multi/Queer/Culture." *Radical America* 24 (4): 27–37.

Hartman, Jed. 2000. "MMM: MORF?" *Words and Stuff*. https://www.kith.org/logos/words/upper3/MMMs.html.

Hearts, Lindsay. 2010. "Lindsay Hearts' Literacy Narrative." Digital Archive of Literacy Narratives. http://www.thedaln.org/#/detail/157ff922-eb6b-425b-a3e4-10b6115abd21.

Jaschik, Scott. 2015. "Fear of New Pronouns." *Inside HigherEd*, September 8. https://www.insidehighered.com/news/2015/09/08/u-tennessee-withdraws-guide-pronouns-preferred-some-transgender-people.

Lesbian Herstory Archives. 2013. http://www.lesbianherstoryarchives.org/.

Lorde, Audre. 2007 (1984). "The Master's Tools Will Never Dismantle the Master's House." In *Sister Outsider: Essays and Speeches*, 110–14. Berkeley, CA: Crossing Press.

Luhmann, Susanna. 1998. "Queering/Querying Pedagogy? Or, Pedagogy Is a Pretty Queer Thing." In *Queer Theory in Education*, edited by William Pinar, 141–56. Mahway, NJ: Lawrence Erlbaum.

Mocilnikar, Earick. 2016. "The Life of Earick Mocilnikar." Digital Archive of Literacy Narratives. http://www.thedaln.org/#/detail/bcfa2fbd-84c2–41fe-a698–68986f66c2d2.

"More Universities Move to Include Gender-Neutral Pronouns." 2015. *All Things Considered.* NPR. November 8. https://www.npr.org/2015/11/08/455202525/more-universities -move-to-include-gender-neutral-pronouns.

Morris, Marla. 1998. "Unresting the Curriculum: Queer Projects, Queer Imaginings." In *Queer Theory in Education,* edited by William Pinar, 227–37. Mahwah, NJ: Lawrence Erlbaum.

Nunberg, Geoff. 2016. "Everyone Uses Singular 'They,' Whether They Realize It or Not." *Fresh Air.* NPR. January 13. https://www.npr.org/2016/01/13/462906419/everyone -uses-singular-they-whether-they-realize-it-or-not.

Pearce-Moses, Robert. 2005. "A Glossary of Archival and Records Terminology." https:// www2.archivists.org/glossary.

Pinar, William. 1998. "Introduction." In *Queer Theory in Education,* edited by WIlliam Pinar, 8–36. Mahwah, NJ: L. Erlbaum Associates.

Plummer, Ken. 2005. "Critical Humanism and Queer Theory." In *The SAGE Handbook of Qualitative Research,* 3rd ed., ed. Nornam Denzin and Yvonna Lincoln. Thousand Oaks: Sage Publications.

QZAP—Queer Zine Archive Project. n.d. https://www.qzap.org/v8/.

Rawson, K. J. 2012. "Archive This! Queering the Archive." In *Practicing Research in Writing Studies,* edited by Katrina Powell and Pamela Takayoshi, 237–50. New York: Hampton.

Reid, Alex. 2009. "Imagining the Online Composition Platform." *Digital Digs,* November 4, 2009. https://alex-reid.net/2009/11/imagining-the-online-composition-platform .html.

Renn, Kristen A. 2010. "LGBT and Queer Research in Higher Education: The State and Status of the Field." *Educational Researcher* 39 (2): 132–41. https://doi.org/10.3102 /0013189X10362579.

Rhodes, Jacqueline. 2004. "*Homo Origo*: A Queertext Manifesto." *Computers and Composition* 21 (3): 385–88. https://doi.org/10.1016/j.compcom.2004.05.001.

Rhodes, Jacqueline, and Jonathan Alexander. 2012. "Queered." *Technoculture* 12. https:// tcjournal.org/vol2/queered.

Ritter, Kelly, and Paul K. Matsuda, eds. 2012. *Exploring Composition Studies: Sites, Issues, and Perspectives.* Logan: Utah State University Press. https://doi.org/10.2307/j.ctt4cgjsj.

Rodriguez, Juana Maria. 2003. *Queer Latinidad: Identity Practices, Discursive Politics.* New York: New York University Press.

Sedgwick, Eve Kosofsky. 1990. *Epistemology of the Closet.* Berkeley: University of California Press.

Selfe, Cynthia L., and DALN Consortium. 2013. "Narrative Theory and Stories that Speak to Us." In *Stories That Speak to Us: Exhibits from the Digital Archive of Literacy Narratives,* edited by H. Lewis Ulman, Scott Lloyd DeWitt, and Cynthia L. Selfe. Logan, UT: Computers and Composition Digital Press. http://ccdigitalpress.org/book/stories /daln1.html.

Selfe, Cynthia L., and Gail E. Hawisher. 2004. *Literate Lives in the Information Age: Narratives of Literacy from the United States.* Mahwah, NJ: Lawrence Erlbaum.

Stuckey, J. Elspeth. 1991. *The Violence of Literacy.* Portsmouth, NH: Boynton/Cook.

Swither, Eli. 2009. "Teaching Genderqueer and Linguistic Determinism." Digital Archive of Literacy Narratives. http://www.thedaln.org/.

Taylor, Kathryn T. 2010. "The CCCC Virtual Underground: Making Sense of My First Cs." Digital Archive of Literacy Narratives. http://www.thedaln.org/.

"2015 Word of the Year is Singular 'They.'" 2016. American Dialect Society. http://www .americandialect.org/2015-word-of-the-year-is-singular-they.

Ulman, H. Louis. 2013. "Reading the DALN Database: Narrative, Metadata, and Interpreta- tion." In *Stories That Speak to Us: Exhibits from the Digital Archive of Literacy Narratives,* edited by H. Lewis Ulman, Scott Llyod DeWitt, and Cynthia L. Selfe. Logan, UT: Computers and Composition Digital Press. http://ccdigitalpress.org/book/stories/ulman.html.

Warner, Michael. 1993. Introduction to *Fear of a Queer Planet: Queer Politics and Social Theory*, edited by Michael Warner, vii–xxxi. Minneapolis: University of Minnesota Press.

Wiegman, Robyn. 2015. "Eve's Triangles, or Queer Studies Beside Itself." *Differences: A Journal of Feminist Cultural Studies* 26 (1): 48–73. https://doi.org/10.1215/10407391-2880600.

Wilchins, Rikki. 1997. *Read My Lips: Sexual Subversion and the End of Gender*. Ithaca, NY: Firebrand Books.

Winans, Amy. 2006. "Queering Pedagogy in the English Classroom: Engaging with the Places Where Thinking Stops." *Pedagogy* 6 (1): 103–22. https://doi.org/10.1215/1531 4200-6-1-103.

Worthen, Meredith, and Danielle Dirks. 2015. "Gender and Deviance." In *The Handbook of Deviance*, edited by Erich Goode, 277–97. Wiley Handbooks on Criminology and Criminal Justice. Hoboken, NJ: Wiley Blackwell. https://doi.org/10.1002/978111870 1386.ch16.

Yancey, Kathleen Blake. 2004. "Made Not Only in Words: Composition in a New Key." *College Composition and Communication* 56 (2): 297–328. https://doi.org/10.2307/4140 651.

10

ASSESSMENT KILLJOYS
Queering the Return for a Writing Studies World-Making Methodology

Nicole I. Caswell and Stephanie West-Puckett

Historically, assessment has functioned as a meritocratic technology that mediates people's access to institutional and social resources and power (Elliot 2005). Meant to facilitate the socially conservative practice of gatekeeping, assessment technologies have sorted, ranked, and ordered bodies, rewarding those who fall in line with dominant ways of knowing, doing, and being while punishing those who don't. As such, assessment technologies have allowed certain kinds of people into the academy and kept others out, creating a hegemonic assemblage of bodies who politely ignore the absence of difference. Coalescing around "happiness," our assessments continue to reproduce normativity through collective investments in objects of schooling such as achievement, success, and standardization.

If someone dares resist these normative objects, questioning investments in both ideologies and the assessment instruments that materialize those ideologies, the individual, not the system, is fingered as the problem. Individuals who dare to doubt the gold standard of the writing portfolio or who problematize what we mean when we say "good writing"—these individuals become assessment killjoys. They create problems for the smooth and frictionless use of assessment instruments and procedures designed to tell us what we already know or to construct single stories about students and their writing. According to queer theorist Sara Ahmed (2010b), "The feminist killjoy 'spoils' the happiness of others; she is a spoilsport because she refuses to convene, to assemble, or to meet up over happiness" (65). For Ahmed, and other queer scholars (Edelman 2004; Palmeri 2015), happiness, like assessment, is a well-trodden path that requires investment in particular heteronormative projects that reproduce the status quo. When bodies fail to invest appropriately, they are marked as willful (Ahmed 2014), attributed with

DOI: 10.7330/9781607328186.c010

creating the conditions they called attention to. The marking of a "kill-joy," then, has historically been a rhetorical move meant to exert pressure on willful bodies in order to bring them back in line.

In this chapter, we argue that those who are committed to assessment as a practice of social justice should embrace the politics and praxis of the feminist killjoy. We offer the practice of queer validity inquiry as a method of ongoing resistance to the normative and normalizing practices of assessment. Building on histories of validity and critical validity that call for ongoing interrogation into the effects of assessment instruments and decisions made from the use of those instruments, queer validity inquiry (QVI) intentionally refuses linear notions of progress and success. Our proposed failure-oriented practices of QVI provide a reorientation toward analyzing previously collected assessment data. As such, QVI revels in the queer pleasures of failure (Halberstam 2011) as it reorients us to other objects, other ways of knowing, doing, and being possible in writing assessment.

WHEN THE ASSESSMENT KILLJOY SPOKE (TO) US

Sara Ahmed's work, particularly *Queer Phenomenology* (2006) and *The Promise of Happiness* (Ahmed 2010b), provides writing studies a queer lens for understanding identity as a product of orientation. To orient, Ahmed reminds us, is to turn toward or away from another body or object in the world; thus, identity orientations are perpetual "happenings" as we are turned around, propelled forward and backward, knocked off course, slowed down or sped up from our embodied engagements with objects, both human and nonhuman. Similarly, in "Feminist Killjoys," Ahmed (2010a) names a particular mode of identity creation that comes from refusal and resistance, arguing that the killjoy emerges as an orientation that creates drag for others, complicating their collective movement toward heteronormative investments like happiness, success, and achievement. For Ahmed, then, identity is not a static experience of self but a moving and malleable assemblage of feeling and investment; it is a layering of accumulated performances that we take on and that are put upon us when our bodies and activities complicate the happiness of others. When we call out and put our bodies in the way of practices that are colonialist, racist, sexist, ableist, homophobic, and so forth, we become the killjoy, the agent who blocks the unquestioned happiness of others.

To briefly trace our own investments, we think it's important to respond to Ahmed's (2010a) question, "When did [X] become a word that spoke not just to you, but spoke of your existence or even spoke you into existence?" For us, that X is *assessment killjoy*, a term that fails to signify monolithically but instead invokes for us a constellation of orientations as writing studies teacher-scholars, writing program administrators, social justice advocates, assessment scholar-practitioners, and feminist/queer theorists. Thus, we trace out a couple of moments here that oriented us *queerly* toward other ways of thinking about and doing assessment as we refused to go along with and invest in particular assessment objects and the ideologies that underpin their use.

1. Refusing a Single Story of Success

For several years, our University Writing Center embodied the typical success narrative told through usage statistics. Over the course of three years, we increased student usage of our services by 265 percent. We were thrilled by such growth, but we also recognized this aggregate percentage offered a limited view of success: we still wanted to know more about the students who comprised those usage statistics. Our registration form provided us the typical demographics of our students: class level, gender, race, ethnicity, and major. As we continued to bring diversity concerns to our staff meetings, the consultants pointed out that we had no clue about how sexuality played into writing and the writing center. After meeting with our LGBT Resource Office and a student affairs educator, who also focused on assessment, we realized one way to be committed to social justice on our campus was to add a question about sexuality to our registration form and move beyond the male/female binary on the gender question. We conducted focus groups with LGBTQ students (Caswell and Banks 2018) to negotiate the wording, and our LGBTQ students, like our consultants, were excited to see this addition to our intake form. Unfortunately, our campus diversity office and the university attorneys were less excited to see the addition, and, through a host of phone calls and meetings, worked aggressively to have us remove all demographic information from our form, arguing that none of it pertained to the services the writing center provides.

The writing program and writing center directors pushed back. They argued that demographic information is pertinent to our larger assessment design in knowing who we are serving and how well we are meeting their needs. When one university attorney suggested other departments and programs meet their students' needs without asking about sexuality, the directors asked, "How do you know that?" They pointed out that just because no other campus office collects information regarding sexuality as part of its assessments does *not* mean LGBTQ students do not have any concerns; nor does it suggest this population has had space to be critical of their experiences. In fact, we believe the lack of information makes our desire to collect the data even stronger because we truly do not know whether our writing center services are meeting their needs. Do LGBTQ students feel welcomed in the writing center? The university was comfortable with a Don't Ask, Don't Tell model of assessment. Eventually, because the program and center directors are respected and valued administrators on campus, a senior administrator stepped in to support them by suggesting they seek IRB approval and consider this collection of data research rather than assessment (a vexed distinction at best, but one that seemed to assuage the concerns of the powers that be and provide some degree of protection for the data collection). In the context of our university, the writing center's desire to collect non-normative assessment data marked the space and its directors as assessment killjoys. It didn't matter that they were going to report the data in aggregate (as the writing center had always done). It didn't matter that they were going to ask critical questions about the work they were doing to see if they could do it better. What did matter was that they wanted to queer programmatic assessment at our university by both privileging queer students and disrupting the assessment categories our university promoted.

2. Failing the Test

In 2014, the state university system elected to partner with a well-known educorp to design and implement a "critical-thinking" test for our university's upper-level students (UNC Board). Administered as a writing test with constructed responses, this assessment would provide a third-party certification of knowledge, giving students who passed a "value-added" diploma. Assessment officials at the university called for no discussion of this new legislative mandate but instead, in order to meet our state-mandated university quota, asked teaching faculty to give their students extra credit for participating in the pilot tests. With serious concerns about how this assessment might (a) pervert our university's construct of postsecondary writing, (b) undermine faculty expertise and institutional autonomy, (c) disproportionately affect students from nondominant demographic groups, and (d) measure our sixteen diverse campuses against one another to provide data that supports an argument for closing our minority-serving institutions, Nikki and Stephanie created a backchannel with other interested colleagues to learn more and share information about the critical-thinking test, creating a small resistance movement that would disrupt the company's attempt to develop baseline and bell-curve scores. Stephanie also shared this information with her students in foundations-level writing courses (FYC), engaging them in critical discussions about the impacts of their participation in the pilot tests and supporting their efforts to voice their concerns to university officials. Because neither Nikki (pretenure faculty) nor Stephanie (non-tenure-track faculty) was in a protected university position, they worked mostly behind the scenes, in the shadows, to disrupt the success of the pilot assessment and, through failure-oriented practices, to create a public concern for the ways this standardized assessment might do real harm to our students, our university, and our state's public university system.

While we can name other moments when the label *assessment killjoy* spoke to us—such as when Stephanie continued to press questions in contingent faculty meetings about the conflation of programmatic assessments and classroom assessment data for a new writing-across-the-disciplines course, rejecting expediency as the value to which assessments should ascribe; and when Nikki refused to participate in the department's negative culture of assessment by working with and through the university's Institutional Planning Assessment and Research office to question and change processes that created undue burdens for faculty—the moments outlined above demonstrate how our experiences have led us to reject normative practices of assessment and pursue disruptive practices and lateral lines of inquiry that can make assessment a vehicle for social justice work in the academy and beyond. What we and others interested in this work need, however, is a framework, grounded in the intersections of queer rhetorics and assessment discourse, to guide that practice. The rest of this chapter provides such a method for intervening in hegemonic assessment practices, working to queer notions of validity through failure-oriented practices.

QUEER VALIDITY INQUIRY

Validation is a normative practice in writing assessment scholarship that we must queer if we are to pursue the work of social justice through assessment. Early definitions of validity allowed us to claim validity if a test measured what it purported to measure. Thus, validity resided in the instrument/test and its ability to correlate to a criterion score (a measurable trait). A criterion score reflected other measures of the construct; so, as long as a test correlated to another test that was measuring the same construct, the test could be considered valid. Current approaches to validity and validation, however, have moved from correlation to argumentation (Kane 2006, 2013). As a normative practice, *validation* is "a process of constructing and evaluating arguments for and against the intended interpretation of test scores and their relevance to the proposed use" whereas *validity* "refers to the degree to which evidence and theory support the interpretations of test scores for proposed uses of tests" (AERA et al. 2014, 11). While this definition of validity emerged from educational measurement, those in writing studies (Huot 2002; Kelly-Riley and Elliot 2014; Perry 2012; White, Elliot, and Peckham 2015) have also taken up the validity inquiry call. For writing studies scholars, validity fits within our wheelhouse as an argument-making (i.e., rhetorical) activity. Validity also aligns with our teaching pedagogy since validity is an ongoing practice, a reflective practice that assesses the assessment. For us, validity represents the argument that teachers and writing program administrators make for an integrated judgment based on relevant theoretical, empirical, and consequential concerns for *how* they are going to use the assessment data. The emphasis shifts validity from the instrument (test, assignment, portfolio) to how teachers and administrators *use* assessment data to make decisions about students. As such, validity can function as a reflexive method that provides a space for social justice work in assessment.

Validity, as a reflexive method, means assessors need to know how they plan to use the scores and then argue for the relevance and appropriateness of that plan. While validity does not have a clear-cut process, it does follow a logical, single loop in which assessors can, and often do, create arguments that suit their agendas. Validity arguments, however, should be able to withstand critical inquiry from others and should help us understand the ways our assessments impact students. Jeff Perry's (2012) work on critical validity inquiry (CVI) provides writing scholars one method for critically examining educational assessment. CVI is designed to uncover power relationships operating in and through assessment technologies by redirecting our focus to the systems (institutional, corporate, political, etc.) in which these technologies operate. CVI is a reflexive validation methodology that redirects our attention to nonnormative areas typically ignored when we focus only on one kind of learner. Thus, one of CVI's main goals is to examine how assessments affect specific groups or individuals traditionally underrepresented in education, pushing us to see "assessment abuse in non-traditional sites of educational demographics that may not emerge in a focused inquiry" (Perry 2012, 199). CVI calls us to move off the path traditional validity inquiry calls for by also looking at social, environmental, and cultural factors. Finally, CVI also calls on us to loop what we learn from our validation studies back into the political and legal arena of educational assessment to change the political climate surrounding educational assessment and help us reconsider the construct of writing.

Drawing from critical discourse analysis, CVI helps uncover the invisible, social, and power structures governing our methods and actions that might direct us to consequences we otherwise would not find. However, we maintain that it falls short in truly disrupting power structures. While we can see CVI working from queer and feminist lenses by focusing primarily on how power operates, we recognize CVI ultimately as an extension of the formative tradition. We propose queer validity inquiry (QVI) to not only identify how power operates (CVI) but also to uncover invisible (ideological) structures and to interrupt the lines we assume provide us the space to operate from the inside (know and work within the discourse). By moving toward QVI, we operate both from within the structure and from a critical stance that allows us to bring new understandings and voices to our work in meaningful ways. QVI moves us toward the messy, scattered, lateral, half-drawn lines that can redirect our attention to inequalities we have yet to name; Nicole Caswell and William P. Banks offer one example of what QVI might uncover by using a set of focus-group conversations with gay male students to discover the impacts local, programmatic, and large-scale writing assessments have on the writing and composing experiences of these students (Caswell and Banks 2018).

What does queer validity inquiry offer writing studies? One, a queer validity argument privileges the voices of those not typically engaged in assessment data: students and teachers. By disrupting notions of expertise and flattening institutional hierarchies, QVI makes way for student voices. Second, by looking back at and involving those most impacted by assessment results, QVI aims to reexamine and rewrite what counts as success in assessment conversations. Third, QVI disrupts the linear, reproductive traditions of writing and assessment; it acts back to queer the construct; it refuses to reify a cognitivist notion of writing that is easy and expedient to assess. Fourth, QVI embraces and enacts a methodology of failure-oriented practices and provides us with a means for reading our assessment instruments, practices, and ideologies *diffractively*. According to Donna Haraway (1997), diffractive readings, unlike reflexive or reflective readings, work to map differences and are interested in the ways objects interact with other objects, paying attention to their collective emergence through relationships born of resistance, refusal, submissiveness, and compliance. Instead of reproducing sameness in a closed loop of interpretation, what Haraway calls "the same reflected—displaced—elsewhere" (268), diffractive interpretations can create multiple trajectories and possibilities for knowledge making through what Ahmed (2006) argues are "object horizons"—lines of queer validity inquiry that can "'point' toward different worlds" (176). As such, we envision QVI as a critical world-making project, one that can serve to reshape traditional notions of writing assessment through an investment in and commitment to social justice.

FAILURE-ORIENTED PRACTICES OF QVI

So much of validity inquiry has historically been about justifying the end use of an instrument through select data points assembled on a trajectory of success or about how data can be used to justify decisions about students (such as placement or graduation requirements). These trajectories reassure us that we are, in fact, orienting in the "right" direction (forward), but for us, the "right" direction does little to move the field beyond restrictive notions of what counts as "good writing." Our interest in QVI, then, reflects a disinvestment in success and a willingness to follow the "wrong" paths of validity inquiry, those that promise to disrupt the demure scholarship of writing assessment. Thus, we turn to the queer rhetoric of failure as a means of reorienting theories and practices of writing assessment. In *The Queer Art of Failure,* Jack Halberstam (2011) writes, "Failure is something queers do and have always done exceptionally well. . . . In fact, if success requires so much effort [and is always already on someone else's terms, we might add], then maybe failure is easier in the long run and offers differing rewards" (3). Thus, we dare to ask, what do we have to let go of in order to grasp those "differing rewards"? How might QVI invite failure? What might failure look like in writing assessment?

To embrace the queer logics of failure, as we've argued, we can fail to promote some people's happiness (which was earned at the expense of others) by asking hard questions to determine how assessment instruments are impacting the teaching and learning context. Following Ahmed, as well as Erin J. Rand (2006), we can acknowledge that our own queer agency as assessment killjoys arises out of the gaps between the known and unknown, between what's intended by an assessment instrument and what happens when that instrument is put to use in a specific context. Rand writes, "Queerness [of agency is] . . . the lack of a necessary or predictable relation between an intending agent and the effects of an action; queerness is how agency emerges" (Rand 2006, 80).

Thus, an assessment killjoy develops agency by dwelling in those gaps, using queer, intersectional approaches to determine how and to what extent assessment practices are best serving stakeholders in a particular context.

1. Failing to Be Successful

This orientation, then, requires that we refuse myths of success, particularly those that claim we have a "gold standard" for writing assessment (White, Elliot, Peckham 2015, 104). So while our widespread use of writing portfolios may well be an improvement over on-demand writing samples, few institutions invest the time and resources to investigate the local impacts of that normative practice despite research and scholarship that suggests portfolios may not be a panacea for our assessment ills. For example, both Tony Scott (2005) and Bill Condon (2012) have critiqued the implementation of portfolio systems, illustrating how instantiations of practice can create normative subject positions as well as promote standardized and mechanized approaches to writing. In addition to gathering observational data and textual portfolio samples, Scott interviewed eleven twelfth-grade students, three teachers, and two administrators participating in the Kentucky statewide portfolio assessment to understand how large-scale assessments influence pedagogy. Though an analysis of fifty-six students' reflective cover letters, Scott revealed how students adopted a generic reflective stance geared toward earning a high portfolio score rather than an individual, self-assessment stance. For students, the reflective letter became a bureaucratic exercise for which they took their instruction from holistic rubric and state-generated models and not an authentic moment for reflecting on their learning. Scott's investigation of the statements made in students' reflective portfolio cover letters uncovered how students can be coerced into adopting false subject positions that reproduce the values of the institution as opposed to putting those values in dialogue with their own aims, purposes, and goals. Similarly, Condon urges the field to avoid making the portfolio assessment into another "test [not] worth taking" (Callahan 1997, 295) by pursuing options for students and teachers to individualize portfolio structures and artifacts and by investigating the use of open portfolios so students' work can be accessible to them and others beyond the course of a semester of their enrollment at a particular institution. As these critiques illustrate, assessment objects act back on us—students, teachers, program administrators, institutions—shaping what is and what is not possible. Thus, by refusing notions of success and turning our attention to other kinds of assessment objects, we might gather up new objects with different horizons of potential that offer us a more capacious view of writing studies practice.

2. Failing to Reproduce

While validity inquiry has served as a gateway for writing program administrators to argue for locally driven, context-specific assessments (Huot 2002) and to participate in larger educational-assessment conversations, we argue it has also placed our work within a reproductive loop that has kept us unaware of other possibilities. Asao Inoue and Maya Poe's early scholarship on diversity and writing assessment (Inoue and Poe's 2012), and more recent work on social justice, writing assessment, and diversity (Poe and Inoue 2016), have made us aware of student populations traditionally disadvantaged by assessment (e.g., students of color, working-class students, gender-nonconforming students, multilingual students). However, researchers/administrators seem to specifically test out those claims and use that information in their validity argument, reproducing a linear loop that follows what has been done before instead of looking outside the loop and taking different paths. The hyperawareness of making sure particular groups of students don't continue to be marginalized by our assessments has prevented us from considering different perspectives, such as the role of intersectionality in identity. We become part of the linear, straight paths of assessment when we engage in validity inquiry to reaffirm values and name known consequences.

A failure-oriented practice would revel in the Deleuzian intensities and folds of new sites of assessment research—open ended, indeterminate, having endless potentiality (Deleuze 1993). To seek out the unknown, QVI asks us to privilege what we don't expect, what we might not seek out, and to disrupt the linear, reproductive loop. As validity arguments are typically constructed after data is collected so as to create the argument for why the data can be used to support particular decision, QVI asks us to look between the numbers. For example, as a grading mechanism, the bell curve distributed student scores so an equal number of students always failed and succeeded regardless of their actual performance. The majority of students fell within the C range, creating and privileging the "average" student so only the elite "earned" the A. The bell curve ignores students' performances and instead forces students into a fixed-average category that doesn't reflect who those students are. Of course, as time unfolded, the bell curve lost prominence in the classroom because it did not actually reflect student performance/

learning but was instead applied to data sets after the fact. However, even though we resist reproducing the bell curve in our classrooms, the bell curve is still used in other research sites. When we engage with QVI to resist reproducing the bell curve, we might question what it means for students when the bell curve is negatively (long tail on the lower scores) or positively (long tail on the higher scores) skewed. When working within the statistical lens, the skewed shapes open up an opportunity to understand what is beneath the redistributed scores and lines. Other distribution shapes—such as a platykurtic distribution (Urdan 2010), which flattens the bell curve and typically has more scores at the ends and fewer in the middle, or a leptokurtic distribution, which has a higher peak with few scores at the ends—open themselves up for interrogation. These shapes violate the normal bell curve, but they also redirect our attention back to our sample populations. Purposefully seeking a systematically biased sample to overrepresent a population of students typically disadvantaged by assessments might create different distribution shapes than would a representative sample of students enrolled at a university. QVI asks us to question the average, summarized data statistics offers us and to run data based on multiple biased and representative samples to make informed interpretations of the data. By working in the nonnormative spaces of demographic data, we can begin to think about fairness (Poe 2013). We can disaggregate demographic data to understand who is privileged by particular kinds of assessments. How might we understand impacts on protected groups? How might intersectionality work to avoid the marginalization of protected concerns (Cox 2018)? Statistics are useful to understand some of these questions, but they only provide the contours and not the twists and turns in which individual student's experiences illuminate the messy, nonlinear construct of writing.

3. Failing to Be Commodified

As Brian Huot and Michael Neal remind us, writing assessment is both political and technical (Huot and Neal 2006). The push for new technologies of assessment in higher education grows out of neoliberal social and economic ideologies, and perpetual educational assessment in higher education contexts is directly tied to the growing commodification of education, a trend that began in K–12 public schools with No Child Left Behind (Moore, O'Neill, and Crow 2016; Rose 2016). Inside a neoliberal ideology, assessments often work as technocratic instruments that aid in promoting individualism and competition while justifying the privatization of public enterprises, the latter of which is demonstrated in

Stephanie's example above. Neoliberal ideologies reject commitments to the public good and promote meritocratic systems in which "success" is configured as achievement gained through individual talent and ability, a frame that ignores imbalances of power, social privilege, and the cumulative effects of oppression, particularly intersectional oppression. According to Lil Brannon, Cynthia Urbanski, Lacy Manship, Lucy Arnold, and Tony Iannone, in a "consumerocracy,"

> literacy is commodified as a "thing" to be "gotten" through the course of one's education and tested to see if its various "components" . . . have been accrued. Those who "have" the components (the set of skills) are named high-achieving and those who do not are low-achieving. The tests are considered "objective"—so the fault of "not having the skills" rests with the individual who did not work hard enough to get them. Individual children are sorted, schools are sorted, and teachers are held accountable for either giving or not giving students what they need to be successful. The sorting/accountability function helps to construct a culture of competition, the hallmark of a capitalist free market economy. Capitalism depends on competition for consumers' funds. (Brannon et al. 2010, 16)

Here, Brannon et al. point to the ways assessments commodify social practices like literacy and writing, rearticulating them as "skills"; skills come to represent modular components of literacy individuals may own more or less of in relation to other skills.

A failure-oriented practice of assessment would fail to be commodified, refusing to participate in these neoliberal ideological frames. As such, it would take a critical stance toward using assessment instruments to build collective capacity in our student populations and in our programs, foregrounding an understanding that writing, learning, and literacy are social practices enacted, shared, and embodied in cultural networks. A queer approach allows us to hold onto the tensions that exist in those networks and value dissensus, acknowledging that no, in fact, we do not all agree on what counts as good writing; it allows us to design our own assessment instruments in participatory (and diffractive) ways that account for and even promote difference.

As such, we argue that QVI can open up opportunities not just on the programmatic level but also to critical conversations in the hyperlocal space of the classroom. By engaging the most transient stakeholders in the system, our students, we can resist easy commodification and work to make learning to write a process of learning to assess (Huot 2002) as we collaboratively negotiate the parameters of what matters in our writing communities and cultures. Practices like dynamic criteria mapping (Broad 2003) and classroom-based assessment (Inoue 2004) have demonstrated the potential of these methods, but few have taken up validity as a critical concern at the hyperlocal or even the programmatic level. Stephanie's work with digital badging, however, demonstrates the ways QVI can thread through writing assessment at all levels, starting at the classroom and "bubbling up" as well as "bubbling out" (West-Puckett 2016). She writes, "[Digital badges] contain the messy baggage of what it means to know, to do, and to learn with particular people and particular resources in particular times and places. As these artifacts move across networks, they are meant to foster negotiation between learners and their learning sponsors or organizations, promoting articulation while resisting standardization" (131). Thus, QVI can help us understand the constraining effects of traditional validity arguments and pursue validity through the marshalling of other kinds of evidences that provide a richer, more capacious view of the work of writers and the textures of writing in the twenty-first century.

4. Failing to Be Mechanized

Though validity inquiry provides a robust framework for current writing assessment, much of the early research on writing assessment focused on establishing reliable scoring methods and creating mechanisms to help teachers reach agreement when they read a piece of student writing. Reliability in writing studies is predicated on notions of appropriateness and the consistent application of a set of values, sometimes formalized in a rubric. To meet standards of appropriateness, assessment instruments must include a range of criteria that meet the stated objective, which commonly asks, does the test measure what it purports to measure? More attention, however, is paid to the consistent application of rules, as readers must be normed and corrected to achieve interrater reliability. As a process of coming to consensus, readers are asked to calibrate their evaluations to insure each reader will make the same kind of value judgement in each category, working to achieve machine-like precision in applying interpretive rules. Samples are typically read twice, and the scoring outcome represents exact agreement, adjacent agreement, or scores differing by two and scores differing by three. Samples whose scores differ by two or more require adjudication by a third reader, whose judgement prevails in an absolute scoring decision.

This process is one well documented as a best practice in educational measurement (Stemler 2004) and writing studies (O'Neill, Moore, and Huot 2009); however, it smooths over human readers' complex and diverse readings of texts. While Diane Kelly-Riley and Norbert Elliot note that "interpretive complexity" (Kelly-Riley and Elliot 2014, 95) makes achieving reliability difficult, a focus on statistical-consistency estimates obscures the diversity, complexity, and range of evaluative responses real readers have to any given text. It is within these folds of "interpretive complexity" that we might begin to see good writing less as a monolithic set of traits and more as a dynamic assemblage of cultural values, one that resists hegemonic notions of knowing, doing, being, and expressing. QVI would work to inhabit these complex spaces and hold onto the syncretic tensions produced there rather than smooth them over through numerical representation. When individuals are interested only in numbers and agreement, it makes sense to allow machines to score writing instead of requiring teachers to read as machines. However, when individuals are interested in the embodied experiences students and teachers have with assessment, we must pay attention to the subjective, emotional components of assessment and scoring. QVI asks us to consider the emotional labor teachers, students, and writing administrators all bring to assessment.

Standardized assessments resist the lived experiences of students. Just as faculty become rubric-reading robots, normed to perform like technology, students act as knowledge repositories required to perform on cue—or on tests. This limited knowledge-to-test-to-performance approach actively resists human individuality and students' bodily responses to the phenomenon of assessment. Standardized assessments operate on the Cartesian mind/body split in which students' emotions have no role in their learning. Education research (Zeidner 2007) has identified the negative emotions students experience when participating in standardized assessments. QVI, in contrast, values the human connection, as well as the knowledges teachers embody about their students, and pushes us to look at both the individual and the aggregate in data. Valuing both ensures the affective, lived experiences of individuals are not erased as data sets undergo multiple analyses.

CONCLUSION

Throughout this chapter we've argued for a methodology that applies a queer lens to validity inquiry. Our arguments rest on our desire for writing and educational assessment to be a practice, or set of practices, rooted in social justice. Ahmed's metaphor of the killjoy has served as an entry for discussing the ways we have resisted the institutional and extra-institutional (e.g., accreditation) pressures to perpetuate assessment "as is" or with minimal interruptions that do little to disrupt the norm. When assessment continues to reproduce the status quo, certain objects and values are upheld as marks of "happiness" and success/achievement. Validity inquiry, as it has been practiced in writing studies, is itself a mark of happiness we work to achieve. It provides us the entry point into larger assessment conversations, legitimizes our programs, and allows us to place objective, quantifiable marks on subjective qualities. When we compose our validity arguments, we do so from the place of privilege that can make us subscribe to traditional, normative values. Thus, our desire to theorize and to engage in QVI marks us again as assessment killjoys.

We hope QVI becomes the means to value the voices of those furthest from the assessment scene. Privileging their voices creates new lines of trajectory for assessment research that might cross curriculum lines or might intersect with students' embodied, creative learning pathways. QVI also forces us to value, name, and count the intersectional identities of students typically not included in assessment reports. If we are to investigate the possible consequences of our assessments, we must look beyond the traditional demographics of students and consider the myriad identity factors that compose an individual student. Paying attention to the embodied, lived experiences of students might offer us new, interesting lines of inquiry around assessment. Ultimately, QVI disrupts the assumed, reproductive nature of writing assessment by queering the return and creating new constructs of writing—what it is, what it can do, when, where, and for whom. By being assessment killjoys, we reframe assessment as a project of possibilities.

REFERENCES

Ahmed, Sara. 2006. *Queer Phenomenology: Orientations, Objects, Others.* Durham, NC: Duke University Press. https://doi.org/10.1215/9780822388074.

Ahmed, Sara. 2010a. "Feminist Killjoys (and Other Willful Subjects)." *Polyphonic Feminisms: Acting in Concert* 8 (3). http://sfonline.barnard.edu/polyphonic/ahmed_01.htm.

Ahmed, Sara. 2010b. *The Promise of Happiness.* Durham, NC: Duke University Press. https://doi.org/10.1215/9780822392781.

Ahmed, Sara. 2014. *Willful Subjects.* Durham, NC: Duke University Press. https://doi.org/10.1215/9780822376101.

AERA (American Educational Research Association), APA (American Psychological Association), NCME (National Council on Measurement in Education), and Joint Committee on Standards for Educational and Psychological Testing. 2014. *Standards for Educational and Psychological Testing.* Washington, DC: American Educational Research Association.

Brannon, Lil, Cynthia Urbanski, Lacy Manship, Lucy Arnold, and Tony Iannone. 2010. "The Ebay-ification of Education: Critical Literacy in a Consumerocracy." *English Journal* 99 (3): 16–21.

Broad, Bob. 2003. *What We Really Value: Beyond Rubrics in Teaching and Assessing Writing.* Logan: Utah State University Press

Callahan, Susan. 1997. "Tests Worth Taking? Using Portfolios for Accountability in Kentucky." *Research in the Teaching of English* 31: 3. 295–336.

Caswell, Nicole I., and William P. Banks. 2018. "Queering Assessment: How Rethinking Our Practices Can Improve LGBT Visibility." In *Writing Assessment as Social Justice,* edited by Asao Inoue, Mya Poe, and Norbert Elliot, 353–77. Anderson, SC: Parlor Press/ WAC Clearinghouse. https://wac.colostate.edu/docs/books/assessment/chapter11 .pdf.

Condon, William. 2012. "The Future of Portfolio-Based Assessment: A Cautionary Tale." In *Writing Assessment in the 21st Century: Essays in Honor of Edward M. White,* edited by Norbert Elliot and Les Perelman, 233–45. New York: Hampton.

Cox, Matthew. 2018. "Shifting Grounds as the New Status Quo: Examining Theoretical Approaches to Diversity and Taxonomy in the Technical Communication Classroom." In *Key Theoretical Concerns in Teaching Technical Communication in the 21st Century,* edited by Angela Haas and Michelle Eble, 287–303. Logan: Utah State University Press.

Deleuze, Gilles. 1993. *The Fold: Leibniz and the Baroque.* London: Athlone.

Edelman, Lee. 2004. *No Future, Queer Theory, and the Death Drive.* Durham, NC: Duke University Press. https://doi.org/10.1215/9780822385981.

Elliot, Norbert. 2005. *On a Scale: A Social History of Writing Assessment in America.* New York: Peter Lang.

Halberstam, Jack. 2011. *The Queer Art of Failure.* Durham, NC: Duke University Press. https://doi.org/10.1215/9780822394358.

Haraway, Donna J. 1997. *Modest_witness@second_millennium.femaleman_meets_ oncomouse: Feminism and Technoscience.* New York: Routledge.

Huot, Brian. 2002. *(Re)Articulating Writing Assessment for Teaching and Learning.* Logan: Utah State University Press.

Huot, Brian, and Michael Neal. 2006. "Writing Assessment: A Techno-History." In *Handbook of Writing Research,* edited by Charles A. MacArthur, Steve Graham, and Jill Fitzgerald, 417–32. New York: Guilford.

Inoue, Asao. 2004. "Community-Based Assessment Pedagogy." *Assessing Writing* 9 (3): 208–38. https://doi.org/10.1016/j.asw.2004.12.001.

Inoue, Asao, and Maya Poe. 2012. *Race and Writing Assessment.* New York: Peter Lang.Kane, Michael. 2006. "Validation." In *Educational Measurement,* 4th ed., edited by Robert L. Brennan, 17–64. Westport, CT: Praeger.

Kane, Michael. 2013. "Validating the Interpretations and Uses of Test Scores." *Journal of Educational Measurement* 50 (1): 1–73. https://doi.org/10.1111/jedm.12000.

Kelly-Riley, Diane, and Norbert Elliot. 2014. "The *WPA Outcomes Statement,* Validation and the Pursuit of Localism." *Assessing Writing* 21:89–103. https://doi.org/10.1016/j.asw .2014.03.004.

Moore, Cindy, Peggy O'Neill, and Angela Crow. 2016. "Assessing for Learning in Age of Comparability: Remembering the Importance of Context." In *Reclaiming Accountability: Improving Writing Programs through Accreditation and Large-Scale Assessments,* edited by Wendy Sharer, Tracy Morse, Michelle Eble, and William P. Banks, 17–35. Logan: Utah State University Press. https://doi.org/10.7330/9781607324355.c001.

O'Neill, Peggy, Cindy Moore, and Brian Huot. 2009. *A Guide to College Writing Assessment.* Logan UT: Utah State University Press.

Palmeri, Jason. 2015. "Rhetorical Disidentification and the Politics of Genre in the 'It Gets Better' Project." Paper presented at the Conference on College Composition and Communication. Tampa, FL. March 20.

Perry, Jeff. 2012. "Critical Validity Theory." In *Practicing Research in Writing Studies: Reflexive and Ethically Responsible Research,* edited by Katrina Powell and Pamela Takayoshi, 187–211. New York: Hampton.

Poe, Mya. 2013. "Making Digital Writing Assessment Fair for Diverse Writers." In *Digital Writing Assessment and Evaluation,* edited by Heidi A. Mckee and Dànielle Nicole DeVoss. Logan: Computers and Composition Digital Press/Utah State University Press. http://ccdigitalpress.org/book/dwae/01_poe.html.

Poe, Mya, and Asao Inoue, eds. 2016. "Toward Writing Assessment as Social Justice." Special issue, *College English* 79 (2).

Rand, Erin J. 2006. *Reclaiming Queer: Activist and Academic Rhetorics of Resistance.* Tuscaloosa: The University of Alabama Press.

Rose, Shirley. 2016. "Understanding Accreditation's History and Role in Higher Education: How It Matters to College Writing Programs." In *Reclaiming Accountability: Improving Writing Programs through Accreditation and Large-Scale Assessments,* edited by Wendy Sharer, Tracy Morse, Michelle Eble, and William P. Banks, 52–63. Logan: Utah State University Press. https://doi.org/10.7330/9781607324355.c003.

Scott, Tony. 2005. "Creating the Subject of Portfolios." *Written Communication* 22 (1): 3–35. https://doi.org/10.1177/0741088304271831.

Stemler, Steven E. 2004. "A Comparison of Consensus, Consistency, and Measurement Approaches to Estimating Interrater Reliability." *Practical Assessment, Research & Evaluation* 9 (4). http://pareonline.net/getvn.asp?v=9&n=4.

West-Puckett, Stephanie. 2016. "Making Writing Assessment More Visible, Equitable, and Portable through Digital Badging." *College English* 79 (2): 123–47.

White, Edward, Norbert Elliot, and Irvin Peckham. 2015. *Very Like a Whale: The Assessment of Writing Programs.* Logan: Utah State University Press.

Urdan, Timothy. 2010. *Statistics in Plain English.* 3rd ed. New York: Routledge.

UNC Board of Governors, Committee on Educational Planning, Policies, and Programs. 2014. *Report from the General Education Council.* http://assessment.uncg.edu/academic/GenEd/documents/2014–01%20UNC%20GEC%20Report.pdf.

Zeidner, Moshe. 2007. "Test Anxiety in Educational Contexts: Concepts, Findings, and Future Directions." In *Emotion in Education,* edited by Paul A. Schutz and Reinhard Pekrun, 165–84. New York: Academic. https://doi.org/10.1016/B978-012372545-5/50011-3.

11

ON QUEERING PROFESSIONAL WRITING

Caroline Dadas and Matthew B. Cox

Queer theory only works side by side with queer practice, otherwise queer theory is straight.
                    —Kate Bornstein

While queer methodologies and rhetorics continue to gain a reliable presence in writing studies journals and conferences, the same does not hold true when we look at professional writing scholarship. As professional writing scholars who work with queer methodologies, we see little evidence scholars are forging intersections between these areas. When we attend the Association of Teachers of Technical Writing (ATTW) conference, we know we will learn about current work taking place in professional writing, and when we attend the Conference on College Composition and Communication (CCCC), we will likely see panels focused on queer methodologies and rhetorics, but these scholarly conversations rarely overlap. This gap leaves us concerned that queer and queered practices, methods, and methodologies are still perceived as irrelevant to the work of professional writing. And yet, professional writing scholars are studying, theorizing, writing, and working at junctures rife with possibility for interplay between these two areas of inquiry. As two of the scholars working at this intersection, we want to make the case that queer methodologies and rhetorics offer needed frameworks for scholarship being done in the professional writing field.

Professional writing is often not associated with the messiness, instability, or boundary crossing inherent in queer scholarship. In fact, these notions seem antithetical to a field that focuses on how work gets done in contexts ranging from large corporations to local grassroots initiatives. As members of both professional writing and queer communities of scholars, we are troubled by this apparent disjuncture. For example, programs from professional writing's two flagship conferences, the

DOI: 10.7330/9781607328186.c011

Association of Teachers of Technical Writing (ATTW) and the Council for Programs in Technical and Scientific Communication (CPTSC), reflect the limited influence of queer methodologies on professional writing practices. In fact, we see our joint interest in these areas as still having limited representation at our primary conferences—ATTW, CPTSC—and even in the journals *Technical Communication Quarterly* (*TCQ*) and *Journal of Business and Technical Communication* (*JBTC*).

Along with our desire to make these fields speak to each other more coherently, we acknowledge the challenges that attend a bridging of such seemingly divergent areas of scholarship. As a field, professional writing has valued quantitative data and certain empirical methods of research that attempt to gain a measure of objectivity, a concept queer theory and queer methods reject as desirable or even possible. Jack Halberstam (2011) argues for the value in resisting mastery and that failure can represent a viable alternative to oppressive structures of success. In addition, many contemporary rhetoric and composition scholars, such as Tony Scott and Nancy Welch (Scott and Welch 2014), Scott and Lillian Brannon (Scott and Brannon 2013), and Chris W. Gallagher (2011) critique neoliberal notions of success-driven educational practices and shine a light on the roles of power, struggle, and dissonance as critical for learning outcomes. As scholars at the intersection of queer theory and professional writing, we believe we need to more rigorously articulate what these alternatives might look like. In particular, how might queer methodologies productively influence the kind of work being done in professional writing, allowing for productive dialogue between these two areas of scholarship? At the same time, we must also ask what cost there may be for making space for queerness in professional writing. In particular, might this move require too much accommodation on the part of queer methodologies in order for this dialogue to work?

In this chapter, we argue that a lack of space for talking about queer theory in professional writing remains, despite longstanding scholarly advances that have complicated professional writing's association with objectivity and standardized conventions and norms. We support our argument with data gathered from a small-scale survey of professional writing scholarship from the past five years, as well as from an interview with Michelle Eble, the current president of ATTW. While we address our study of professional writing scholarship in detail later in this chapter, we integrate Eble's insights throughout. Through both collections of data, we demonstrate that while an interest in queer rhetorics seems to be emerging in professional writing, there is still little representation of queer rhetorics within the field. We then offer suggestions and heuristics for including queered methodologies and methodological practices in professional writing research. In doing so, we seek to make clear—especially to newer scholars in rhetoric and writing studies—that professional writing is not a space for hypernormativity or hypernormativizing rhetorics. Rather, we see the field as a context in which queer rhetorics and queer bodies can make significant contributions.

DEFINING OUR TERMS

In this chapter, we draw on specific terminology to describe the gap we see in professional writing scholarship while acknowledging that part of the work we must do involves establishing ways of talking about queer methodological approaches within professional writing. We draw our definition of *queer* from David Halperin (1990), who notes that "queer is by definition whatever is at odds with the normal, the legitimate, the dominant" (62). This idea of queer grew out of the LGBT and queer civil rights movements of the 1960s and 1970s. The experiences, viewpoints, discourses, and wisdom of the LGBT and queer communities gave rise to queer as a scholarly and theoretical approach in the late 1980s. Queer theory asks us to consider the ways identities are "constructed and validated," (Jack Halberstam 2011) as well as both how discourses of sexuality "circulate and reaffirm or reassert power" and how "queers or other marginalized sexual and gendered beings engage in 'world-making'" (Warner 2005). Queer theory work by these and other scholars (such as Eve Kosofky Sedgwick [1990], Judith Butler [2011], and José Esteban Muñoz [1999]) became visible in the field of writing studies during the first two decades of the new millennium. Writing studies scholars such as Connie Monson and Jacqueline Rhodes (Monson and Rhodes 2004), Harriet Malinowitz (1995), and Jonathan Alexander and William P. Banks (Alexander and Banks 2004) are credited as having been part of the first rhetoric and writing cohort to take the theoretical advances of queer theory and apply them to rhetorical contexts concerning sexuality, identity, literacy, and methodologies. An action-oriented, rhetorically infused version of queer theory, a queer theory in action as described in the introduction to this collection, queer rhetorics has grown rapidly in recent years at the level of graduate instruction, with increasing numbers of queer rhetorics graduate seminars finding root in programs across the country. We attribute this growth in part to the influence of cultural rhetorics, or "culturally located practice and study" (CR Theory Lab 2011). According to the Cultural Rhetorics Theory Lab at Michigan

State University (2011), cultural rhetorics demonstrates "how rhetoric and culture are interconnected through a focus on the processes by which language, texts, as well as other discursive practices like performance, embodied rhetorics, and material rhetorics, create meaning." Because of the influence of cultural rhetorics, we are seeing scholarship in writing studies that devotes attention to the material and embodied rhetorical practices that emerge from shared experience.

The influence of cultural rhetorics in professional writing has not necessarily been a welcome shift, however; some professional writing scholars believe any kind of cultural work falls outside the purview of the field. In fact, as Matt has talked to doctoral students at conferences and elsewhere, many have confided in him that their mentors are actively dissuading them from culturally aware PW scholarship because, as some of their professors tell them, it does not represent "real research." While some members of the discipline hold to strict interpretations of what constitutes work in the field, ATTW's official mission and statement of purpose do not articulate boundaries for what counts as valid scholastic contributions (http://www.attw.org/). According to its website's mission statement, "The Association of Teachers of Technical Writing was formed in 1973 to encourage dialogue among teachers of technical communication and to develop technical communication as an academic discipline. ATTW today has approximately 1,000 members and includes both graduate and undergraduate students of technical communication as well as professional technical communicators in business and industry." The lack of boundaries in this statement both opens possibilities for defining what constitutes professional writing and represents a missed opportunity for the field to officially mark cultural rhetorics and other advances of recent decades as valid frames for inquiry. We mention this source of disciplinary tension both to celebrate significant contributions in the field and to point out that cultural rhetorics, specifically queer rhetorics and methodologies, has yet to be codified in any highly visible way we can see as constituting a significant research agenda in the field. Among the most significant achievements, to our minds, the *Journal of Business and Technical Communication*'s 2012 special issue, "Race, Ethnicity, and Technical Communication," includes pieces such as Angela Haas's "Race, Rhetoric, and Technology: A Case Study of Decolonial Technical Communication Theory, Methodology, and Pedagogy." Haas (2012) investigates the ways in which all communication—even in technical and professional realms—is influenced by normative discourses of race, class, gender, sex, and ability. We are eager to read more scholarship that builds on this insight, scholarship that specifically focuses on how queer methods and methodologies seek to disrupt normative discourses. How are queer communities (e.g., company-sponsored LGBTQ employee professional organizations like those that exist at Disney, Target Corporation, or Microsoft) using language, texts, and discursive practices to create queer/ed meanings within professional writing?[1]

WHAT DO QUEER RHETORICS AND METHODOLOGIES OFFER?

We believe this broader turn toward cultural and queer rhetorics (Cox and Faris 2015) has laid the groundwork for the development of queer methodological approaches within professional writing and writing studies more broadly. Queering the field's methodological lenses will involve exploring how queer theory can be used to disrupt objectivity, neutrality, and normativity. Because professional writing research has historically been associated with objectivity, we believe it is all the more important that we draw on queer notions of disruption or "messiness" to reorient that work. In focusing more intently on whose experiences are privileged and by questioning the way things are, we can disrupt the perspective that neutrality is achievable or even desirable. We highlight normativity as an especially pernicious concept, one that, unlike objectivity or neutrality, has not been addressed at length in the field of professional writing. Queer methodologies would prove useful in this regard because they seek to disrupt normativity by exploding binaries and other systems that hypernormalize reality. While professional writing scholarship has been impacted by postmodernity's interrogation of objectivity, the field has not offered a sustained interrogation of normativity; in particular, we see certain conceptualizations of "success" being forwarded as the norm within workplace, academic, and community contexts. For this reason, we believe queer methodologies can prove especially useful in challenging what we consider the norm in the wide variety of rhetorical situations professional writing concerns itself with.

While queer methodologies are defined in the introduction to this collection, in this chapter we provide a direct application to professional writing by highlighting how queer methodologies challenge the concept of normativity, providing a useful frame for professional writing. We draw on the work of Michael Warner (2005), who has posited queer counterpublics as a "world-making project" that eschews Habermasian ideals of community. Warner's conception of a counterpublic appeals to us because of his emphasis on how counterpublics, by operating outside heteronormativity, honor alternative ways of relating to each other: alternative to biological familial structures, corporate entities, political alliances, geographic boundaries, and so forth. His critique of intimacies being equated with private spaces creates a fuzzier boundary between public and private (also referenced in Bersani and Phillips 2008). As feminists and queer theorists have argued for decades, delineating the private as apolitical and outside the realm of social justice places a heavy burden on marginalized populations. In response to heteronormative expectations for what constitutes privacy, Warner (2005) argues that "making a queer world has required the development of kinds of intimacy that bear no necessary relation to domestic space, to kinship, to the couple form, to property, or to the nation" (199). In other words, a queer methodological lens can envision—in fact, may require—alternate ways of working with one another to solve problems: a central concern of professional writing.

Rejecting heteronormativity through a queer methodological lens means fostering an awareness of all the cultural practices and systems aside from sexuality that unfold with normative expectations. As Warner (2005) maintains, "Heterosexuality involves so many practices that are not sex that a world in which this hegemonic cluster would not be dominant is, at this point, unimaginable" (198). In the years since his writing, scholars have indeed begun to imagine a world not organized by heteronormativity. While the term itself is often deployed in relation to sexuality, *heteronormativity* implies much more:

> A whole field of social relations becomes intelligible as heterosexuality, and this privatized sexual culture bestows on its sexual practices a tacit sense of rightness and normalcy. This sense of rightness—embedded in things and not just sex—is what we call heteronormativity. Heteronormativity is more than ideology, or prejudice, or phobia against gays and lesbians; it is produced in almost every aspect of the forms and arrangements of social life: nationality, the state, and the law; commerce; medicine; education; plus the conventions and affects of narrativity, romance, and other protected spaces of culture. (Warner 2005, 194)

We can see a "tacit sense of rightness" in many structures that concern professional writing scholars: workplace hierarchies, procedures concerning usability, social media integration into organizations, and even what counts as professional writing work/scholarship. By rejecting heteronormative constructions of rightness and privacy, we can expand our thinking about collaboration and innovation within the field.

To be more clear about what such a shift in thinking and practice might look like, we reimagine one piece of professional writing scholarship through this lens to illustrate what queer methodologies may offer. Consider the study described by Stephen Doheny-Farina (1986) in "Writing in an Emerging Organization," a fairly recognizable professional writing context in which Doheny-Farina examined how colleagues worked together to write a business plan. While Dohney-Farina focused on power dynamics between a group of writers and their boss, the writing processes they engaged in, and the complex social dynamics that led to the final version of the business plan, a queer methodology might offer different emphases for this study. For example, in the data-collection section of his chapter, Doheny-Farina explains that he drew on both open-ended interviews about the history of the company and discourse-based interviews pertaining to the actual drafting of the business plan. Via a queer methodology, a researcher conducting a similar study might also/instead conduct interviews concerning participants' perspectives on the social dynamics of the work group and how those dynamics affected the writing task. A central concern of queer rhetorics involves how certain identities, practices, and structures are categorized into normative and deviant; in tracing the power dynamics among this group of writers—and between them and their boss—a researcher could focus on behaviors marked as deviant within this context, how others addressed them, what the consequences were for a collaborative project, and what the ongoing repercussions were for those who were the source of the behaviors. Such an analysis could offer a researcher a more detailed sense of the social dynamics that bore upon a writing context. This critique, of course, is not intended to suggest Doheny-Farina's study is flawed; rather, we want to posit that this same study might have have led to different conclusions if a queer methodology were involved. Shifting our frames is essential to reorienting writing studies, to recognizing the ways our research methodologies work to reproduce the same knowledge in the same frameworks we're already comfortable exploring.

Offering participants the opportunity to more directly discuss interpersonal dynamics might be viewed by some as being too personal, or as fitting within the realm of what is considered private. A queer methodology, however, acknowledges that intimacies come in many forms, including those that exist between coworkers or collaborators. Acknowledging the role those intimacies play in a writing task requires different methods and frameworks than we often see in workplace studies. In addition, while Doheny-Farina's (1986) study predated the rise of mobile technologies, examining how participants' uses of text messaging and other mobile capabilities influence their collaborative processes represents another way of troubling public/private boundaries. Texting and applications like GroupMe factor heavily into collaborative groups' authoring processes, and we need robust studies that incorporate those communications as fully as more familiar documents such as e-mails or memos. While scholars have engaged in research about distributed technologies, we encourage additional attention to how "private" communications such as text messages influence collaborative workplace writing tasks.

By troubling a public/private binary, queer methodologies can also open up opportunities for more in-depth studies of gender, sexuality, and performativity. Professional writing can intervene to address how current topics in the public discourse bear on private industry. For example, 2016 saw much legislation and discussion surrounding bathroom use for transgender individuals. Particularly in states where legislators have enacted discriminatory policies surrounding bathroom use, it would be fruitful to explore the ramifications of these policies in private industry. The lines of public/private become increasingly blurred when examining issues such as this one—and it is this haziness that queer methodologies are poised to address. As Warner (2005) has argued, "Intimate life is the endlessly cited elsewhere of public political discourse, a promised haven that distracts citizens from the unequal conditions of their political and economic lives, consoles them for the damaged humanity of mass society, and shames them for any divergence between their lives and the intimate sphere that is alleged to be simple personhood" (193). Professional writing scholarship should explore intimate spaces and topics as inherently political, particularly when it comes to marginalized populations. Queer rhetorics have done this kind of work in writing studies at large, reaching back to Harriet Malinowitz's 1995 examination of how queer students experience "personal" classroom writing as a political and sometimes risky activity. Queer rhetorics and methodologies reach beyond the politics of representation, though that is important as well, to offer new frameworks and orientations for professional writing.

CALLS TO ACTION AND MISSED OPPORTUNITIES

Before articulating ways forward when it comes to increased engagement between professional writing and queer rhetorics, we want to offer a brief overview of both professional writing and queer scholarship that opens the door for the kinds of conceptual collaborations we believe are important and overdue. Our overview is not exhaustive; we focus in depth on a few pieces of scholarship we believe are representative of a cultural rhetorics-inflected approach to professional writing. While the messiness and fluidity of queer theory at first may appear incompatible with professional writing, we argue that recent scholarship in professional writing has offered productive critiques of institutional constraints and power structures that align with queer methodological approaches (Frost 2016; Haas 2012; Palmeri 2006). These approaches support Kath Browne, Catherine J. Nash, and Sally Hines's argument that "'queer research' can be any form of research positioned within conceptual frameworks that highlight the instability of taken-for-granted meanings and resulting power relations" (Browne, Nash, and Hines 2010, 574). The questioning of taken-for-granted meanings and power relations has always been present in the field of professional writing but, according to Angela Haas (2012), became a more explicit focus as a result of Bernadette Longo's 1998 call for more scholarship that draws on cultural studies methods of inquiry. The years following this call saw the publication of the widely used *Critical Power Tools*, edited by J. Blake Scott, Bernadette Longo, and Katherine V. Wills, a collection that identifies "approaches that are openly critical of nonegalitarian, unethical practices and subject positions, that promote values other than conformity, efficiency, and effectiveness" as one of its organizing forces (Scott, Longo, and Wills 2006, 1). Haas (2012) herself acknowledged that while cultural studies has much to offer professional writing, very few scholars are producing work that interrogates race and ethnicity (and we add sexuality) in this context—so few that she writes about how she was unable to design a graduate syllabus without drawing from other disciplines. Haas's (2012) aforementioned "Race, Rhetoric, and Technology: A Case Study of Decolonial Technical Communication Theory, Methodology, and Pedagogy" argues for the value of infusing decolonial methodologies into the field via introductory courses in technical communication with assignments such as her cultural identity map and a cultural and technological artifact analysis. Through these efforts, Haas reminds professional writing that we must attend carefully to the exercise of power along interstices of difference.

Building on Haas's (2012) attention to decolonial methodologies, Erin Frost (2016) introduces an "apparent feminist methodology" she argues is needed "in order to intervene in situations in which technical documentation unfairly and uncritically engages in oppression while feigning objectivity" (4). Frost's mention of objectivity reinforces the notion that writing in professional, technical, or scientific contexts is no more objective than any other type of writing—objectivity being a tenet that continues to adhere to professional writing. Frost's "apparent feminist methodology" draws on previous work by theorists working in cultural studies, indigenous environmental activism, anthropology, and queer theory, a move that demonstrates the richness of perspectives we in professional writing should consider when it comes to our scholarship. While Frost cites at length past feminist work in the field, she also calls attention to its decline over the past fifteen years, a trend that contributes to the exigence for her project. For Frost (2016), an apparent feminist methodology "encourages a response to social justice exigencies, invites participation from allies who do not explicitly identify as feminist but do work that complements feminist goals, and makes apparent the ways in which efficient work actually depends on the existence and input of diverse audiences" (5). With this methodological approach, Frost addresses current issues in the public sphere—recent legislation related to the policing of women's bodies—by arguing that professional writing has much to offer to heated cultural debates about feminism and women's civic/civil rights.

While this work has indicated a purposeful recent turn in the field toward the exercise of power against nonprivileged populations—a move we view as resonant with queer theory—we wonder whether some of our colleagues might counter that such work has always been present in professional writing, rendering our critique moot. Indeed, we acknowledge early work by Carolyn Miller (1979) that argues for professional writing as an inherently humanistic enterprise, one that rejects positivistic perspectives of language and positions "good technical writing" as "a persuasive version of experience" (50). Although she does not explicitly address notions of difference, these versions of experience imply the question of *whose* experience. In other words, when we ignore the implications of difference, we are complicit in the attempt to posit dominant subject positions' experiences as simply the way things are. While we have often cited and anthologized her work, we as a field have not fully brought to bear Miller's vision.

THE LACK OF QUEERNESS IN RECENT SCHOLARSHIP

We locate our evidence for this critique in the recent programs for both the ATTW and CPTSC conferences and the articles published in the *Journal of Business and Technical Communication* (*JBTC*) and *Technical Communication Quarterly* (*TCQ*), the two flagship journals in professional and technical communication. We searched all titles and abstracts from these conferences and journals from the years 2012–2016 for evidence of queer-related topics. We focused on this time frame because we are interested in surveying the most recent scholarship in the field.

Specifically, we coded for the following terms: *lesbian, gay, bisexual, queer, trans, transgender, sexuality, sex,* LGBT, GLBT, LGBTQ, *gender.* We chose these terms as reflective of a queer focus, though these terms are, of course, slippery. The term *gender,* in particular, can be part of a line of inquiry that has nothing to do with queerness. Conversely, a speaker or writer may address queer topics in a talk/article that does not contain one of these terms in the title or abstract. In addition, by including *LGBT(Q)* in this coding schema, we do not mean to imply that we see the terms *LGBT(Q)* and *queer* as being synonymous. A goal of this edited collection is to demonstrate the multiple contexts in which queerness can be applied to research and writing; the term *LGBT(Q),* on the other hand, connotes a more direct reference to sexuality. Because many people still use these terms interchangeably, however, we thought it appropriate to include *LGBT(Q)* in our coding schema. We recognize titles and abstracts are not representative of the content of a presentation or article—but titles are often what prospective attendees/readers use to evaluate whether they want to engage further with the speaker/writer's ideas. Especially when it comes to conferences, presenters may change the focus of their presentations after the publication of the conference program, or audience questions may steer conversations in particular ways. At the same time, conference titles and abstracts are often all attendees have to go by as they choose which panels they will attend. Article titles and abstracts, as well as presentation titles for conferences, serve as an incomplete but official record of what topics were being discussed in a given year in a field.

Despite the fact that professional writing scholars have been arguing for quite some time that the field should demonstrate greater acknowledgment of cultural studies-related concerns, we found little evidence of scholarship that attends to queer rhetorics and/or methodologies.

We see several terms we coded for appearing most frequently at the past two ATTW conferences in 2016 and 2015. Both the terms *queer* and *LGBT* surfaced in conference titles each year, one title per year stemming from Matt's work. While we are heartened to see this increased visibility of queer work over the previous years of 2012–2014, we also caution that two panels out of twenty-seven (in 2016) at a conference does not make for a large-scale or nuanced conversation. Nonetheless, it is worth mentioning that several of these recent presentations appear to have taken up queer methodologies and rhetorics in the kinds of ways we see as particularly useful for professional writing. At ATTW 2015, Beth Keller participated in a panel entitled "Mentoring as Relationship Building: Identity, Performance, and Value in Technical Communication." As

	ATTW	CPTSC	TCQ	JBTC
2016	2 [1 *queer*, 1 *LGBT*]*	n/a	1 [*gender*]	0
2015	2 [1 *queer*, 1 *LGBT*]*	0	0	1 [*gender*]
2014	1 [*gender*]	0	0	0
2013	1 [*gender*]	1 [*gender*]	0	0
2012	1 [*LGBTQ*]*	N/A	1 [*gender*]	0

*The data includes a presentation by Matt.

part of her description in the conference program, Keller (2015) stated she would address "the ways in which professional development happens within workplaces, with emphases on feminist, queered, and de-centralized ideas, performances, and practices of mentoring." That same year, Matt Cox, Michelle Eble, Erin Frost, and Meredith Johnson offered a panel titled "Not Normally Valued: Queering Methodologies, Risky Research, and Institutional Review Boards" (Cox et al. 2015). The description for this panel reads, "We propose a queer methodological framework for valuing knowledge about research ethics and practices in the field of technical communication. We mean queering as troubling, disrupting, at-odds with the dominant (Ahmed 2006)." While Matt specifically focused on LGBTQ identities, both Eble and Frost used the notion of queerness as a framing device to talk about Institutional Research Boards' tracking of nonnormative bodies. It is this use of queerness as a lens, a methodology, an ontological frame that we find especially encouraging, found both in Keller's examination of mentoring practices and Eble and Frost's focus on IRB practices.

An additional reason to be encouraged by this data is that Michelle Eble, who addressed queer methodologies in her presentation, is the current president of ATTW. Eble's leadership in this regard helps establish a tone that queer rhetorics and methodologies are worthy areas of inquiry within professional writing. During our interview, Eble addressed her role as an ally in using queer rhetorics and methodologies in her research:

> I think early in any kind of work that is identity driven . . . we can't depend on just that group of scholars to do that work. We have to have allies. You'll never have the mass you need if you always depend on a minority population. So if it only depends on GLBTQ individuals to help us change and queer tech comm, that's likely not going to happen because you will never have the amount needed. That's why you need allies. That's why things need to be named, theories need to be named. So that people can then think about how that work, how they can use methodologies and

theoretical frameworks to do work that they're interested in as allies even if they're not themselves identified as queer. (pers. comm.)

Eble's point reinforces the notion that scholarship (like this collection) functions to disseminate ideas pertaining to queer methodologies among scholars in the wider field. It is our job as scholars who work with queer methodologies to offer guidance for those scholars who may be reticent to use such a theoretical framework for fear of appropriating it (a concern that is not unusual when it comes to cultural rhetorics or, to use Eble's language, "work that is identity driven"). Part of the work that must be done before we can see professional writing taking up queer methodologies in a significant way involves "naming" what queerness can bring to professional writing (and vice versa).

Perhaps because this naming work has not yet occurred to the degree needed, we see that CPTSC, according to our coding scheme, did not show any evidence of discussing queer rhetorics in the past five years. While one presentation in 2013 addressed gender, we hoped to see further evidence of queer rhetorics at the programmatic level than is represented by this conference. Considering that ideas tend to make their way to the programmatic level after broad circulation within the field, it is not surprising to see that a conference focusing on professional writing programs does not show engagement with queer rhetorics. Even so, the work of including queer rhetorics (or cultural rhetorics more broadly) in professional writing programs can be undertaken at the local level. Caroline, for example, has worked in her capacity as a director of a professional writing minor to include courses such as Writing Women Safe: Writing, Rape, Prevention, Advocacy as electives in her university's program. While at first glance, a course focused on rape might seem outside the scope of professional writing, the course's orientation toward writing as a means of social action fits squarely within the program's goal to have students view writing as a form of action and activism. We hope to see further evidence of these kinds of courses—and evidence of queer rhetorics and methodologies in particular—at the programmatic level in the coming years.

While the scholarship being presented at professional writing conferences does not show much queer influence, there is even less evidence of such influence in two major journals of professional writing: the *Journal of Business and Technical Communication* and *Technical Communication Quarterly*. Our study revealed only three mentions of the word *gender* in article titles for the past five years—and no mention of *queer*. As stated previously, we are heartened by the 2012 special issue of *JBTC* devoted to ethnicity and race in technical communication.

We hope that, moving forward, cultural rhetorical approaches will expand beyond special issues to become more fully integrated into the scholarship being published in these journals. In our interview, Eble addressed the relationship between professional writing's conferences and journals by suggesting that "what we need to see and maybe foster are those . . . little things that are happening at conferences, that they find their way into the journal[s]" (pers. comm.). Indeed, as we see more discussion of queer rhetorics and methodologies happening at conferences, we should expect to see those discussions materialize more frequently in print.

Although our small-scale study appears to surface largely disappointing evidence about the state of queer rhetorics and methodologies within professional writing, we want also to acknowledge the importance of less visible kinds of queer work. In particular, graduate programs hold a significant amount of influence in shaping the field. The training of graduate students has always shaped any discipline in terms of how students perceive the contours of the field—and how they decide to push against those contours once they reach the professorate. We call particular attention to Michigan State University in this regard, whose doctoral program, through its emphasis on cultural rhetorics, has pushed professional writing (and writing studies in general) to devote more attention to how race, gender, ability, class, and sexuality influence and are influenced by various writing contexts. In our coding of professional writing conference presentations and articles, we repeatedly saw graduates from this program producing scholarship that views professional writing through a lens of what we refer to above as *cultural rhetorics.* Michigan State is not alone in this regard, as other doctoral programs such as Miami University and East Carolina University regularly integrate queer methodologies into their research-methods courses. While a comprehensive study of the structure of writing studies graduate programs is beyond the scope of this chapter, we nonetheless want to emphasize the importance of this integrative work at the graduate level. If queer methodologies and rhetorics are never placed into dialogue with professional writing and other areas of inquiry, graduate programs are tacitly ignoring queer theory's applicability to a range of workplace and nonprofit contexts. Just as writing studies has embraced feminist methodologies as appropriate for myriad sites of research, we look forward to watching queer theory travel beyond contexts that focus specifically on sexuality. The scholarly attention we hope to see emerge in professional writing's conferences and journals can be fostered in a sustained way via instruction at the graduate and undergraduate levels.

Another less visible opportunity for those of us eager to see more integrated work between professional writing and queer rhetorics and methodologies might involve inviting visiting scholars to campus in order to push at the boundaries of these scholastic areas. In the fall of 2015, Caroline, who sits on Montclair State's Gender, Sexuality, and Women's Studies (GSWS) steering committee, suggested inviting Professor Shelly Eversley of Baruch College to her campus. Eversley had recently launched the Equality Archive (www.equalityarchive.com), a multimodal collection of artifacts documenting ongoing work for queer and women's rights. Though Eversley does not affiliate herself with professional writing (or writing studies in general), Caroline saw an opportunity to highlight the kind of multimodal work instructors have been teaching in the professional writing minor, particularly in the Digital Writing course. From Caroline's perspective, this speaker would offer as much to Montclair State University's professional writing students as she would to GSWS majors. As a result, Eversley presented her multimodal archive to students in the Digital Writing course as a concrete example of how multimodal approaches to activism offer rich opportunities to readers. While such gestures seem small, opportunities to open students and faculty to new work being done across the country can serve as important moments in encouraging dialogue among areas of scholastic inquiry. We remain optimistic that deliberate steps such as these will accumulate in productive ways.

FORGING ALLIANCES BETWEEN QUEER METHODOLOGIES AND PROFESSIONAL WRITING

How, then, can we in professional writing make queer work more visible in the field? Here, we offer a series of concrete actions those of us invested in this kind of work might take. We hope, of course, that others will add to these actions moving forward.

Build on the Informal Discussions Occurring at Conferences and Represent Them in Journals

Our examination of professional writing conference programs and journals indicates queer rhetorics and methodologies have found limited representation at ATTW and none yet in *JBTC* and *TCQ*. Considering that many of us use conferences as a means for getting feedback on new ideas or written drafts, it is important that we then work to represent that material in print. Because the field's journals and books remain the primary source of idea distribution, reaching a broad audience in professional writing will not happen until queer work finds its way into print. Relatedly, we call on editorial boards to work with scholars who seek to move the field in this direction; we also encourage journals to invite more guest editors who might put out a call that encourages queer work. As mentioned in her interview, Eble believes important conversations are already happening at conferences. She also alluded to being aware of several dissertations that have engaged in this kind of queer work but added it takes time for scholars to publish their scholarship in journals. She explained, "You see a lag time. And while Technical/Professional Communication, depending on which history you want to discuss, is still a relatively young discipline of its own, I think you see diversification of disciplines happening over time and adjacent to fields similar to them. I think and I hope we'll see more work in queer rhetorics and tech comm" (pers. comm.). We might view Eble's mention of "adjacent fields" in relation to writing studies more broadly, a field in which, as we mentioned earlier in this chapter, scholars have steadily initiated discussions of queer rhetorics over the past twenty years. Despite the existence of ATTW, the CCCC leadership might consider ways of integrating more professional writing work into the conference; a professional writing caucus might be a good place to start. The proximity of these two fields bodes well for professional writing's commitment to queer work; we believe the time has come for professional writing to begin to show growth in this direction similar to what we have seen in writing studies. At the same time, as Alexander and Banks note in their introduction to a special issue of *Computers and Composition* (2004), to wait for queer scholars to achieve tenure and then propose a special issue of a journal is yet another way we disempower the already disenfranchised. We believe *TCQ* and *JBTC* should both be actively pursuing queer scholars who can help them to bring focused issues into print. After all, why should pretenure faculty take a chance on diversifying the field if it isn't interested in supporting them as they work toward tenure? While we do not necessarily claim this to be the case, we worry that a field waiting for young scholars to be brave enough to step forward is, in fact, a field actively discouraging that movement.

Be Attentive to the Programmatic Level, Particularly Graduate Courses

In addition to the attention we must devote to journals and conferences, those of us interested in furthering queer work within professional writing must also examine the structure of our graduate programs and the curricula of our graduate courses. For example, do queer methodologies have a presence in a program's professional and technical communication courses? Is there a regular rotation of special-topics courses in which professors and students can explore more recent developments in professional writing? Are queer methodologies—if they are addressed at all—relegated to an isolated article in a class, or are they presented as a major recent theoretical development and integrated throughout the curriculum? Most important, how have queer methods and methodologies become part of the standard research-methods coursework? For example, a number of PhD programs include a Studies in Rhetoric-type course; special topics courses such as these can create an opening for queer rhetorics in the curriculum.

While our survey is not exhaustive, we believe any research-methods course in professional writing, as this point in history, should at least consider topics such as the professional practices of marginalized populations that have been used to undercut or bypass colonial, misogynistic, or patriarchal structures; workplace narratives that complicate notions of success; pedagogical reflections on how to incorporate a cultural rhetorical focus into traditional professional writing courses such as Technical Writing and Business/Workplace Writing; and methodological frameworks that draw on queer and feminist traditions to trouble objectivity. We want to highlight several articles and monographs located within professional writing and writing studies that take up some of these topics and would make excellent additions to a graduate research-methods course in professional writing:

- Melody Bowdon's (2004) "Technical Communication and the Role of the Public Intellectual: A Community HIV-Prevention Case Study"
- Angela Haas's (2012) "Race, Rhetoric, and Technology: A Case Study of Decolonial Technical Communication Theory, Methodology, and Pedagogy"
- Jeffrey Grabill's (2000) "Shaping Local HIV/AIDS Services Policy through Activist Research: The Problem of Client Involvement"
- Blake Scott's (2003) *Risky Rhetoric: AIDS and the Cultural Practices of HIV Testing*
- Jonathan Alexander and William P. Banks's (2004) "Sexualities, Technologies, and the Teaching of Writing: A Critical Overview"
- Erin Frost's (2016) "Apparent Feminism as a Methodology for Technical Communication and Rhetoric"
- Eric Darnell Pritchard's (2017) *Fashioning Lives: Black Queers and the Politics of Literacy*

In addition, graduate faculty should be willing—as Haas was for her previously mentioned article—to go afield to find appropriate queer material for graduate methods courses. Until the field has built up a solid collection of articles and monographs that address queer methodologies, those of us who teach graduate students may have to reach into other disciplines to amass material for courses. In pursuing this course of action, we are also driving home the point that professional writing as a field needs more engagement with queer methodologies; upon completing these courses, our students will then be prepared to do so. Making our readings more inclusive for graduate-level methods courses can yield significant rewards as graduate students move into the professorate and publish.

Be Specific about Ways Allies Can Implement Queer Methodological Frameworks

We want to emphasize Eble's point that integrating queer work into professional writing will require our helping allies to become conversant in queer rhetorics and methodologies while avoiding the possibility of appropriation. Those of us who have written about queer methodologies must offer terminology and theoretical frames others can take up in their own work (consider how feminist methodologies have become more present in writing studies in recent years). As Eble explained, "There's a branding thing too. We want to know how you all who are doing this work want us in the field to talk about the work" (pers. comm.). To take up the work Eble references, we can think of several steps: one, include readings like the ones mentioned in the previous section and ask how they challenge the status quo. Two, when graduate students are engaging with identities as part of their surveys, focus groups, or interviews, ask them to articulate how they plan to engage with nonnormative identities. Three, reach outside the field when necessary to offer readings that address nonnormative methodologies and projects. Four, collaborate with those scholars who identify themselves as allies and want to learn more about what queer methodologies can offer. We might think about venues such as the annual Women in Technical Communication Lunch at ATTW, or roundtable discussions at CCCC, where scholars interested in queer methodologies and rhetorics could have the opportunity to learn more about the "branding" of queer rhetorics and methodologies—and subsequently, how to be allies. While this list is not exhaustive, we hope it will get our colleagues thinking carefully about how they can make queer methods and methodologies more central to their work.

Look for Less Visible Ways of Integrating Queerness and Professional Writing
In addition to programmatic and curricular innovations, we should also be attentive to less visible moments when we might participate in integrative work. In particular, women and gender studies programs often function as rich sites of interdisciplinarity; experts in queer theory and gender studies might be invited to present their research in the context of professional writing programs. Critical theorists are eager to prove their relevance; forging a connection with professional writing can be mutually beneficial for all involved. In addition to inviting visiting scholars, when meeting with students in formal and informal advising sessions, we should consider ways of helping students discover and formulate intersections between queer work and professional writing.

As we offer some concluding thoughts, we want to emphasize that the writing and rhetorical practices that take place in our field are professional communication practices and are professionalizing activities. In this way, not just the content of our work but also the context and conveyance matter. To us, this very volume, drawing on queered methodological practices from early-career queer scholars, shows the ways these practices are increasing in number, scope, and visibility. We both, also, have built queered methods and methodologies into our research practices.

In his 2012 dissertation, *Through Working Closets: Examining Rhetorical and Narrative Approaches to Building LGBTQ and Professional Identity Inside a Corporate Workplace*, Matt tried to build these queer frameworks and practices in his case studies of LGBTQ workers. For him, one approach was to save a more detailed methodological discussion for his sixth and final chapter—an unexpected place for most dissertation structures. Matt noted that this was, for him and his participants, the way "our stories actually unfolded. First, we told them to each other, then we sought, together, to make meaning of what we'd revealed" (Cox 2012, 28). In this organic and collaborative way, Matt and his research participants were able to draw from their myriad life experiences as lenses and frameworks for making knowledge together (frameworks that were queer, lesbian, gay, bi, and trans). In addition, it was crucial to Matt to be transparent and visible in his own research work. He notes, "I didn't want to hide or even hold back my own positionality as a gay professional. I also wanted to be able to include as much of my participants' stories and agency in this dissertation as I could while still contributing analysis and additional meaning where I could" (Cox 2012, 147). Of course this meant an open admission that the work would, at times and to certain audiences and individuals, feel messy and also that the

dissertation work would necessarily have shortcomings and places needing future work (of course, Matt believes this is true of all works, but the
open, visible embracing of this "weakness" was a form of queer practice
and queer failure).

Caroline's dissertation, *Writing Civic Spaces: A Theory of Civic Rhetorics
in a Digital Age* (Dadas 2011), contains a methodology chapter that
sketches out a queer methodological approach for ethically researching social media websites such as Facebook. Detailing her experiences
researching marriage equality on Facebook, she argues that queer
theory can help researchers negotiate the public/private continuum
that figures so heavily into digital research (and also professional writing research). During her study, she turned to queer theory to negotiate ethical quandaries regarding her relationship with participants,
recruitment, and data collection. She details how, on the one hand,
she identified as queer to potential participants in an effort at being
transparent with them; on the other hand, she grew uneasy that some
of her Facebook friends would be confused by the fact that she was
joining homophobic Facebook groups for the purpose of her research.
Ultimately, she argues that a queer methodology enables an understanding of how the public/private continuum influences multiple parts of
the research process; complicates accepted methodological practices
in productive ways; and provides a productive lens for exploring social
media as a research method (as she continues to do in Dadas 2016, as
do Pigg 2014 and Sun 2012).

Considering that the workplace and social media represent two
common areas of research within professional writing, we highlight
these two dissertations in order to emphasize the ways in which queer
rhetorics and professional writing can inform one another. Disrupting
expected structures, making self and relationships visible, calling attention to normative structures, and embracing failure and unexpected
processes and outcomes are just a few ways of queering professional
writing spaces. While these queered approaches must be undertaken
mindfully and with an awareness of potential consequences, we believe
the strategies we mention above can help guide scholars as we think
more queerly about methodologies for studies in professional writing.

NOTE

1.   Throughout this chapter we also refer to professional writing as the field that
      represents scholars who attend ATTW and CPTSC and who publish in *JBTC* and
      TCQ. While terms such as *technical communication* and *professional and technical*

communication are often used interchangeably, we recognize particular terms connote different foci within the field. Our choice in this chapter is primarily driven by the terminology used in steadily proliferating professional writing programs across the country. While these programs often include a technical writing course, they also more broadly encompass writing for business contexts and science writing, among other contexts. We have chosen professional writing as shorthand for the field whose scholarship addresses many professional, civic, and governmental contexts, ultimately making the point that queer methodologies can prove useful when studying/working within all these contexts.

REFERENCES

Ahmed, Sara. 2006. *Queer Phenomenology: Orientations, Objects, Others.* Durham, NC: Duke University Press. https://doi.org/10.1215/9780822388074.

Alexander, Jonathan, and William P. Banks. 2004. "Sexualities, Technologies, and the Teaching of Writing: A Critical Overview." In "Sexualities, Technologies, and the Teaching of Writing," edited by Jonathan Alexander and William P. Banks, special issue, *Computers and Composition* 21 (3): 273–93.

Association of Teachers of Technical Writing. n.d. "History." http://www.attw.org.

Bersani, Leo, and Adam Phillips. 2008. *Intimacies.* Chicago, IL: University of Chicago Press. https://doi.org/10.7208/chicago/9780226043562.001.0001.

Bowdon, Melody. 2004. "Technical Communication and the Role of the Public Intellectual: A Community HIV-Prevention Case Study." *Technical Communication Quarterly* 13 (3): 325–40. https://doi.org/10.1207/s15427625tcq1303_6.

Browne, Kath, Catherine J. Nash, and Sally Hines. 2010. "Introduction: Towards Trans Geographies." *Gender, Place and Culture* 17 (5): 573–77. https://doi.org/10.1080/096 6369X.2010.503104.

Butler, Judith. 2011. *Gender Trouble: Feminism and the Subversion of Identity.* New York: Routledge.

Cox, Matthew B. 2012. "Through Working Closets: Examining Rhetorical and Narrative Approaches to Building LGBTQ and Professional Identity Inside a Corporate Workplace." PhD diss., Michigan State University.

Cox, Matthew B., Michelle Eble, Erin Frost, and Meredith Johnson. 2015. "Not Normally Valued: Queering Methodologies, Risky Research, and Institutional Review Boards." Presentation at the Annual Association of Teachers of Technical Writing (ATTW) Conference, Tampa, FL, March.

Cox, Matthew B., and Michael Faris. 2015. "An Annotated Bibliography of LGBTQ Rhetorics." *Present Tense: A Journal of Rhetoric in Society* 2 (4). http://www.presenttense journal.org/volume-4/an-annotated-bibliography-of-lgbtq-rhetorics/.

Cultural Rhetorics Theory Lab at Michigan State University. 2011. *The Cultural Rhetorics Startup Guide (1e).* East Lansing, MI: Cultural Rhetorics Theory Lab.

Dadas, Caroline. 2011. "Writing Civic Spaces: A Theory of Civic Rhetorics in a Digital Age." PhD diss., Miami University.

Dadas, Caroline. 2016. "Messy Methods: Queer Methodological Approaches to Researching Social Media." *Computers and Composition* 40:60–72. https://doi.org/10.1016/j .compcom.2016.03.007.

Doheny-Farina, Stephen. 1986. "Writing in an Emerging Organization: An Ethnographic Study." *Written Communication* 3 (2): 158–85. https://doi.org/10.1177/074108838600 3002002.

Frost, Erin. 2016. "Apparent Feminism as a Methodology for Technical Communication and Rhetoric." *Journal of Business and Technical Communication* 30 (1): 3–28. https://doi .org/10.1177/1050651915602295.

Gallagher, Chris W. 2011. "Being There: (Re)Making the Assessment Scene." *College Composition and Communication* 62 (3): 450–76.

Grabill, Jeffrey T. 2000. "Shaping Local HIV/AIDS Services Policy through Activist Research: The Problem of Client Involvement." *Technical Communication Quarterly* 9 (1): 29–50. https://doi.org/10.1080/10572250009364684.

Haas, Angela. 2012. "Race, Rhetoric, and Technology: A Case Study of Decolonial Technical Communication Theory, Methodology, and Pedagogy." *Journal of Business and Technical Communication* 26 (3): 277–310. https://doi.org/10.1177/1050651912439539.

Halberstam, Jack. 2011. *The Queer Art of Failure.* Durham, NC: Duke University Press. https://doi.org/10.1215/9780822394358.

Halperin, David. 1990. *One Hundred Years of Homosexuality and Other Essays on Greek Love.* London: Routledge.

Keller, Elizabeth Jean. 2015. "Mentoring as Relationship Building: Identity, Performance, and Value in Technical Communication." Presentation, 2015 ATTW.

Longo, Bernadette. 1998. "An Approach for Applying Cultural Study Theory to Technical Writing Research." *Technical Communication Quarterly* 7 (1): 53–73. https://doi.org/10.1080/10572259809364617.

Malinowitz, Harriet. 1995. *Textual Orientations: Lesbian and Gay Students and the Making of Discourse Communities.* Portsmouth, NH: Heinemann.

Miller, Carolyn. 1979. "A Humanistic Rationale for Technical Writing." *College English* 40 (6): 610–17. https://doi.org/10.2307/375964.

Monson, Connie, and Jacqueline Rhodes. 2004. "Risking Queer: Pedagogy, Performativity, and Desire in Writing Classrooms." *JAC* 24 (1): 79–91.

Muñoz, José Esteban. 1999. *Disidentifications: Queers of Color and the Performance of Politics.* Minneapolis: University of Minnesota Press.

Palmeri, Jason. 2006. "Disability Studies, Cultural Analysis, and the Critical Practice of Technical Communication Pedagogy." *Technical Communication Quarterly* 15 (1): 49–65. https://doi.org/10.1207/s15427625tcq1501_5.

Pigg, Stacey. 2014. "Coordinating Constant Invention: Social Media's Role in Distributed Work." *Technical Communication Quarterly* 23 (2): 69–87. https://doi.org/10.1080/1057 2252.2013.796545.

Pritchard, Eric Darnell. 2017. *Fashioning Lives: Black Queers and the Politics of Literacy.* Carbondale: Southern Illinois University Press.

Scott, J. Blake. 2003. *Risky Rhetoric: AIDS and the Cultural Practices of HIV Testing.* Carbondale: Southern Illinois University Press.

Scott, J. Blake, Bernadette Longo, and Katherine V. Wills, eds. 2006. *Critical Power Tools: Technical Communication and Cultural Studies.* Albany: SUNY Press.

Scott, Tony, and Lillian Brannon. 2013. "Democracy, Struggle, and the Praxis of Assessment." *College Composition and Communication* 65 (2): 273–98.

Scott, Tony, and Nancy Welch. 2014. "One Train Can Hide Another: Critical Materialism for Public Composition." *College English* 76 (6): 562–79.

Sedgwick, Eve Kosofsky. 1990. *Epistemology of the Closet.* Berkeley: University of California Press.

Sun, Huatong. 2012. *Cross-Cultural Technology Design: Creating Culture-Sensitive Technology for Local Users.* Oxford: Oxford University Press. https://doi.org/10.1093/acprof:oso /9780199744763.001.0001.

Warner, Michael. 2005. *Publics and Counterpublics.* New York: Zone.

ABOUT THE AUTHORS

Editors' Note: One of the ways queer rhetorics have re/oriented writing studies is through the disruption of binary gender categories, which matter significantly in the contexts of research with human participants. In recognizing that scholars, like research participants, have the right to choose the pronouns that best represent them, we asked our contributors to include their preferred pronouns. However, several also pushed back and noted they were uncertain that any particular pronoun worked for them; others noted that the pronouns they offered at this time might not work at a later point. As editors, we mention this because it is yet another thing about which researchers should be mindful—when developing demographic data sets, when selecting research participants, when interviewing research participants. We must also recognize that scholars in queer rhetorics are not universally agreed on either the value of pronoun statements or how best to represent the diversity of genders available to us through the limited pronouns the English language currently provides. These are important conversations for researchers to continue having as they do their work.

Chanon Adsanatham (pronouns: he, him, his)
Chanon Adsanatham, assistant professor of rhetoric and writing, researches and teaches comparative rhetoric, digital writing, and multimodality at the Thammasat University. His current book project recovers conduct as an important form of rhetoric in the Thai tradition. Several of his works have appeared in *Computers and Composition* and in edited collections in Asia and the United States. He was the recipient of the James Berlin Memorial Outstanding Dissertation Award in 2015.

William P. Banks (pronouns: he, him, his)
Will Banks is director of the University Writing Program and the Tar River Writing Project and is professor of rhetoric and writing at East Carolina University, where he teaches courses in writing, research, pedagogy, and young adult literature. His essays on digital rhetorics, queer rhetorics, pedagogy, and writing program administration have appeared in several recent books, as well as in *College Composition and Communication, College English,* and *Computers and Composition.* He is coeditor of *Reclaiming Accountability: Improving Writing Programs through Accreditation and Large-Scale Assessments* (Utah State UP, 2016).

Jean Bessette (pronouns: she, her, hers)
Jean Bessette is an assistant professor at the University of Vermont, where she teaches rhetoric and writing courses that address issues in gender and sexuality, historiography, and multimodality. She is the author of *Retroactivism in the Lesbian Archives: Composing Pasts and Futures* (Southern Illinois UP, 2017). Her work has also appeared in *Rhetoric*

Review, College Composition and Communication, Rhetoric Society Quarterly, and *Computers and Composition.*

Nicole I. Caswell (pronouns: she, her, hers)
Nicole is an associate professor at East Carolina University, where she directs the University Writing Center. Her articles have appeared in the *Journal of Writing Assessment, Composition Forum,* and *Academic Exchange Quarterly,* as well as in multiple edited collections. She coauthored the book *The Working Lives of New Writing Center Directors* (Utah State UP, 2016).

Matthew B. Cox (pronouns: he, him, his)
Matthew is an associate professor at East Carolina University, where he teaches graduate and undergraduate courses in rhetorical theory, cultural rhetorics, queer theory and rhetorics, and technical and professional writing. His articles have appeared in *Present Tense: A Journal of Rhetoric in Society,* the *Journal of Technical Writing and Communication,* and *Computers and Composition.*

Caroline Dadas (pronouns: she, her, hers)
Caroline is an associate professor in the Department of Writing Studies at Montclair State University, where she teaches courses in the women, gender, and sexuality major and the professional and public writing minor. Her articles on queer methodologies, citizen participation in digital environments, and ethical practices for the rhetoric and composition job market have appeared in *College Composition and Communication, Computers and Composition, New Media and Society, Literacy in Composition Studies, Composition Forum,* and *Computers and Composition Online.*

Michael J. Faris (pronouns: generally he, him, his, but totally cool with they, them, their, and she, her, hers)
Michael is an assistant professor in the technical communication and rhetoric program, housed in the English Department, at Texas Tech University. He directed the department's Media Lab from 2015 to 2017 and teaches graduate courses in new media, digital rhetoric, composition studies, and queer theory. He has published on digital technologies, composition and technical communication pedagogy, and queer rhetoric in the *Journal of Business and Technical Communication, College Composition and Communication, Composition Forum, Present Tense: A Journal of Rhetoric in Society,* and *Kairos: A Journal of Rhetoric, Technology, and Pedagogy.*

Hillery Glasby (pronouns: she, her, hers)
Hillery is an assistant professor in Michigan State University's Department of Writing, Rhetoric, and American Cultures. She teaches writing courses focused on sexual literacy, environmental sustainability, social justice, and handmade/DIY multimodality. Her research interests include LGBTQ movements; digital, DIY, and queer rhetorics; and writing center and writing program administration. Hillery's work has been published in *Harlot, Liminalities,* the *Writing Networks for Social Justice* zine, and *Constellations: A Cultural Rhetorics Publishing Space,* featured in 2014's *Best of the Independent Rhetoric and Composition Journals,* and reviewed in the Sweetland Digital Rhetoric Collaborative. She is currently coediting a collection on queer Appalachia, forthcoming from West Virginia University Press.

Deborah Kuzawa (pronouns: she, her, hers)
Deborah is a senior lecturer with Engineering Education at The Ohio State University. She teaches engineering technical communications, which explores STEM topics using rhetorical, social, and reflective lenses, with attention to the ways social diversity in the United States impacts STEM in all areas. Her research focuses on diversity and inclusion in engineering education, technical communications, queerness, pedagogies and

classrooms, and archives. Her most recent publication is a collaborative chapter in the edited collection *Creative Ways of Knowing in Engineering* (Springer, 2017).

Maria Novotny (pronouns: she, her, hers)
Maria is an assistant professor of English at the University of Wisconsin Oshkosh, where she teaches courses in professional and digital writing. Her research and teaching focus on cultural projects related to reproductive rights in healthcare. Her scholarship has been published in *Peitho, Communication Design Quarterly,* and *Harlot.* In addition, she is the co-founder and co-director of The ART of Infertility, a traveling art and infertility exhibit, which aims to make visible nonnormative reproductive experiences.

G (GPat) Patterson (pronouns: they, them, their)
GPat is an assistant professor of English at Kent State University Tuscarawas. Their research interests include curriculum development, rhetorics of social justice, and queer and transgender studies. GPat is the editor of Facing LGBTQ+ Pride Project (2018), an anthologized collection of queer and trans stories from East Central Indiana. Their scholarship has been featured in the *Journal of LGBT Youth,* Women and Language, *Queer Media Studies in Popular Culture,* and *Constellations: A Cultural Rhetorics Publishing Space,* as well as in three edited collections focused on contemporary issues in rhetoric. In 2014, GPat was awarded the CCCC Lavender Rhetorics Dissertation Award for their pedagogical research on the intersections of sexuality, gender identity, and religious discourse. GPat served as the cochair of the CCCC Queer Caucus from 2016 to 2018.

Pamela Takayoshi (pronouns: she, her, hers)
Pamela Takayoshi is professor of English at Kent State University, where she researches the ways people use writing in academic and non-academic contexts to make meaning in their lives, with a particular interest in research methodologies, the digital mediation of written communication, and feminist epistemologies. She is the co-editor of four collections of research, most recently *Literacy in Practice: Writing in Public, Private, and Working Lives* (2015 with Patrick Thomas), and articles and chapters that have appeared in *College Composition and Communication, Computers and Composition, Rhetoric Review, Research in the Teaching of English,* and numerous edited collections.

Stacey Waite (pronouns: depends on context)
Stacey Waite is associate professor of English and director of composition at the University of Nebraska–Lincoln and has taught courses in writing, pedagogy, queer rhetorics, and poetry. Waite has published four collections of poems: *Choke, Love Poem to Androgyny, the lake has no saint,* and *Butch Geography* and has had articles appear most recently in *College Composition and Communication, Writing on the Edge,* and *Literacy in Composition Studies.* Waite's newest book is *Teaching Queer: Radical Possibilities for Writing and Knowing* (University of Pittsburgh Press, 2017).

Stephanie West-Puckett (pronouns: she, her, hers)
Stephanie is assistant professor of writing and rhetoric and director of first-year writing at the University of Rhode Island. Her scholarship focuses on digital, queer, and maker-centered composition practices and writing program administration. She has published peer-reviewed scholarship on writing assessment, National Writing Project administration, and digital writing in journals such as *College English* and *Educational Sciences* and in a number of recent edited collections.

INDEX